D0086988

TRAINING PROGRAM WORKBOOK AND KIT

Carolyn Nilson

PRENTICE HALL
Englewood Cliffs, New Jersey 07632

Prentice-Hall International (UK) Limited, *London*
Prentice-Hall of Australia Pty. Limited, *Sydney*
Prentice-Hall Canada, Inc., *Toronto*
Prentice-Hall Hispanoamericana, S.A., *Mexico*
Prentice-Hall of India Private Limited, *New Delhi*
Prentice-Hall of Japan, Inc., *Tokyo*
Simon & Schuster Asia Pte. Ltd., *Singapore*
Editora Prentice-Hall do Brasil, Ltda., *Rio de Janeiro*

© 1989 *by*

PRENTICE-HALL, Inc.

Englewood Cliffs, NJ

All rights reserved. No part of this
book may be reproduced in any form or
by any means, without permission in
writing from the publisher.

A James Peter Book

10 9 8 7 6 5 4 3

*(Names of persons and companies used in examples in this book are fictitious.
Any resemblance to real people or actual companies is not intentional.)*

Library of Congress Cataloging-in-Publication Data

Nilson, Carolyn D.
    Training program workbook and kit/Carolyn Nilson.
      p. cm.
    "A James Peter book."·
    Includes bibliographical references.
    ISBN 0-13-926247-4
    1. Employees—Training of—Handbooks, manuals, etc. I. Title.
HF5549.5.T7N53 1989
658.3' 124—dc20   89–16210
                                               CIP

ISBN 0-13-926247-4

PRENTICE HALL
BUSINESS & PROFESSIONAL DIVISION
A division of Simon & Schuster
Englewood Cliffs, New Jersey 07632

Printed in the United States of America

Mark Moon
15 Appleford Road
St. Catharines, Ont.
L2P 3M2

688-3326

Mark Moon
15 Appleford Road
St. Catharines, Ont.

ABOUT THE AUTHOR

CAROLYN NILSON, Ed.D., is a veteran in training design, instructional delivery, and training management. Her special interest is standards for and evaluation of technical training programs.

Dr. Nilson is a training consultant for corporations and agencies. Among the corporations she has served are RJR Nabisco, National Westminster Bank USA, New Jersey Bell, Southern New England Telephone Company, AT&T Consumer Products, the Rockefeller Foundation, the New Haven Foundation, and the National Occupational Competency Testing Institute. She also did independent evaluation work for the U.S. Department of Education, Office of Vocational and Adult Education, the New Jersey State Department of Education, and the Connecticut Advisory Council on Vocational and Career Education. For three years she was a field agent in Connecticut for the National Institute of Education, and for two years she worked in the New Jersey Vocational-Technical Education Curriculum Laboratory at Rutgers University. Her work has been characterized by a concern for equal employment opportunity, competency development, and technology transfer.

Dr. Nilson held the position of Product Manager for Simulation Training at Combustion Engineering, where she was responsible for design, delivery, and management of computer-based training (CBT) simulations for the chemical process industry. At Combustion Engineering, she also was part of a corporate design team in Artificial Intelligence, with specific responsibilities for design of an expert system in learning and evaluation.

She also was a Member of Technical Staff (MTS) at AT&T Bell Laboratories' Systems Training Center, where she was part of the Standards, Audits, and Inspections group. At Bell Labs, she worked as an instructional designer in concert with engineers and software experts to produce courses, seminars, and conferences for the AT&T R&D and technical communities. She taught the Bell Labs' course, *Techniques of Instruction.*

Carolyn Nilson received her doctorate from Rutgers University with a specialty in measurement and evaluation in vocational and technical education. She has been active in professional associations through presentation of papers and publication in journals. She is currently a member of the National Society for Performance and Instruction.

ACKNOWLEDGMENT _____

I would like to thank Marc Dorio for his contributions to Chapter 1 on needs assessment, Chapter 5 on course design, and Chapter 10 on delivery methods.

WHAT THE TRAINING PROGRAM WORKBOOK AND KIT WILL DO FOR YOU _____

The Training Program Workbook and Kit is a new, breakthrough guide to training design, delivery, and management. In one handy volume, you'll find a wealth of worksheets, checklists, and guidelines designed to walk you step by step through every key aspect of planning and carrying out training. With the help of this workbook, you can streamline and simplify the training process and, at the same time, rest assured that your program is based on sound training principles—and that nothing has been overlooked.

Here are just a few of the reasons why you'll turn to this *Workbook* again and again for help in training planning, instruction, and management.

If You Are a Training Designer

Good training programs begin with careful design. The *Training Program Workbook and Kit* is built around a systems approach to training that takes you logically through the steps of training needs assessment, job and task analysis, course and test design, selection of the right training media, and evaluation of what you've done in order to make improvements.

You'll also find a completely worked-out system for writing a training proposal, complete with fill-in-the-blank budgeting worksheets and a sample presentation layout. The *Workbook* automatically takes care of the mechanics for you, leaving you free to concentrate on the particular needs of your company and its trainees.

If You Are an Instructor

The *Training Program Workbook and Kit* spells out tried-and-true techniques for teaching trainees new skills and improving productivity. Its guidelines and worksheets make it easier to select the best training method for your course and students, manage a classroom, give feedback to trainees—even plan your lecture notes!

You'll also find step-by-step instructions for choosing and using Computer-Based Instruction (CBI), checklists for streamlining workshop and conference planning, and valuable help in buying new training equipment. Because the *Workbook* hands you an organized framework for training delivery, you'll spend less time on paperwork and more on your students.

If You Are Involved in Publicity

In this *Workbook* you'll find everything you need to get employees involved in your training programs. Here's how to write brochure copy . . . a catalog entry . . . a course announcement . . . even an article for your company newsletter! The *Workbook* outlines each step for you, complete with fill-in-the-blank worksheets and sample publicity materials you can use as models.

If You Are a Training Manager

Training managers are under growing pressure to run their departments like a business, keeping a sharp eye on the bottom line. The *Training Program Workbook and Kit* gives you the tools you need to do just that. You'll find a worked-out system for writing a business plan, including fill-in-the-blank worksheets, examples, and a sample layout; a "roadmap" for project management that helps you track costs and keep projects on schedule and under control; budget worksheets specially designed to complement your company's budgeting system; even ways to prepare for—and survive—an operational audit.

You'll also find more than a dozen worksheets, checklists, and forms for streamlining the day-to-day aspects of training administration, from hiring training personnel to handling course enrollment.

Whether you're installing an entirely new training system or enhancing your company's present program, or are part of a large corporation or a small training consulting firm, the *Training Program Workbook and Kit* offers you invaluable help at every stage of design, delivery, and management.

HOW TO USE THIS WORKBOOK

The *Training Program Workbook and Kit* has been carefully organized to make it easy to use. It includes:

- *Detailed instructions* to help you prepare a wide variety of training documents, reports, and other materials; from job and task analyses, tests, and publicity to training proposals, budgets, and project status reports.

- *Worksheets*, including fill-in-the blank forms, step-by-step guidelines, and comprehensive checklists. Worksheets are located next to instructions for quick and easy reference. Depending on the topic and your training needs, worksheets can be prepared singly or in combination. (Check the sections titled "How to Use the Worksheets in This Chapter" before you begin.)

- When you've finished the worksheets, you'll have in hand a complete document or training tool: a course outline, equipment inventory, business plan, cost analysis, lecture planning notes, course delivery schedule, and much more.

- *Examples.* Throughout the *Workbook,* you'll find hundreds of examples and even sample documents that clearly illustrate how to complete the worksheets. You can use them as models to follow whenever you're preparing training materials.

Each chapter in the *Workbook* begins with a concise explanation of training design techniques, training delivery methods, or training management tools. The *Workbook* also contains a detailed table of contents and a comprehensive index so you can locate the worksheets you need at a glance.

TIPS FOR GETTING THE MOST FROM THIS WORKBOOK

Here are some tips that will help you benefit fully from the *Workbook*:

- *Define your planning period up front.* Know what time frame you have in which to operate, whether it's three months, one year, or five years. This *Workbook* is useful in all situations, but you'll benefit most if your timelines are clear.
- *Use words appropriate for your company and industry* when you adopt a form or set of guidelines. Be sensitive to local favorite terms. Your management might prefer "student" to "trainee," "test" rather than "exercise," or "salesperson" rather than "account executive."
- *Avoid shortcuts.* When you complete a worksheet or follow guidelines, don't eliminate a step. It's there for a reason. Instead, adapt that step to your situation, making it more useful.
- *Get supervisors and managers involved* when you design training programs. While managers tend to be more concerned with carrying out training, you'll need their input during the design stage to make training work well for your company.
- *Get your colleagues involved.* Have them review and comment on your training program plans before you submit them to management. Peer review can point out roadblocks that might not have been apparent to you or to your manager.

Above all, be flexible. Use this *Workbook* to encourage creativity and adaptability, not rigidity. Training is a people business, and people require flexibility.

CONTENTS _____

How to Use the Worksheets in This Chapter 159

CHAPTER 8
HOW TO PACKAGE TRAINING: MANUALS AND JOB AIDS ————————

How to Use the Worksheets in This Chapter 173

CHAPTER 9
HOW TO CONDUCT A FIELD TEST ———————————————————

How to Use the Worksheets in This Chapter 183

CHAPTER 10
HOW TO DELIVER TRAINING ———————————————————————

How to Use the Worksheets in This Chapter 198

CHAPTER 13
GUIDELINES FOR PURCHASING AND MAINTAINING TRAINING
EQUIPMENT AND FACILITIES _____ 265

CHAPTER 14
HOW TO ATTRACT EMPLOYEES TO YOUR TRAINING PROGRAMS _____ 287

CHAPTER 18
HOW TO SURVIVE AN OPERATIONAL AUDIT _____ 373

Be Aware of Sages and Stakeholders   373
Build In a Bias for Action   374

How to Use the Worksheets in This Chapter   374

CHAPTER 19
WAYS TO STREAMLINE TRAINING ADMINISTRATION _____ 395

How to Use the Worksheets in This Chapter   395

CHAPTER 1

HOW TO ASSESS TRAINING NEEDS

In training program design, what might seem to be the beginning may not be. Behind your sparkling first morning of class are months of individuals, ideas, numbers, processes, and organizations that have shaped your reason for being there. The way in which all of these precursors of training are hooked together and managed gives your training program its strength and its justification. Behind the apparent beginning is Needs Assessment.

FIND IT AND FIX IT

Training program design has a circular nature about it of "finding and fixing and finding and fixing" problems that affect the performance of people at work. That first smiling encounter between instructor and trainee is only the beginning of the "fix it" phase. What comes before this structured learning activity is a "find it" phase, commonly known in the language of training design as Needs Assessment.[1]

This chapter presents only the big picture of Needs Assessment, defining and elaborating on some of its parameters with worksheets and guidelines. The following chapters on Job Analysis and Task Analysis provide specific tools for implementing these specialized analysis processes that are useful during most Needs Assessment projects.

KEY FACTORS TO CONSIDER WHEN PLANNING A NEEDS ASSESSMENT

How you plan and carry out a Needs Assessment depends on many factors. Consider the following.

"An Ounce of Prevention . . ."

Needs Assessment is akin to the old adage, "An ounce of prevention is worth a pound of cure." In training Needs Assessment, that "ounce of prevention" is

---

[1] Professional literature in training is full of books on Needs Assessment. A particularly comprehensive and easily read book is Allison Rossett's *Training Needs Assessment* (Englewood Cliffs, NJ: Educational Technology Publications, 1987).

best described as the time, personnel, and resources required to accurately describe a performance problem that can be solved by training. That seemingly small task of finding just the right problem or exactly the critical issue can save you many hours of discussion and days of design effort as you prepare your course or program. Whether you buy a course from a vendor or create your own, a little Needs Assessment up front guarantees better results in the end.

Organizational Layers and How They Interact

When you think about planning and carrying out a Needs Assessment, it is important to consider the organization as a multi-dimensional entity. A thorough and fair Needs Assessment divides the organization into as many pieces as seem fit to describe your particular company. It's important to think of these pieces as interacting; as being necessary to the cohesiveness of the whole.

Some of these interacting pieces, or layers, might be individual employees, departments, lines of business, field offices, central offices, customers, laws, new technologies, outdated technologies, policies, the corporate image, or stockholders. Planning a Needs Assessment begins with drawing a clear picture of the interacting layers of an organization that seem to have some effect on the reason why you need training.

You can look for help within each of these layers of your organization from key informers, or persons to whom you can go to get straight answers. Within each of these layers you can probably find individuals or small groups who can function as your partners in your Needs Assessment as it becomes formalized into interviews, questionnaires, or document searches. If you've defined your layers correctly, you'll also find within each layer persons who have a stake in the outcomes of the training you eventually will produce. It's those key informers, partners, and stakeholders who can help you define the right problem and set you off on the right track to solve it. Define their facilitative roles within and between the layers you've drawn.

"What Should Be": Look for Training Needs Here

What should be is related to what is. The difference between what is and what should be is probably a good area for possibly needing training. During Needs Assessment, all the "what should bes" are good clues in an organization. A person engaged in Needs Assessment, after listing all the what should bes, then has the tougher job of finding out what is.

In most companies, it's easy to find standards. In customer-driven businesses, sometimes the company's standards have become obscured by customer standards, and the customer standards then become the new company standards. The careful Needs Assessor will exercise a good amount of intuition when searching for standards. He or she will also verify the reality of current performance; that is, check around!

When that discrepancy is found and defined accurately, the Needs Assessor's next job is to determine if training is the appropriate action to eliminate the discrepancy and cause the standard to be met. (Often, training is not the only way—sometimes a policy change will solve the problem, a change in personnel will solve the problem, a bonus or incentive will make the standard attainable, changing the structure of the organization will solve the problem, a working model on the floor or a job aid posted on the wall will help improve performance as workers become more accessible to step-by-step procedures.)

In business, the goals are generally the big three—improved performance, increased productivity, and more profit. Needs Assessment uncovers the needs that can be addressed by training in order to accomplish these three major goals. Thinking "what should be" helps the Needs Assessor to focus on goals.

Don't Overlook Soft Data

Because organizations are made up of human beings interacting with each other, the realm of soft data is important in shaping problems and defining needs for help. Needs Assessors pay attention to the feelings, beliefs, reactions, and attitudes of persons in the Needs Assessment target group. Attitude questionnaires, for example, are often used during Needs Assessment phases. These subjective areas of response are generally known as soft data. Good soft data collection is done using the same care and safeguards as is good hard data collection, and can provide the Needs Assessor with the "fleshed out" picture of training needs that is not possible with hard data alone.

Locating and Using Hard Data

Many Needs Assessors think first of getting the hard data—that is, the facts, figures, statistics, and charts that represent the unequivocal truth about an organization. Hard data is found in annual reports and file drawers, minutes of meetings, videotaped presentations, auditors' reports, tax returns, business plans, attendance records, parts-per-minute counts, quality control reports, sales figures, and a host of other quantified sets of information. The Needs Assessor's major task regarding hard data is to verify it and to use it in a way that has meaning for the task of defining a very specific problem that might be solved through training. Don't make the mistake of becoming buried in hard data that has no relationship to the task at hand. Engage in a hard data hunt only after you've thought about Needs Assessment in all of the other ways suggested above.

Identifying Problems and Setting Priorities

The final phase of a Needs Assessment is a decision-making phase in which specific problems are defined and prioritized. This phase comes only after all the planning, collaborating, and collecting of data have been done and verified at every major revelation or decision point along the way. The end product of a Needs Assessment should be an annotated list of training solutions to specific performance problems.

Worksheets in this chapter help put into action these ways of thinking about

Needs Assessment. Worksheets in the next two chapters can also contribute to an effective Needs Assessment.

TIPS FOR CONDUCTING AN EFFECTIVE NEEDS ASSESSMENT

Keep the following in mind when assessing training needs:

1. *Estimate how much of your resources will be required.* Figure out the amount of management involvement and cost, employee involvement and cost, total person-hours, lapsed time (start date to end date), expenses such as travel, rented conference rooms away from the office, telephone, video supplies, and equipment.

2. *Vary your methods of seeking information.* Use instruments that record written information from individuals as well as those that document personal interactions among people in groups. In addition to questionnaires and checklists, consider using audio tapes and videotapes.

3. *Keep it simple.* Needs Assessment tools should be easy to use and analyze. Seek only the kind of information that focuses on the performance problem you think you have; don't confuse your respondents with too many questions. Aim to be able to quantify, group, weight, and prioritize the responses you get.

4. *Tell the people whom you interview how you expect to use the information they supply.* Give clear instructions, tell them when you will give them some feedback on the Needs Assessment process, briefly describe "the big picture" of why this is necessary (performance, productivity, profit), and be clear in your own mind what kinds of information you intend to release at the conclusion of the Needs Assessment. Be confident that you will get useful information, and be clear about when and how you will disseminate it.

5. *Develop your own Needs Assessment instruments.* You know your company better than an outside evaluator does. You and your colleagues are the best ones to design information-gathering tools that will not waste time and that will be accepted within your corporate culture.

6. *Look for spin-off benefits.* A good Needs Assessment will spark people's imaginations, will often result in discussions or task forces, and will have the potential for changing attitudes, even before a training program is designed. Persons who are involved in the analysis of needs often "buy into" the solutions to those needs more readily.

7. *Focus on results.* As you collect information, stay focused on results, not on efforts. Most people try to do a good job. If there's a reason for slipping performance to be uncovered, you'll find it faster by working backwards from results. Results generally are facts—numbers that have been accepted already. Cooperative attitudes are easier to achieve when you start from these generally agreed-upon results.

HOW TO USE THE WORKSHEETS IN THIS CHAPTER

Worksheet 1–1: The Big Picture: Where to Look for Information

Use this worksheet as you begin to plan your Needs Assessment. A checklist of likely information sources follows statements of what triggered the Needs Assessment and what its goal is.

Worksheet 1–2: Graphic Representation of Organization Relationships

Use this worksheet to identify the interrelationships among groups that seem to have some effect on the reason why you need to develop new training. A graphic representation often points up areas of overlap or relationships that can signal opportunities for cost savings later as training is implemented.

Worksheet 1–3: Key Informers

Use this worksheet to list the most important individuals to whom you can turn for support, straight answers, and relevant commentary.

Worksheet 1–4: Self Assessment Questionnaire

Use this generic self assessment questionnaire either as a "take home" written survey to be mailed back to you or as an interview schedule which you administer face-to-face with each respondent. This kind of instrument is helpful in defining the content of your potential new training.

Worksheet 1–5: What Should Be Versus What Is

Use this worksheet as a first step in defining the realistic condition that you want to achieve. This worksheet structures your thinking to encourage you to rule out training in some situations as a means of reaching "what should be," thereby reserving the appropriate training solutions for the problems that can be solved most effectively by training.

Worksheet 1–6: Needs Assessment Results

Using the training information from Worksheet 1–5 as input, use Worksheet 1–6 to define and prioritize the training solutions your Needs Assessment has indicated. The addition of a first-cut at implementation dates will start you on the training design and development phase of your training program.

THE BIG PICTURE: WHERE TO LOOK FOR INFORMATION

This worksheet will help you get started on your search for the kinds of information you'll need to verify that you have a need for training. In this search, don't be surprised if you find out that some problem that you have identified can be solved by something other than training. One of the major reasons for doing a Needs Assessment is to precisely define those problems for which training is the only—and the best—way to achieve a solution. The training that you eventually design, develop, and deliver will be more effective and less costly if all along you are aware of what training is and what training is not.

The Trigger and the Goal

Begin your Needs Assessment by stating exactly what has triggered someone to believe that there's a problem that can be solved by training. Next, state the goal of that probable training.

Example #1: Trigger

Recent legislation has been passed to ensure a safe work environment for persons who work in front of a CRT computer screen.

Example #1: Goal

To find out what this target group of computer operators, data entry clerks, and others needs to know or to do in order to be safe at work.

Example #2: Trigger

Our company was bought out by another company. In order to achieve consistency in personnel record-keeping procedures, we now have to do everything their way.

Example #2: Goal

To learn a completely new set of procedures to use with different personnel forms. To automate/computerize many former procedures that were done by hand.

Selected Sources of Information

Once you have stated both the trigger and the goal for your probable training program, you'll need to locate the sources of information that will provide you with the facts and opinions you'll need to define training more precisely. Place a check (√) next to any items that identify the parts of the organization in which information for the training Needs Assessment can be found. Other items may be added.

Example

Selected Sources of Information	Notes
1. ☐ customers	
2. ☑ policies	Who is writing the policy?
3. ☑ laws	Check both corporate attorneys.
4. ☑ management practices	What do we need in addition to the grievance procedure? See John.

WORKSHEET 1–1

THE BIG PICTURE: WHERE TO LOOK FOR INFORMATION

The Trigger: _____

_____

The Goal: _____

_____

_____

Selected Sources of Information	Notes
1. ☐ customers	
2. ☐ policies	
3. ☐ laws	
4. ☐ management practices	
5. ☐ budgets	
6. ☐ financial results	
7. ☐ annual plans	
8. ☐ schedules	
9. ☐ procedures	
10. ☐ equipment/hardware	
11. ☐ systems/software	
12. ☐ performance appraisals	
13. ☐ productivity reports	
14. ☐ departments	
15. ☐ work groups	
16. ☐ informal cliques	
17. ☐ individuals affected by Needs Assessment results	
18. ☐ physical environment	
19. ☐ specifications	
20. ☐ current courses	

(Add more pages or substitute other information sources as needed.)

GRAPHIC REPRESENTATION OF ORGANIZATION RELATIONSHIPS

Most Needs Assessments involve a large number of people both in your organization and in other organizations affected by the consequences of the Needs Assessment. It's a good idea to make a drawing of the interacting organizations that will contribute to your Needs Assessment early in your planning. This often helps you to see overlapping or intersecting influences, or to identify where cost savings can be realized, as training is planned and developed.

Use the checklist of Selected Sources of Information on Worksheet 1–1 for ideas. Verify your drawing with several colleagues, and review it periodically to add to or modify it with new relationships as they become obvious as your Needs Assessment progresses.

Example #1

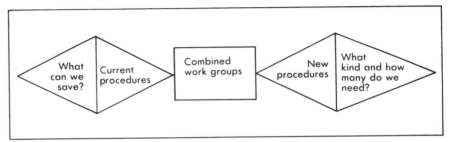

Example #2

Example #3

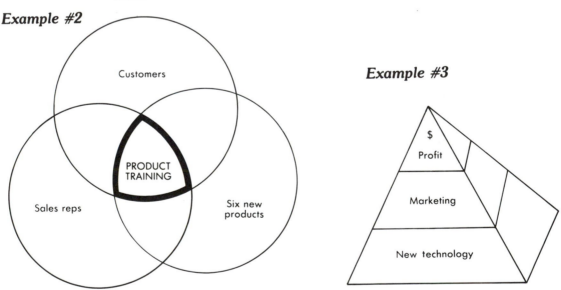

TRAINING TIP: Use this graphic as an overhead transparency or slide in presentations about your Needs Assessment. This kind of graphic often helps people understand the concept of Needs Assessment and helps dispel fears that everyone is being watched!

WORKSHEET 1–2

GRAPHIC REPRESENTATION OF ORGANIZATION
RELATIONSHIPS

KEY INFORMERS

Use this worksheet to list the most important individuals to whom you can turn for support, straight answers, and relevant commentary.

In your listing, be sure to identify your Key Informer's organization correctly. This information can be extremely useful later as you begin the implementation of your training program. Create this Key Informers worksheet so that it is useful now in the beginning of your Needs Assessment as well as later.

Example

Name	Organization	Address	Telephone
Lana Jeanneau (Executive Secretary)	Advertising Distribution Org.# 1028	Building 19– 440	x 2144

WORKSHEET 1–3

KEY INFORMERS

Name	Organization	Address	Telephone
(Add more pages as needed.)			

SELF-ASSESSMENT QUESTIONNAIRE

Use this generic self-assessment questionnaire either as a "take home" written survey to be mailed back to you or as an interview schedule that you administer face to face with each respondent. During this process, individuals rate themselves.

Reasons for This Kind of Questionnaire

This kind of questionnaire yields information about both people and content. The people who respond to such a questionnaire are often the ones for whom training is targeted. Their responses can give you both hard and soft data and a good picture of individual needs regarding performance improvement.

One Way to Tabulate Results of this Kind of Questionnaire

Use a "Need to Know Table" to list the individuals who say that they need help in performing certain skills. One option is to build a "1,2,3" table including any person who rated himself/herself a 1,2, or 3 on any item. This table will give you a clear picture of which skills need improvement and who needs to learn them.

	Need to Know Table for Data Entry Clerk		
	2. Reading coded data	7. Moving text	9. Managing files
Jennifer	X		X
Sue	X	X	X
Marnie			X
Robin	X		X

Three Typical Skills Lists

Construct your questionnaire so that one specific skill is listed after each number. Define and list as many skills as are appropriate to the performance on which you are seeking assessment information. Be sure that each skill listed can be taught, learned, and measured. Follow each skill with space for comments.

Listed below are some typical skills that you can use as a start:

Supervisor	Account Representative	Data Entry Clerk
1. Administering paperwork	1. Prospecting	1. Reading tables
2. Managing performance	2. Qualifying leads	2. Reading coded data
3. Solving problems	3. Planning work	3. Keyboarding
4. Making decisions	4. Keeping records	4. Using menus
5. Resolving conflicts	5. Completing paperwork	5. Formatting text
6. Motivating employees	6. Making presentations	6. Using on-line speller
7. Communicating	7. Probing for information	7. Moving text and data

12

WORKSHEET 1–4

SELF-ASSESSMENT QUESTIONNAIRE

Name: _____   Telephone: _____

Job title: _____   Date: _____

Directions: Please rate yourself on the specific skills listed below by circling the appropriate number on the rating scale, ranging from poor to excellent. Briefly explain your rating for each item. Your responses will be used to plan training programs.

Skills	**Poor**				**Excellent**
	1	2	3	4	5

1. _____   1 2 3 4 5

   Comment:

   _____

   _____

   _____

2. _____   1 2 3 4 5

   Comment:

   _____

   _____

   _____

3. _____   1 2 3 4 5

   Comment:

   _____

   _____

   _____

4. _____   1 2 3 4 5

   Comment:

   _____

   _____

   _____

5. _____   1 2 3 4 5

   Comment:

   _____

   _____

   _____

6. _____   1 2 3 4 5

   Comment:

   _____

   _____

   _____

(Add more pages as needed.)

WHAT SHOULD BE VERSUS WHAT IS

Use this worksheet as a first step in defining the realistic condition that you want to achieve. All sources of information and methods of gathering information provide input to this definition of "what should be."[2]

Begin this worksheet by repeating the "Trigger" and the "Goal" from Worksheet 1–1. Consider how all of your input data from documents, observations, interviews, and written questionnaires applies to that desired "what should be" condition.

On the worksheet, also briefly describe "what is," based on the facts and opinions you believe are true.

Next, decide if that discrepancy between "what should be" and "what is" can best be corrected by training or by some other means. Comment briefly on your decision.

The example below illustrates what this kind of planning worksheet might look like:

Trigger: An increase in drug abuse in the region has prompted the pharmaceutical manufacturer to institute a program of account representative accountability for drug samples.

Goal: To have local managers perform a daily accounting of the whereabouts of all drug samples for a period of six months as a pilot program. Managers will have to monitor their account reps' accountability regarding samples given to private practice physicians, emergency walk-in centers, hospital staff physicians, and any other persons. Managers will report to the Vice-President of Advertising.

What Should Be	What Is	Training Needed	Other Solution Suggested	Comment
Exact correspondence of samples distributed to samples manufactured on a daily basis.	Monthly tally sheets.	X	X	Need new forms as well as training in how to use them. (Get the forms before designing the training.)
Local Advertising Manager responsibility for his/her account reps' accountability.	Advertising Director's Administrative Assistant has been responsible. Reps all phone in weekly to him.		X	Executive Brief needs to come from VP explaining the change and setting start date for new accountability procedures.
Local Managers, Account Reps, the Director's staff, and VP's staff all have to understand new roles and how to perform new procedures.	Only two levels are currently involved: Acct. Rep and Director's staff.	X		We have to figure out how to inform and train equally— consider videotape plus cross-level workshops within a 3-week time span.

---

[2] A classic work in the field of performance technology is *Analyzing Performance Problems or 'You Really Oughta Wanna'* by Mager and Pipe. (Belmont, CA: Fearon Pitman, 1970.)

WORKSHEET 1–5

WHAT SHOULD BE VERSUS WHAT IS

Trigger: _____

_____

_____

Goal: _____

_____

_____

What Should Be	What Is	Training Needed	Other Solution Suggested	Comment

(Add more pages as needed.)

15

NEEDS ASSESSMENT RESULTS

Using the training information from Worksheet 1–5 as input, use Worksheet 1–6 to define and prioritize the training solutions your Needs Assessment has indicated. The addition of a first-cut at implementation dates will start you on the training design and development phase of your training program.

The example below has been derived from a Needs Assessment triggered by legislation to ensure a safe work environment for persons who work in front of a CRT (Cathode Ray Tube) computer screen.

Prioritized Training Solutions	Performance Problem Addressed	Start Date	Notes
1. Make a videotape about how we use ergonomics to create a safer work environment. Use our own people as actors. Use it in every training program during the next year. Invite discussion to clarify perceptions.	Nobody has any idea of the practical applications of "ergonomics."	1/5	Allow 2 months for shooting, editing, and copying.
2. Sponsor a "Vertical Conference" of all workers, supervisors, and top management. Break into 4 rotating small groups to design implementation plans.	No mechanisms exist for workers to implement the four new policies.	3/1	Try to get facilitators from the OD organization.
3. Run a one-day supervisor training program. Use role play and video feedback.	Supervisors are inconsistent in their safety training methods and messages.	3/15	Verify availability of cameraman by 3/1.
4. Design and train individuals to self-administer a Vision Checklist on a daily basis. (Provide weekly feedback.)	Vision and lighting standards are met by only 15% of the target population.	2/20	
5. Work group "hands-on" 2-hour workshops in The Importance of Body Movement conducted at group workstations.	Safety standards regarding body movement have been ignored.	4/1	Invite company doctor to participate.

WORKSHEET 1–6

NEEDS ASSESSMENT RESULTS

Prioritized Training Solutions	Performance Problem Addressed	Start Date	Notes
1.			
2.			
3.			
4.			
5.			

(Add more pages as needed.)

CHAPTER 2 _____

HOW TO DO JOB _____
ANALYSIS _____

A job is what an individual does at work to satisfy an employer's needs and expectations in exchange for pay. A job consists of responsibilities, duties, and tasks that are defined and can be accomplished, measured, and rated.

USING JOB ANALYSIS IN TRAINING AND
PERSONNEL ADMINISTRATION

Job definitions are fundamental personnel tools. A job is an employment tool for classifying work and for selecting employees, for planning one's own career development and training, and for facilitating growth and change in an organization through promotion or termination. A job is a basic personnel unit around which policies, programs, and procedures revolve.

The term *job* is a familiar one in American business. We talk about people's jobs, job descriptions, job advertisements, job advancement, and being on the job.

JOB VERSUS OCCUPATION

Jobs that are related to each other belong to an occupation. Two examples of occupational fields are health services and insurance. Within each of these occupations, the following sample jobs are classified:

Health Services Occupation Jobs	Insurance Occupations Jobs
neurosurgeon	chief operating officer
operating room nurse	attorney
nurse practitioner	office manager
home health aide	agent
lab technician	appraiser
laundry aide	claims adjuster
hospital administrator	accounts payable clerk

Health Services Occupation Jobs   *Insurance Occupations Jobs*

ambulance driver   accounts receivable clerk
medical secretary   word processing specialist
dietician   internal auditor

How a Job Fits Within an Occupation

The circle shown in Figure 2–1 represents the nature of a job within an occupation. If you are responsible for designing effective training to improve performance, you will generally begin your course design with an analysis of a job—and the duties and tasks that job is broken down into.

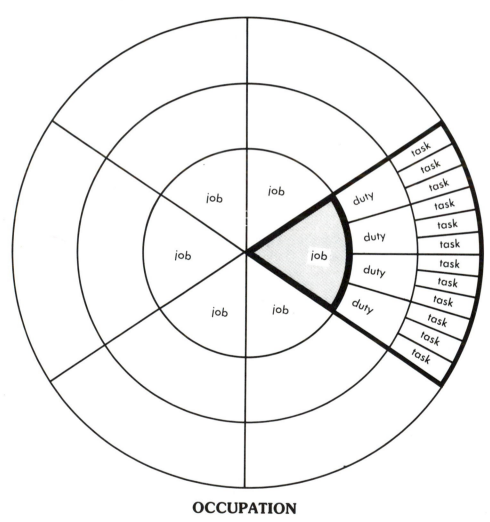

OCCUPATION

Figure 2–1

HOW JOB ANALYSIS LAYS THE GROUNDWORK FOR EFFECTIVE TRAINING

Trainers perform job analysis as part of the systematic design of a course or training program. Performing a job analysis is the fundamental step that distinguishes training—designing for improvement or behavioral change—from presentation, or designing simply for information or show.

Trainers do job analysis to make training as spare and as cost-effective as possible. By performing a good job analysis before designing a course, you can demonstrate that training development costs are worth the investment of corporate resources. Training designed to improve or optimize a specific job can affect business in a positive way.

WHAT'S INVOLVED IN JOB ANALYSIS?

Job analysis breaks down the complexity of a person's job into logical parts, identifying and organizing the knowledge, skills, and attitudes required to perform the job correctly.

Job analysis is frequently concerned with the subjective elements of a job—that is, expectations and attitudes. It is vitally important to document and quantify measures of these subjective elements. Careful analysis of expectations and attitudes is often the key to appropriate training design—and sometimes, it may point to alternatives to training.

Job analysis typically includes these elements:

1. Performance standards
2. Accomplishments and competencies, and
3. Deficiencies.

Job analysis takes into account both the nature of the job and the nature of the person doing the job.

FIVE KEY TOOLS TO USE WHEN CONDUCTING A JOB ANALYSIS

Training designers have a variety of tools (e.g., checklists, charts, and questionnaires) to assist them in doing a job analysis. A sample of these tools is featured in this chapter. These tools can be used alone or in combination, depending on the training designer's situation and preference.

1. *People-Data-Things Job Analysis*

Jobs are often characterized by proportions of time spent focused on people, on data, and on things. Performance deficiencies often result from a mismatch between the true nature of the job and the employee's preference for focus on people, data, or things.

Here's an example. A hospital laundry aide accepted a job because he thought that 90 percent of his time would be spent operating washing and drying machinery and stacking laundry. However, it turned out that his particular job required him to spend 60 percent of his time filling out forms and adding columns of numbers. The result? A performance problem, caused by a mismatch between the expectation of a "things" job and the reality of a "data" job.

Job analysis uncovers such discrepancies. Jobs are performed well when knowledge, skills, attitudes, and personal preferences are adequate and in balance.

When to use this technique. People-data-things job analysis is especially useful for retraining or when performance problems plague an organization. This kind of job analysis quickly pinpoints discrepancies in performance against standards of existing jobs.

People-data-things job analysis is also useful when new jobs are created and a workforce has to be trained to perform them. You can easily design lessons around each of the analysis categories: people lessons, data lessons, and things lessons.

People-data-things job analysis has been used by the U. S. Department of Labor for several decades to categorize and list jobs. See the *Dictionary of Occupational Titles*, and periodic updates, found in the reference section of most public libraries.

2. *Structured Employee Interview Job Analysis*

Employees like to be heard. They want the opportunity to improve their situation at work and to improve the work they do. A structured employee interview gives you some direct employee input regarding improvement.

Employee interviews can be conducted using both open questions and closed questions. These questions are structured to elicit information from employees concerning:

- Performance standards
- Costs of doing the job
- Quality of work life
- Procedures and methods of doing the job
- Resources available or needed

Using employee's responses, you can create training opportunities that address employees' stated concerns.

When to use this technique. This tool is especially useful when training is required to introduce updated methods and procedures, when quality and productivity are training issues, and when additional resources seem to be needed to enhance morale.

3. *The Expert's Critical Task/Training Matrix*

In recent years, the use of analysis of experts at work has garnered an increasingly solid base in training research and development. Potential uses for job analysis through expert models will be found in competency studies, mastery skills and testing design, certification and credentialling, setting performance standards, and in expert systems design.

Expert behavior is not just superstar or whiz kid competency. Expert behavior happens because the expert consciously performs certain critical tasks on the job, often because that expert has mastered certain kinds of training.

When you want to design a course to incorporate the insights of experts (and, hopefully, to help trainees to become experts themselves), you seek the expert's self analysis in a formal, systematic fashion. One way to do this is by asking the expert to complete a Critical Task/Training Matrix.

When to use this technique. This job analysis tool is especially appropriate for analyzing management, sales, training, and research and development jobs.

4. *Job Analysis by Observing the Expert*

This is a systematic way of describing the on-the-job behavior of an expert at that job. Each trainee observes the expert at work. After all trainees have had the opportunity to observe, they meet for group discussion.

Your role as trainer is to brief the expert(s) and the observers regarding the observation process, schedule observation sessions, lead discussion groups, and design subsequent training for the observers based on results of the discussion.

When to use this technique. This job analysis tool uses the principle of modeling behavior. It is suited to any job and focuses on specific requirements for performing a job well.

5. *Job Analysis Through Career Path Discussion*

This job analysis tool gives credence to the current realization that persons at work have important beliefs about their jobs and are striving to accomplish certain personal goals through work. These beliefs and goals shape the way in which employees perform their jobs. Most employees want to do a job well. They benefit from periodic discussions about the nature of their jobs and their career aspirations. The entire corporation benefits when career path discussions are turned into training programs that improve job performance.

During career path discussions, an employee and supervisor talk about ways in which the employee can contribute his or her skills and knowledge to advance corporate growth. These discussions often pinpoint training as a means to enhance productivity and job satisfaction. As training manager or designer, you can actively participate in the career development process by designing forms used during career path discussions and acting on the results of those discussions.[1]

HOW TO USE THE WORKSHEETS IN THIS CHAPTER

Job analysis is a trainer's fundamental training design tool, and trainers can choose the type of job analysis best suited to particular situations and groups of

[1] Additional information on collecting and analyzing job data can be found in Chapter 5 of *Designing Training and Development Systems* by William R. Tracey. (New York, AMACOM, 1984.)

employees. The worksheets in this chapter are designed to help you collect information that is useful to your particular organization. These worksheets can be used singly and in combination.

Worksheet 2–1: Job Analysis of Job Description Using People-Data-Things Approach

Use this worksheet to categorize the duties and responsibilities of a job according to their focus on people, data, and things. ·

Worksheet 2–2: Bar Chart Representing Job Analysis of Job Description Using People-Data-Things Approach

Use this worksheet to create a bar chart estimating the percentage of time focused on people, data, and things. A bar chart can be useful in presentations to management, individual discussions with persons currently holding a job, and discussions with job candidates.

Worksheet 2–3: Job Analysis Using a Structured Employee Interview: Closed Question Technique

Use this worksheet during the closed question phase of a structured employee interview. Closed questions are those which can be answered with "yes," "no," or a single correct fill-in-the-blank type of answer.

Worksheet 2–4: Job Analysis Using a Structured Employee Interview: Open Question Technique

Use this worksheet during the open question phase of a structured employee interview. Open questions require an explanatory or descriptive answer and are meant to lead to more discussion.

Worksheet 2–5: Job Analysis Using the Expert's Critical Task/Training Matrix

Use this worksheet to survey experts to determine elements of success on the job and identify the factors that constitute competent behavior.

Worksheet 2–6: The Expert Model Observation Form and Task Force Discussion Guide

Use this worksheet to help trainees take notes during observation of experts sessions. It also should be used during group discussion following the observation session.

Worksheet 2–7: Know Yourself Checklist: Career Path Analysis

Use this worksheet to help employees focus on specifics concerning their needs, aspirations, and beliefs about work. Employees should bring the completed worksheet to career path discussions with their supervisors.

Worksheet 2–8: Employee Career Path Profile

Use this worksheet to help employees express their opinions about their jobs. These profiles allow management to determine quickly where problems or successes are evident.

Worksheet 2–9: Supervisor's Career Path Profile

Use this worksheet in tandem with Worksheet 2–8 to help supervisors assess an employee's skills and suggest training that will improve skills and productivity.

HOW TO DO JOB ANALYSIS OF JOB DESCRIPTION USING PEOPLE-DATA-THINGS-APPROACH

1. *Identify the Job.*

Fill in the date of your analysis and the exact title of the job as it appears on the written job description. Job titles often change with changing times, so it is important to include the date as part of your identification of the job being analyzed. Get the job description from the Personnel Office or from managers' files.

Example

Date: January 30, 19XX

Job Title: Vice President, Investments

2. *Analyze the Responsibilities/Duties of the Job.*

Categorize the responsibilities/duties of the job into the appropriate people-data-things columns. Critically read the job description for clues that guide you in organizing the duties of the job.

Look for the following "tell-tale" verbs to assist you:

people duties: facilitates, coordinates, conducts, implements, plans
data duties: documents, prepares, designs, monitors, calculates
things duties: assembles, transports, operates, repairs, demonstrates

Example

People Duties	Data Duties	Things Duties
manages office staff	chooses stocks for purchase	operates personal computer
interacts with clients	calculates returns and profits	provides word processing hardware and printers
presents investment seminars	develops formulas	produces materials to distribute at seminars
represents firm on the Chairman's Council	analyzes weekly reports	decorates offices in VP suite

WORKSHEET 2–1

JOB ANALYSIS OF JOB DESCRIPTION
USING PEOPLE-DATA-THINGS APPROACH

1. Date: _____

   Job Title: _____

2. <u>Instructions</u>: Using the written job description for this job, categorize the responsibilities/duties of the job into the appropriate columns.

People Duties	Data Duties	Things Duties

SAMPLE

JOB ANALYSIS OF JOB DESCRIPTION
USING PEOPLE-DATA-THINGS APPROACH

Date: December 19, 19XX

Job Title: Operations Manager

Instructions: Using the written job description for this job, categorize the responsibilities/duties of the job into the appropriate columns

People Duties	Data Duties	Things Duties
conducts operational reviews	tracks sales and service results	manages van fleet
implements corrective programs	evaluates methods and procedures	maintains automated tracking system
sponsors promotional programs	monitors quality assurance efforts	maintains product introduction center
coordinates product introductions	prepares budget and balance sheet	
conducts service audits		
supervises staff		
attends headquarters staff meetings		
serves on corporate Affirmative Action Group		

TRAINING TIP: Share results of job analyses with the personnel department. Although the techniques and tools of job analysis are primarily training's, folks in the personnel operation will probably find the results of using these tools useful in their work too.

The people-data-things approach to job analysis can be especially useful in employment interviewing and career counseling, functions typically carried out by the personnel department.

Check out your organization chart—if Training and Personnel both report to the same vice president, that's all the more reason for sharing information.

HOW TO CREATE A BAR CHART REPRESENTING JOB ANALYSIS OF JOB DESCRIPTION USING PEOPLE-DATA-THINGS APPROACH

This bar chart is a rough approximation of the job. It can be useful in presentations to management regarding training analysis and program design, and in individual discussions with persons currently holding this specific job or with persons being interviewed for this job. Because it is based on your company's specific job description and way of doing business, it will, of course, be your particular way of doing this job.

The bar chart is a helpful tool when you need to roughly estimate the efforts required to design training built around the people, data, and things that are unique to this specific job.

Instructions: Draw a horizontal line in each bar representing the percentage of the job that falls in each category—people, data, and things. Make this decision based on information on and analysis of the job description, as recorded on Worksheet 2–1. Fill in the bars below this line, so that each bar can be seen clearly in relationship to the other bars. Fill in the corresponding percentages on each blank line, for another graphic way of looking at the job.

Example

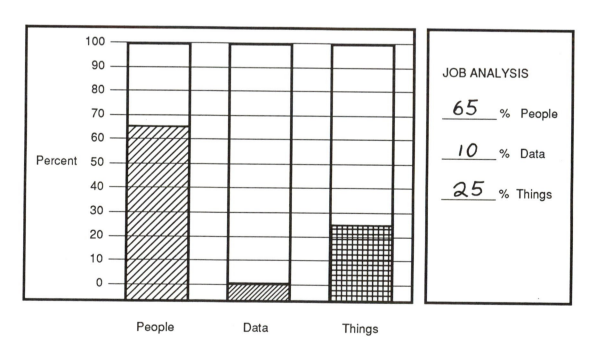

Job Title_____COSMETOLOGIST_____

WORKSHEET 2–2

BAR CHART REPRESENTING JOB ANALYSIS OF JOB DESCRIPTION USING PEOPLE-DATA-THINGS APPROACH

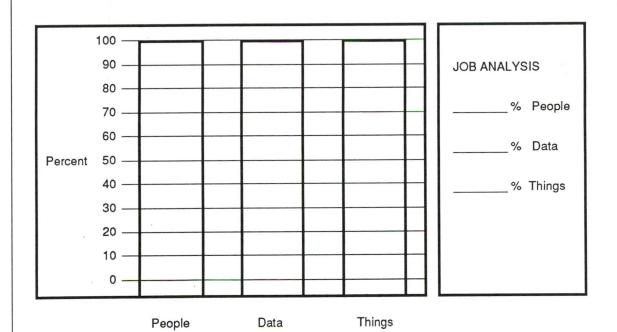

Job Title_____

HOW TO CONDUCT A JOB ANALYSIS USING A STRUCTURED
EMPLOYEE INTERVIEW: CLOSED QUESTION TECHNIQUE

For the purpose of job analysis, the structured employee interview consists of two phases:

1. a closed question phase, and
2. an open question phase.

Both kinds of questions are necessary when interviewing an employee during job analysis. Remember that the purpose of the job analysis is to get information to use in designing training.

The following instructions are for the closed question phase. Closed questions are those which can be answered with "yes," "no," or a single correct fill-in-the-blank type of answer.

TRAINING TIP: Most people find closed questions easier to answer than open questions, especially in a personnel context. It is, therefore, a good idea to begin an employee interview with closed questions. Limit the number of questions to no more than ten.

---

1. *Identify the job, the employee, and yourself.*
   Read from the interview form if you are doing a face-to-face interview. Be sure to verify the correct job title with the employee. If only you are writing the answers, give a copy of the interview form to the employee as a courtesy during the questioning.
2. *Structure the questions so that the answers will be short, unequivocal, and unambiguous.*

Examples

- Do you use word processing software in your job? _____
- What is your social security number? ____ ____ ____
- Are you a Certified Financial Planner (CFP)? _____

TRAINING TIP: A closed question interview form can be administered orally one to one, to a group during a staff meeting, or individually as a "take back to your desk" task.

WORKSHEET 2–3

JOB ANALYSIS USING
A STRUCTURED EMPLOYEE INTERVIEW:
CLOSED QUESTION TECHNIQUE

① _____   _____

                Job Title   Employee Being Interviewed

                                           _____ _____

                                          Interviewer   Date

② 1. On a scale of 1 to 10, how do you rate yourself in quality of your performance on this job? 1 is low; 10 is high. (Circle one number.)

                            (low)   1   2   3   4   5   6   7   8   9   10   (high)

    2. How long have you been in this specific job? _____

    3. What systems and equipment do you use on the job? _____

      _____

      _____

    4. What training have you had to help you do this job better? Give dates if possible.

      _____

      _____

    5. What courses, programs, or training aids do you think you need to help you do this job better? _____

      _____

      _____

    6. etc.

TEN GOOD REASONS FOR USING CLOSED QUESTIONS

1. They tend to be easy to answer.
2. They generally lead to "the facts."
3. There is usually no argument about the answer.
4. They generally do not intimidate.
5. They generally do not confuse.
6. They usually can be answered quickly.
7. They generally yield correct answers.
8. They generally do not need explanation.
9. They help build the respondent's confidence regarding answering questionnaires.
10. Responses to them are generally usable immediately.

JOB ANALYSIS USING
A STRUCTURED EMPLOYEE INTERVIEW:
CLOSED QUESTION TECHNIQUE

Laboratory Assistant	Jeffrey Field
Job Title	Employee Being Interviewed

Neil Wood	7/12/XX
Interviewer	Date

1. On a scale of 1 to 10, how do you rate yourself in quality of your performance on this job? 1 is low; 10 is high. (Circle one number.)

    (low)   1   2   3   4   5   6   ⑦   8   9   10   (high)

2. How long have you been in this specific job: 18 months

3. What systems and equipment do you use on the job? microscope, scalpel, culture dishes, glass slides, incubator, LSC statistical software package, mini computer, personal computer

4. What training have you had to help you do this job better? Give dates if possible. Lab Safety 2/XX; Basic Tissue Sampling 3/XX; Advanced Culture Techniques 6/XX

5. What courses, programs, or training aids do you think you need to help you do this job better? a newer model microscope with greater power, another course in using LSC software, a demonstration by Prism Company of their new staining dyes

HOW TO CONDUCT A JOB ANALYSIS USING A STRUCTURED EMPLOYEE INTERVIEW: OPEN QUESTION TECHNIQUE

For the purpose of job analysis, the structured employee interview consists of two phases:

1. a closed question phase, and
2. an open question phase.

Both kinds of questions are necessary when interviewing an employee during job analysis. Remember that the purpose of the job analysis is to get information to use in designing training.

The following instructions are for the open question phase. Open questions are those which require an explanatory or descriptive answer. Open questions lead to more discussion.

Open questioning is a valuable information-gathering technique. When you use it, be careful not to "close" the response prematurely. People like to be listened to—give your respondent the last word! You'll be surprised how much you'll learn by active listening and open questioning.

TRAINING TIP: Limit open question interviews to about 30 minutes in order to keep responses on target and to avoid fatigue. The employee's comfort level can be increased by holding a closed question interview immediately preceding open questioning.

---

1. *Ask questions in a friendly, relaxed, but serious way.*

    Examples of open questions:

    *   What was this factory like 15 years ago when you joined the company?
    *   Why do you find this brand of word processing software superior to other brands?

2. *Allow at least three minutes per response, and encourage the employee to "say more."*

3. *Record responses in an organized way.* Worksheet 2–4 is one way to do it.

    As the employee responds to an open question, listen carefully in order to analyze the response. Fill in the appropriate people, data, or things box across each row. Note important elements of the response in the Responses column.

4. *Summarize the interview at the end of it.* The people-data-things approach is one way. Get employee agreement.

    Example: It looks like we've defined this job as about a 90 percent "data" job. Do you agree?

WORKSHEET 2-4

JOB ANALYSIS USING A
STRUCTURED EMPLOYEE INTERVIEW:
OPEN QUESTION TECHNIQUE

_____   _____
Job Title   Employee Being Interviewed

                             _____ _____
                             Interviewer   Date

①.	People	Data	Things ③.	Responses ②.
1.				
2.				
3.				
4.				
5.				

④ *Summary*: It looks like we've defined this job as about a
_____ percent "_____" job. Do you agree?

37

FIVE RULES OF THUMB TO HELP YOU GET GOOD INFORMATION DURING OPEN QUESTIONING

1. Keep the questioning and responding going when you are getting good responses—use short, positive words of encouragement at short intervals such as "good," "I appreciate where you're coming from," "yes," "that's a valuable insight," "your comments are excellent."

2. Maintain smiling eye contact during questions and answers—don't let your respondent wander. Your eye contact can help motivate the respondent to keep focused on the question at hand.

3. Don't allow responses to degenerate into gripes. If your respondent begins to lose focus and starts to complain or "dump" on you, gently bring the respondent back on tack by asking him or her to "define that a little better," or to "explain that more, please." Use the terms "define" and "explain" to focus attention on a specific subject, thereby helping the respondent elaborate rather than digress into a gripe.

4. Keep your opinions to yourself. Don't be tempted to indicate agreement or disagreement with your respondent. Your role is to encourage the respondent's free response—be careful not to jeopardize this.

5. Verify any response that seems different or potentially controversial. Read it back to the respondent and say, "Do I have this response recorded correctly?"

JOB ANALYSIS USING A
STRUCTURED EMPLOYEE INTERVIEW:
OPEN QUESTION TECHNIQUE

Word Processing Correspondence
Secretary

         Job Title

Dawn Andrews

Employee Being Interviewed

Mary McDonald   3/11/XX

Interviewer   Date

	People	Data	Things	Responses
1. What factors contribute most to enabling you to do a good job?	80%	20%	—	—no interruptions —friendly co-workers —get the boss off my back —adequate training
2. How would you describe your interface with the equipment?	35%	—	65%	—half the stuff is obsolete —others hog the best terminals —too much glare in my corner
3. What do you think of the productivity measurement system currently in place?	80%	20%	—	—good standards —not communicated well enough —poor rewards —people who administer tests are too serious
4. Is this job what you expected it to be this year?	100%	—	—	—yes; boss is tough —yes; company is growing; lots of work —account reps get too much attention —no time for training

Summary: It looks like we've defined this job as about a
75 percent "people" job. Do you agree?

HOW TO ANALYZE A JOB BY USING THE EXPERT'S CRITICAL TASK/TRAINING MATRIX

Job analysis through analysis of expert performance is one way to identify elements of success on the job and to pinpoint what constitutes competent behavior.

While an expert's judgment is only one person's point of view, remember that expert performance is largely determined by others—experts are seldom only self-proclaimed. Experts have managed to uphold or elevate corporate or job standards, to demonstrate a consistently high performance level over time, to positively impact the work of those around them, and to significantly contribute to corporate profits.

Because of the expert's role in business relationships, the expert's self analysis can be a useful job analysis tool, especially if a survey form is presented as a Critical Task/Training Matrix.

The trainer's task is to design the survey form, to distribute it to the selected expert(s), and to collect and use the results of the expert analysis to design a training course or program.

Examples of how an expert might fill out a Critical Task/Training Matrix follow.

For the job of *Dispatcher*:

Critical Tasks	Creativity	Math/Number Facility	Memorization/Recall	Muscle Coordination	Oral/Verbal Expression	Organization	Reasoning	Speed	Teamwork	Written Expression
	Kinds of Training Needed									
1. Verify everyone's schedule every six hours						✓			✓	
2. Know at least four pieces of personal information about each driver			✓		✓	✓				
3. Know how to troubleshoot all communication equipment			✓				✓	✓		
4. Maintain computer-based assignment and tracking system						✓	✓		✓	

TRAINING TIP: Give the expert your personal attention. Include a personal note or cover letter with the survey form. Follow up the form with a phone call to be sure the expert understands what you want. Offer to review the survey in person if the expert prefers. Experts generally know that they're special, and they like to be treated that way.

WORKSHEET 2–5

JOB ANALYSIS USING THE EXPERT'S
CRITICAL TASK/TRAINING MATRIX

To the survey respondent:

You have been selected by our Training Department's job analysis team as a person with expertise in the job of _____ .

We need your help in accurately describing your job. Please respond to the items below so that your response describes the job as it is performed by an expert. This data will be used to design training programs.

Instructions:

Step 1: List 10–20 critical tasks of doing this job.

Step 2: Complete the matrix by checking the boxes appropriate to the kind of training needed to accomplish each task.

Please return completed matrix to _____

by _____ 19XX. Thank you very much.

Critical Tasks	Creativity	Math/Number Facility	Memorization/ Recall	Muscle Coordination	Oral/Verbal Expression	Organization	Reasoning	Speed	Teamwork	Written Expression	
					Kinds of Training Needed						
1.											
2.											
3.											
4.											
5.											
6.											

LIST OF POTENTIAL AREAS OF BEHAVIOR IN WHICH EXPERT TRAINING MIGHT BE REQUIRED

(Any of these could be used as a column heading on your Matrix.)

- Attitude towards self
- Attitude towards others
- Creativity
- Elaboration skill
- Estimation skill
- Evaluation skill
- Expansive thinking
- Flexibility
- Illustration skill
- Independence
- Inference skill
- Leadership
- Management
- Math facility
- Memorization and recall
- Muscle coordination
- Organization
- Originality
- Oral/verbal expression
- Prioritizing
- Reasoning
- Summarizing skill
- Speed
- Symbolic thinking
- Synthesizing skill
- Teamwork
- Translating/transforming
- Visualizing skill
- Written expression

JOB ANALYSIS USING THE EXPERT'S
CRITICAL TASK/TRAINING MATRIX

<u>To the survey respondent:</u>

You have been selected by our Training Department's job analysis team as a person with expertise in the job of <u>programmer</u>.

We need your help in accurately describing your job. Please respond to the items below so that your response describes the job as it is performed by an expert. This data will be used to design training programs.

<u>Instructions:</u>

Step 1: List 10–20 critical tasks of doing this job.

Step 2: Complete the matrix by checking the boxes appropriate to the kind of training needed to accomplish each task.

Please return completed matrix to <u>Training Manager</u> by <u>Friday 8/10/XX</u>. Thank you very much.

Critical Tasks	Creativity	Math/Number Facility	Memorization/Recall	Muscle Coordination	Oral/Verbal Expression	Organization	Reasoning	Speed	Teamwork	Written Expression
				Kinds of Training Needed						
1. choose the precisely appropriate language for the job	✓	✓	✓			✓				✓
2. flowchart the program to establish logic, although it takes time						✓	✓	✓		✓
3. maintain regular, periodic personal contact with orginator of the request for program					✓				✓	
4. seek regular periodic review of code, especially at decision points					✓		✓		✓	
5. verify system specs with peers and management as parts of the program are finished					✓		✓		✓	✓
6. analyze all expressions for clarity, leanness, and sufficiency	✓	✓				✓	✓			✓
7. construct a spare program	✓	✓				✓	✓	✓		✓
8. produce code sheets that are clean and neat										✓
9. pre-test completed sections before system test						✓	✓			

THE EXPERT MODEL: HOW TO ANALYZE A JOB BY OBSERVING AN EXPERT AT WORK

This method of analyzing a job is a systematic way of describing the on-the-job behavior of a person who is considered an expert at that job. The observer is a person who aspires to be an expert in a similar job. The trainer's role is to set the process in motion, briefing both the observer(s) and the expert regarding the intended outcome of the observation: a carefully designed training program to improve work and to maximize human resources. The trainer also functions as discussion facilitator after observations have been completed.

The method works best when at least three similar experts are observed on the job by three different aspiring experts. Or at minimum, the same expert is observed by three different aspiring experts. Each observation is conducted for the same amount of time, for example, three hours.

After the observations, the observers become a task force who meet with the training designer, who functions as discussion facilitator. Each observer takes a blank form to the observation session, and makes notes in the first two columns. Upon retrospection after the observation session, or during the task force discussion, the observer fills in the third column. It is this third column, "Possible Ways to Model Expert Behavior," from which training is designed.

Remember to brief observers to focus on expert behavior. Tell them to be alert to special things that experts do on the job. The observation form requires that critical behaviors be defined and advanced skills be listed. This form then becomes the task force guide.

The following is an example of how an observer might document an expert's behavior:

Job Title _____Retail Clerk_____

Broad Categories of Critical Expert Behavior	List of Advanced Skills Exhibited	Possible Ways to Model Expert Behavior
• maintains contact with all customers	• remembers stated interest of each browser • speaks to each customer as she or he enters area • maintains eye contact with each customer as she or he browses	• increase my verbal and nonverbal skills—practice on peers and with supervisor
• recalls inventory	• suggests alternatives from large stock items • describes best sellers	• learn more about inventory system

WORKSHEET 2–6

THE EXPERT MODEL:
OBSERVATION FORM AND TASK FORCE DISCUSSION GUIDE

Job Title _____

_____

Observer's Name   Date

_____

Expert's Name

_____

Expert's Address

_____

_____

Broad Categories of Critical Expert Behavior	List of Advanced Skills Exhibited	Possible Ways to Model Expert Behavior

A FEW POSTSCRIPTS ABOUT EXPERTS

PS #1.   Experts are found everywhere—among receptionists, file clerks, custo-
          dians, bus drivers, data entry operators—not just among highly edu-
          cated, highly paid, or highly skilled workers. Be careful not to restrict
          your search for expert behavior because of a potential bias in favor
          of high-end jobs.

PS #2.   Experts do things differently from other workers in the same job.
          Often this difference is found in small ways such as the frequency
          of an action (often vs. sometimes), the detail of an action (20 vs. 10,
          five fingers vs. three fingers, all dials vs. some dials), the use of
          elaboration and illustration (using analogies, examples, diagrams
          rather than lists only), or the way in which that person organizes
          and manages work (always starts meetings on time, handles paper
          only once, always ties up loose ends).

          When you observe an expert, look for the places where small
          differences are found.

PS #3.   Experts often have better preparation for work than others in similar
          jobs. Look for signs of this preparation edge in the two important
          areas of quality and quantity.

          Has the expert had the advantage of a mentor? an internship?
          an apprenticeship? a supervised independent project? a career-build-
          ing rotation assignment? paid leave to attend courses? a better univer-
          sity degree?

          Has the expert had more years on the job? more education? more
          focused job experience? more bosses? fewer bosses? more or fewer
          of anything that might make a difference in the expert's way of doing
          the job?

THE EXPERT MODEL:
OBSERVATION FORM AND TASK FORCE DISCUSSION GUIDE

Job Title Statistics

Instructor

Sandra Zimmer   May 15, 19XX
Observer's Name   **Date**
    Constantine Malcis

Expert's Name
    Quality Control Department

Expert's Address
    TTA and Company
    Newtown, NJ   00000

Broad Categories of Critical Expert Behavior	List of Advanced Skills Exhibited	Possible Ways to Model Expert Behavior
• shows personal interest in each student	• greets each by name as he or she enters classroom • during first hour of class, finds out each student's major job concern • remembers job concern of each student and uses it in various ways during the course • remembers first name of each student and addresses each student at least three times each hour	• learn and practice mnemonics and other memory and recall techniques • allow enough time before class to get and memorize the list of registered students
• uses feedback	• gives guidance and feedback on learning accomplishments to class or individuals at least once every 15 minutes • seeks and incorporates comments from class in subsequent lessons	• practice giving feedback on a class of "fake" students—get someone to monitor and time me—and give me feedback
• presents content using analogies and examples	• uses a variety of presentation techniques • compares and contrasts • gives examples of what the topics are not, as well as what they are	• revise my course to include more examples from actual business situations

HOW TO ANALYZE A JOB THROUGH CAREER PATH DISCUSSION

Most employees welcome the opportunity to discuss their career path with supervisors. In order for trainers to benefit from this personnel management process, they need to work with supervisors and employees before career path discussions occur.

The trainer's task is one of helping the employee focus on specifics of his or her own actions, understandings, and beliefs about work. Career path analysis and discussion yield information about what training an individual would like to have in order to improve the job. Information is also produced during career path discussions that define a particular employee's sense of what the company can give him or her in order to continue to nurture a productive employee.

This kind of job analysis has limitations because it is highly specific to one individual, but it often yields insights about job improvement that cannot be uncovered in other more behaviorally oriented job analysis methods.

Career path discussions are subjective because they deal with attitudes, beliefs, plans, and outcomes. The trainer's best hope for getting usable information for development of training comes with being involved in the design and distribution of recording forms used during career path discussions.

Three worksheets are included on the following pages to help the trainer. These are:

- Worksheet 2–7 Know Yourself Checklist (for the employee)
- Worksheet 2–8 Employee Career Path Profile (for the employee)
- Worksheet 2–9 Supervisor's Career Path Profile (for the supervisor).

After the career path discussion has occurred, it is the supervisor's responsibility to share the checklist and profile information with the training designer. It is the training manager's responsibility to see to it that this happens.

TRAINING TIP: Before career path discussion occurs, provide the employee with some structure for thinking about the job so that the discussion with his or her supervisor doesn't become a gripe session. (The Know Yourself Checklist is one kind of structure.) Help the employee to focus on opportunities for career growth through training.

JOB ANALYSIS THROUGH CAREER PATH DISCUSSION: KNOW YOURSELF CHECKLIST

Make sure the employee understands the instructions before completing this form.

Examples for the trainer

Following are some examples of kinds of responses you can expect employees to make. Encourage the employee to record responses on another sheet of paper if he or she wants to say more.

	Comments
1. What results do I want?	1. 20 percent over the average
2. How much recognition do I need?	2. daily compliments from either supervisor or peers; at least once a week from supervisor
3. How much energy do I have?	3. probably not enough to consistently perform the lifting tasks of the job without eventual injury
4. What factors release my energy?	4. bonus; opportunity for overtime—I like to work
5. How does working environment affect me?	5. dark warehouse makes me want to fall asleep

TRAINING TIP: As you review the employee's comments, look for responses that give you ideas for action. In this example, comment 3 should alert you that perhaps a quick course in safe lifting is required for at least this person. Be alert for similar responses from other employees: Perhaps an entire group of employees could benefit from a safe lifting course.

On the other hand, comments 4 and 5 suggest action, but not training action. It is your responsibility to pass along these comments to other departments that might be interested in them or that can make a correction (e.g., more lighting in the warehouse) in order to improve productivity. Remember that training is not always the only way!

A WORD TO THE WISE—

Supervisors and personnel representatives will probably be somewhat reluctant to have trainers involved in employees' career path discussions. As a trainer, your best shot at getting the information you need from these discussions is to be helpful to the supervisor.

Give the supervisor some carefully written questions that you'd like included in any career path discussions, and do this far enough ahead so that your questions can be incorporated into any existing personnel questionnaires—and far enough ahead to get necessary personnel department approval regarding language, EEO concerns, and so on. Make it a point to sit down with the supervisor to explain why it is that you want information, and how this information regarding training will be useful to the company through more productive employees.

The supervisor is your key to success. Offer information and real support early in the process—share your secretary to help revise existing questionnaires, pay for duplicating out of your budget, help schedule career path discussions or make followup reminder phone calls, help distribute and explain the new forms, be available if employees have questions, offer to help tally results, offer to co-author and draft a report to the personnel manager on the career path discussion process. Work with the supervisor to make training be seen as a viable opportunity of employment.

WORKSHEET 2–7

KNOW YOURSELF CHECKLIST: CAREER PATH ANALYSIS

To the employee: Prior to career path or job advancement discussions with your supervisor, review this checklist by yourself. Use the "comments" column to record any ideas that can jog your memory or help you focus your thoughts. Take this checklist with you to use during discussion with your supervisor, and leave it for your supervisor to forward to the Training Department. Knowing yourself and being able to articulate this knowledge to others is often the key to successful career planning and advancement.

This information will be shared with the Training Department in order to maximize opportunities for your growth and to improve the work of this corporation.

		Comments
1. What results do I want?	1.	
2. How much recognition do I need?	2.	
3. How much energy do I have?	3.	
4. What factors release my energy?	4.	
5. How does working environment affect me?	5.	
6. Do I work best alone or in groups?	6.	
7. How do I respond to criticism?	7.	
8. What do I do to turn others off?	8.	
9. Am I a good listener?	9.	
10. Do I work slowly or quickly?	10.	
11. Do I like to learn?	11.	
12. What is my best learning style?	12.	
13. What do I value on the job?	13.	
14. Can I give and receive feedback?	14.	
15. Do I like to compete?	15.	
16. Why should the company value me?	16.	
17. What are my personal goals?	17.	
18. Do I prefer to lead or be led?	18.	
19. What are my weaknesses?	19.	
20. What are my strengths?	20.	

JOB ANALYSIS THROUGH CAREER PATH DISCUSSION: EMPLOYEE CAREER PATH PROFILE AND SUPERVISOR'S CAREER PATH PROFILE

The next two worksheets make up the Career Path Profile. One worksheet is completed by the employee; the other by the supervisor. Both worksheets are forwarded to the Training Department after the career path discussion has occurred between employee and supervisor.

Using a rating scale helps the supervisor see at a glance an employee's profile of opinion about the job. The profiles of all employees within a supervisory unit taken together can be a vivid graphic representation of areas of satisfaction or dissatisfaction, allowing management to see quickly where problems or successes are evident. Trainers can find useful information for development of training programs in the Career Path Profile.

Note that the Supervisor's Career Path Profile requires the supervisor to collect and record training information. The reasons for supervisory involvement in training documentation during career path discussion are several:

- Supervisors have to release employees from regular work to attend training
- Training fees are borne by a supervisor's budget
- Promotion is generally tied to acquiring new skills; supervisors need to know where the employee stands regarding skill level
- Companies often have policies regarding training and Affirmative Action; upper management and federal monitors want to know what training plan is in place for individuals.

The following pages contain a blank worksheet and a completed sample for each Career Path Profile:

- Worksheet 2–8: Employee Career Path Profile
- Worksheet 2–9: Supervisor's Career Path Profile

WORKSHEET 2–8

EMPLOYEE CAREER PATH PROFILE

To the employee: This Career Path Profile will be used to help you progress beyond your current level of productivity through training opportunities during the next 24 months.

Please complete the profile and return it to your supervisor by _____ 19XX. Within two weeks, your supervisor will review your responses and meet with you to discuss the completed Career Path Profile. Thank you for your attention.

Biographical Information

Name _____   Date _____

Job Title _____   Social Security # _____

Highest Degree or Diploma _____   Birth Date _____   Sex _____

Number of Years in Current Job _____   Number of Years in This Company _____

Desired Job Within 24 Months _____

Job Satisfaction Information

Place an X on the rating scale after each item indicating your satisfaction with that item.

	Dissatisfied	Mildly Dissatisfied	Neutral	Mildly Satisfied	Satisfied
1. Pay					
2. Benefits					
3. Bonuses and awards					
4. Promotion policies and practices					
5. Job description					
6. Working conditions					
7. Relationship with peers					
8. Support from supervisor					
9. Computer and systems support					
10. Clerical and staff support					
11. Career guidance					
12. Professional growth opportunities					
13. Training opportunities					
14. Recognition					

EMPLOYEE CAREER PATH PROFILE

To the employee: This Career Path Profile will be used to help you progress beyond your current level of productivity through training opportunities during the next 24 months.

Please complete the Profile and return it to your supervisor by January 4, 19XX. Within two weeks, your supervisor will review your responses and meet with you to discuss the completed Career Path Profile. Thank you for your attention.

Biographical Information

Kathleen O'Brien	December 14, 19XX
Name	**Date**

Manager of Applications Engineers	XXX XX XXXX
Job Title	**Social Security #**

MS Chemical Engineering	3/17/XX	F
Highest Degree or Diploma	**Birth Date**	**Sex**

four	eight
Number of Years in Current Job	**Number of Years in This Company**

Director of Engineering
Desired Job Within 24 Months

Job Satisfaction Information

Place an X on the rating scale after each item indicating your satisfaction with that item.

	Dissatisfied	Mildly Dissatisfied	Neutral	Mildly Satisfied	Satisfied
1. Pay			X		
2. Benefits					X
3. Bonuses and awards				X	
4. Promotion policies and practices				X	
5. Job description					X
6. Working conditions		X			
7. Relationship with peers				X	
8. Support from supervisor				X	
9. Computer and systems support	X				
10. Clerical and staff support		X			
11. Career guidance		X			
12. Professional growth opportunities				X	
13. Training opportunities			X		
14. Recognition			X		

WORKSHEET 2–9

SUPERVISOR'S CAREER PATH PROFILE

To the supervisor: Please complete this Career Path Profile indicating your assessment of this employee's training skill levels and training needs for the next 24 months. This data will be used to improve training and enhance productivity. This profile is intended to be used after discussion with the employee regarding the Employee Career Path Profile. Please forward to the Training Manager by _____ 19XX. Thank you very much.

_____   _____

Employee's Name   **Date**

_____

Supervisor's Name

_____

Employee's Current Job Title/Classification

Employee's Desired Job Within 24 Months:

_____

Employee's Relevant Prior Training or Testing:

_____

_____

_____

List of Required Entry-Level Skills for Desired Job	Employee's Skill Status		Training Suggested During Next 24 Months
	Yes	No	

SUPERVISOR'S CAREER PATH PROFILE

To the Supervisor: Please complete this Career Path Profile indicating your assessment of this employee's training skill levels and training needs for the next 24 months. This data will be used to improve training and enhance productivity. This profile is intended to be used after discussion with the employee regarding the Employee Career Path Profile. Please forward to the Training Manager by September 1, 19XX. Thank you very much.

Alfonso Vincenzi   8/16/XX

Employee's Name   **Date**

Gloria Urbano

Supervisor's Name

Account Representative, Small Accounts

Employee Current Job Title/Classification

Employee's Desired Job Within 24 Months: Regional Sales Manager
Employee's Relevant Prior Training or Testing: fluent in Italian, recently completed course in conversational French, taught in-house course in Basic Salesmanship for all new account reps for 3 years

List of Required Entry-Level Skills for Desired Job	Employee's Skill Status		Training Suggested During Next 24 Months
	Yes	**No**	
• conversational Italian	X		
• written Italian	X		
• conversational French	X		
• written French		X	French Immersion Weekend at Language Institute
• issue contracts between companies across political borders		X	International Contracting at World Trade Center
• manage account reps in regional office		X	Company courses: • Benefits and Bonuses • Motivational Systems • Consulting Accounting

CHAPTER 3 _____

HOW TO DO TASK _____
ANALYSIS _____

Good training aims to improve the way a job is done. Two basic kinds of learned behavior are cognitive (knowledge-based) behavior and motor (skills-based) behavior. When skillfully designed and delivered, training improves both.

Training lessons, exercises, courses, and programs are built around the tasks that make up these two kinds of job behavior. The goal of training design and delivery is to enable trainees to do something differently—to change their behavior—in order to improve the way a job is done. Techniques for teaching and learning motor tasks are different from techniques for teaching and learning cognitive tasks.

Training for Cognitive Tasks

Training designed around cognitive tasks is more difficult than other types of training. It is hard to measure success in accomplishing cognitive tasks during the training session itself, since success may only be evident long after training is over. Take, for example, a training program designed to help managers conduct better performance evaluations of employees. The success of the training cannot be finally determined until each manager has actually evaluated an employee's performance during his or her annual (or semi-annual) review. The actual performance evaluation may take place months after the training program has ended.

Advanced-level training in cognitive tasks focuses on analysis, synthesis, application, evaluation—in short, on problem-solving and decision-making.

Training for Motor Tasks

Training for motor tasks is sometimes called "hands-on" training. It is best done on the actual equipment used on the job—a word processor or a piece of machinery, for example. If this is not possible, tasks can be taught on simulated equipment. Practice is often the key to successful performance of motor tasks.

WHAT CONSTITUTES A TASK?

As they develop training programs, instructional designers focus on the smallest essential part of a job. This element is known as a *task*.

A task is a discrete, meaningful part of doing a job. It can be described in simple terms. It has a starting point and an ending point. A task is usually related to a standard, so that its accomplishment can be measured. Good training designers think about how to measure task performance while they design lessons.

Examples of tasks include:

Cognitive Tasks	*Motor Tasks*
• Add the column of figures	• Dry-mop the corridor
• Translate the press release into Spanish	• Align the pins
• Recall the five points of the manager's presentation	• Rotate the wheel
• De-bug the program	• Three-hole punch the document
	• Sign checks

WHAT'S INVOLVED IN TASK ANALYSIS

Task analysis is the process of finding out what tasks are necessary to do a job right. Task analysis is always done in the context of a specific job. It usually involves interviews with people who are doing or trying to do a specific job. The analysis provides the raw material for designing training lessons.

You can perform task analysis in a number of ways:

- talking to experts
- analyzing survey results
- analyzing documentation such as performance reviews
- analyzing equipment and usage logs
- checking error rates
- checking frequency counts
- looking at output and productivity measures
- systematically observing someone at work.

The end result of task analysis is a task list for a particular job. You write learning objectives for course participants based on this list of tasks, and the list represents the range of content for the training experience.

Task lists are often presented in chart or matrix form. They generally are presented in one of several ways:

- as groupings of tasks
- in hierarchical order beginning with the most important task
- by assigned weighting factors in terms of their importance to the job.

In addition, tasks are often assigned a difficulty index or coded for frequency of use on the job.

HOW TASK ANALYSIS FACILITATES GOOD TRAINING
PROGRAM DESIGN

Task analysis facilitates training program design by providing you with a description of the fundamental elements of a job. You write training lessons and exercises based on these actual job elements.

Here's an example:

Task: The worker lifts off transfer letter(s) without
leaving any marks.

Training exercise for doing this:

1. Position the transfer sheet over the blank area of your page, aligning the rows of transfer guide marks.
2. Grasp the transfer stylus as you would grasp a pencil.
3. Hold the transfer sheet onto your page firmly with your other hand, or with masking tape at the corners, so that the pages do not slide.
4. Press the transfer stylus firmly at the top of the letter(s) to be transferred, in order to establish contact between the transfer sheet and your page.
5. Gently pull the transfer stylus down over the letter(s) to be transferred. (With a firm contact at the top, the phenomenon of friction transfer will allow the letter to "jump" from the transfer sheet to your blank page with only a gentle pulling motion, and will not leave any marks.)
6. Burnish the newly transferred letter lightly through a silicon sheet with the flat end of the transfer stylus. Once is enough.

As you can see from this example, it is not enough to simply say to a trainee, "Lift off the letter from the transfer sheet." You have to spell out a specific, detailed method for doing this in the training manual. By breaking down each observed task into parts that can be taught and learned, you help trainees accomplish the task. A classroom full of trainees can master all parts of the task, and the instructor can provide help and guidance to individuals on various parts of the task with which they might have difficulty.

Task analysis is important to good training design because it provides the structure for accounting for individual differences among trainees. When task analysis is part of training design, training is fairer in terms of opportunity of employment and employee development.

In the example above, all six steps—actually discrete tasks in themselves—are motor tasks. They require dexterity and coordination of eye and hand muscles. Step five also requires mastery of the cognitive task of "translating" the concept of friction to the situation of transferring lettering. You could probably teach this cognitive task using question and answer dialogue, drawings on a flip chart, or demonstration. You could probably teach the motor tasks by having trainees practice the steps until they get each step right. Before practicing the motor tasks, you might also have to teach the cognitive task of identifying the equipment and supplies to be used. To do this, you might use a wall chart or slide identifying the equipment and supplies, allowing the trainee to refer to the description as often as needed in order to feel secure about the identity of the materials being used.

HOW TO USE TASK ANALYSIS IN TRAINING DESIGN

There are a number of ways you can use task analysis as the basis for good training design. The first step, of course, is to actually identify, group, and index the tasks of a job. From there, you can sort tasks by type and level of difficulty in order to design appropriate training exercises.

Designing Training Around Knowledge-Based (Cognitive) Tasks

By classifying or sorting cognitive tasks, you will find it is much easier to set up learning situations that reinforce each other and are cost-effective for your organization.

For example, let's say that a trainer knows that about two-thirds of all the tasks of a job require only simple cognitive skills, such as reading labels on items or recognizing a color code. He or she can probably carry out the training in an instructional setting that is not very demanding on the instructor. Classes could be large, very little trainee interaction would be required, a lecture format could be used, less experienced instructors could be used, and so forth.

On the other hand, let's consider more complex cognitive tasks, such as monitoring complex chemical processes and troubleshooting deviations from standard, or applying a newly-learned formula to a seemingly insolvable math problem. In cases like these, the trainer would have to devise a learning situation where individual trainees received maximum feedback from the instructor and had ample opportunity to explore ideas in a laboratory, a workshop, or through dialogue with peers and experts.

When you classify the cognitive tasks of a job before designing a lesson or course, you have a very good chance of creating training around those tasks that employees will say is exciting, challenging, stimulating, and right on target.

Designing Training Around Skills-Based (Motor) Tasks

Tasks within the motor (sometimes called the *psychomotor*) domain are classified or sorted by level of difficulty. This sorting by level helps you to design training appropriate to each level of task.

In all training, your goal is to make the resources expended have a positive impact on the corporate bottom line. With motor skills training in particular, the payoff can be swift and dramatic if you teach new skills appropriately, focusing on the correct skill level.

Motor skills training can also be particularly satisfying to you as a training designer because of its cause-and-effect nature. For example, teaching a receptionist to efficiency route phone calls has measurable results in terms of numbers of completed call transfers and satisfied customers. Similarly, training an entire shop floor of workers to evacuate the building quickly in a fire has measurable impact that shows up in safety records, insurance costs, and OSHA ratings. In both cases, good training results in good performance.

Discrepancy Analysis

Discrepancy analysis is done in order to find out exactly where training is needed. It should always be done in a nonthreatening way—never by a person's supervisor or anyone having authority over an employee's pay. A member of the training staff is the best choice for an observer.

By observing an employee perform his or her job, you can determine whether he or she is performing a specific task at 100 percent standard. If not, your discrepancy analysis will help determine where specific training is needed.

Discrepancy analysis is conducted in order to identify tasks that can be improved by training. Keep in mind, however, that training is not always the solution to performance problems. Sometimes poor performance is an attitudinal or compensation problem, or is related to poor health or personal factors. In cases like these, training may not be the solution of choice.

HOW TO USE THE WORKSHEETS IN THIS CHAPTER

The following worksheets for doing task analysis present options in training design.

Worksheets 3–1 through 3–4: Breaking a Job Down Into Tasks

Worksheets 3–1 through 3–4 are meant to be used together to form a task analysis. In this set of worksheets, the tasks of a job first are identified, then grouped, and then indexed. Each succeeding worksheet builds upon the previous worksheet. Together, they make up the task analysis.

Worksheet 3–5: Knowledge-Based (Cognitive) Tasks

Worksheet 3–5 is used to classify or sort cognitive tasks in order to design appropriate training.

Worksheet 3–6: Skills-Based (Motor) Tasks

Worksheet 3–6 is used to classify or sort tasks within the motor domain in order to facilitate training design.

Worksheet 3–7: Discrepancy Analysis: Performance Discrepancy Observer's Checklist

Worksheet 3–7 is an observer's checklist form to be used during observation of a person at work. It is constructed from a grouped task list such as the one created on Worksheet 3–3.

HOW TO BREAK A JOB DOWN INTO TASKS:
BACKGROUND INFORMATION

Worksheets 3–1 through 3–4, taken together, comprise a task analysis when completed. By the time Worksheet 3–4, "Indexed Task List," is completed, the training designer has a good idea of what kinds of tasks make up a particular job and what kind of emphasis might be indicated during training of persons in jobs like that one.

In practice, trainers generally have five ways of doing task analysis:

- analysis of job description and extrapolation of tasks from verbiage of the job description
- analysis of job-related documents
- observation of people at work, directly or on videotape
- discussion with people about specific jobs
- extrapolation of tasks from a customer's stated training need.

It is critical that any source of data used for task analysis is considered valid by all parties concerned with the outcome of training.

TRAINING TIP: The wise training designer will always seek multiple opinions about which source of data to use for any task analysis. If direct observation of a worker is chosen, be sure to arrange for at least two observers; if analysis of documents is chosen, arrange for a review of the results of analysis by colleagues; if you choose to rely on a customer's stated need, be sure that the statement is not just one person's opinion.

Background Information

1. Identify the job by its correct job title.
2. Identify the source(s) of data used in the task analysis by checking all appropriate boxes.
3. Tell how you actually did the task analysis.
   Example: Watched six one-hour videotapes made on four different days. Analyzed the tasks into three categories of cognitive behavior and two categories of motor behavior.
4. List several other jobs closely related to this job. This often helps clarify which tasks distinguish the job you are reviewing.

WORKSHEET 3–1

BREAKING A JOB DOWN INTO TASKS: BACKGROUND INFORMATION

1. Name of Job _____

2. Source of Data: (check as many as apply)*

   · Interview with job performer ☐   · Mailed survey/questionnaire ☐
   · Interview with expert ☐   · Performance review document ☐
   · Interview with supervisor ☐   · Equipment usage log ☐
   · Direct observation ☐   · Schematic, prints ☐
   · Video observation ☐   · Other ☐

   _____

3. Brief narrative describing method of analysis: _____

   _____

   _____

   _____

   _____

4. Three other jobs closely related to this job:

   _____

   _____

   _____

* Attach raw data to your task list as an appendix.

HOW TO BREAK A JOB DOWN INTO TASKS: COMPOSITE LIST OF TASKS

This is the first working document to use during the observation or analysis of paperwork. You will probably find it easier simply to list any task you observe being exhibited, in more or less a chronological order, during the course of the observation or analysis session. Later you will go back to this worksheet and reorganize the tasks listed here.

Remember to watch for the smallest element of behavior on the job which is necessary to successful performance of the job. The goal is to provide information on which to build training. Don't record tasks that are unnecessary.

Instructions: Begin each task with an active verb. Keep the description of the task short. Add many more pages if you need them.

Examples

LIST OF TASKS

1. Smile at the customer.
2. Open the bag.
3. Place the bag on the shelf.
4. Begin bagging as soon as about half of the order is rung up.
5. Put large cans and bottles on the bottom.
6. Put meats, fish, and poultry in plastic bags.
7. Put breads on the top.
8. Put frozen foods in freezer bags.
9. Place produce where it won't be crushed.
10. Put a "Paid" sticker on items too big for bags.

Each of the above tasks can be taught and learned. Some trainees will learn some tasks faster than other trainees, some trainees will get it right the first time they try to do a task, and some trainees will do it right sometimes and not do it right other times. Training that is designed around accomplishing very specific, small tasks provides the best assurance that most trainees will learn to do most tasks of the job.

WORKSHEET 3–2

BREAKING A JOB DOWN INTO TASKS: COMPOSITE LIST
OF TASKS

Name of Job _____

Date of Task Listing _____

LIST OF TASKS
(Begin each with an active verb)

1.	21.
2.	22.
3.	23.
4.	24.
5.	25.
6.	26.
7.	27.
8.	28.
9.	29.
10.	30.
11.	31.
12.	32.
13.	33.
14.	34.
15.	35.
16.	36.
17.	37.
18.	38.
19.	39.
20.	40.

(Add more pages if necessary to complete the composite list.)

HOW TO BREAK A JOB DOWN INTO TASKS: GROUPINGS OF TASKS

Worksheet 3–3 is used after the composite list of tasks has been completed. If a direct observation is used in order to generate that composite list, chances are that the list will be in chronological order—not necessarily in any logical order or order of difficulty or importance to the whole job.

The training designer now has the job of grouping the tasks recorded on Worksheet 3–2 into some logical categories. The reason for this reorganization is to provide a structure for the eventual creation of "units" of training. At this point of analysis, the training designer is beginning to plan for one- or two-hour sessions, or 15- or 30-minute lessons. Each category of grouped tasks could possibly become a unit of instruction.

Instructions: *Re-list all tasks on the composite list (Worksheet 3–2) on Worksheet 3–3*. Include at least five tasks in each category. (If there are fewer than five tasks in a category, it probably isn't a separate category. Take another look at the task—perhaps it is actually more than one task.)

Example

The job of *Receptionist* includes logical groupings such as:

Group 1 Tasks

Category: greeting tasks
1.
2.
3.
4.
5.

Group 2 Tasks

Category: message taking tasks
1.
2.
3.
4.
5.

Group 3 Tasks

Category: filing tasks
1.
2.
3.
4.
5.

Group 4 Tasks

Category: office maintenance tasks
1.
2.
3.
4.
5.

WORKSHEET 3–3

BREAKING A JOB DOWN INTO TASKS:
GROUPINGS OF TASKS

Name of Job _____

Group 1 Tasks

Category: _____

1.

2.

3.

4.

5.

Group 2 Tasks

Category: _____

1.

2.

3.

4.

5.

Group 3 Tasks

Category: _____

1.

2.

3.

4.

5.

Group 4 Tasks

Category: _____

1.

2.

3.

4.

5.

(Add more pages if necessary to complete the groupings of tasks.)

BREAKING A JOB DOWN INTO TASKS: GROUPINGS OF TASKS

Name of Job Financial Counselor

Group 1 Tasks

Category: Client interface tasks

1. List at least three bits of personal information per client.
2. Begin each day by writing thank you notes to at least three clients.
3. Schedule appointments in the client's office whenever possible.
4. Introduce one new service at each client meeting.
5. Get client agreement within the first 10 minutes of the meeting.
6. Allow client to lead the dialogue for two-thirds of the meeting.
7. Go for the close after client has made five assenting comments.

Group 2 Tasks

Category: Marketing tasks

1. Attend civic and professional group meetings to make contacts.
2. Enter potential client information on formatted cards.
3. Prepare periodic mailings.
4. Develop coded file of referrals.
5. Telephone seven "cold calls" each day.
6. Meet four potential clients for lunch each week.
7. Follow up each contact within 10 days.

Group 3 Tasks

Category: Data-crunching tasks

1. Prepare protocol for client to use to organize data.
2. Review protocol with client in person or by phone.
3. Get client to sign pension information release form.
4. Get copies of client's tax returns for five years.
5. Verify adequacy of software to handle data on a case by case basis.
6. Code all input data on input form (from software company).
7. Key in data using client protocol and input form.
8. Do a trial run on inexpensive paper.

ALTERNATE METHOD FOR GROUPING OF TASKS— CARD SYSTEM

Some task analysts prefer to use index cards during this grouping stage of task analysis. to do this, place each task from the composite list (Worksheet 3–2) on a separate index card. Lay out all the cards on a big table and separate them into logical categories. Then make your list (Worksheet 3–3) from the cards. It is often useful to have a colleague discuss the cards with you to verify the composition of each group of tasks.

Example

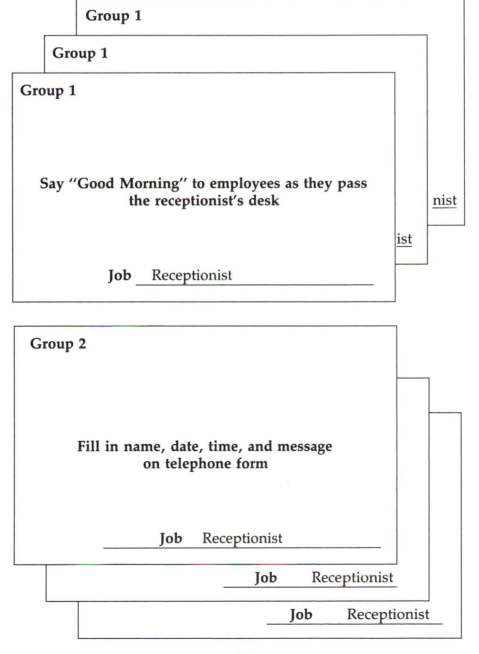

HOW TO BREAK A JOB DOWN INTO TASKS: INDEXED TASK LIST

Worksheet 3–4 is used in the final phase of task analysis. Use the groupings of tasks compiled on Worksheet 3–3 to fill out this worksheet.

Your task here is to determine several indexes that can apply to all categories of tasks. Indexes will vary from job to job. From the analysis of each task according to these indexes, you will be able to write lessons and lab exercises in the correct proportion for training to be efficient and effective. It does no good, for example, to spend an hour of training time to teach a task which has very little value to management or is very easy to learn. Remember, in training design, you write lessons for adults to accomplish some business improvement.

Instructions

1. Using Worksheet 3–3, determine several appropriate indexes for the groupings of tasks.
2. Analyze each task according to these indexes and record the analysis on the chart.

Example

INDEXED TASK LIST

Name of Job Receptionist

Index 1 frequency of task in 2-hour period (8–10 A.M.)

Index 2 difficulty level (hard, medium, easy)

Index 3 value to client (high, medium, low)

Index 4 value to superior (high, medium, low)

Group 1 Tasks

Category: Greeting tasks

	Index 1 Frequency in 2 Hours	Index 2 Difficulty h,m,e	Index 3 Client Value h,m,l	Index 4 Supervisor Value h,m,l
1. Say "Good Morning" to employees	ⅢⅢ ///	easy	low	high
2. Greet clients who phone in	////	medium	high	high
3. Take employee sick calls	//	medium	low	medium
4. Get business cards of walk-ins	/	easy	high	high
5. Wear appropriate dress/grooming	NA	medium	high	high

BREAKING A JOB DOWN INTO TASKS: INDEXED TASK LIST

INDEXED TASK LIST

Name of Job _____

    Index 1 _____

    Index 2 _____ ① _____

    Index 3 _____

    Index 4 _____

Group 1 Tasks

Category: _____   *Index 1*   *Index 2*   *Index 3*   *Index 4*

1.

2.

3.

4.   ②

5.

6.

7.

8.

9.

10.

(Add more pages for additional groups of tasks.)

HOW TO IDENTIFY KNOWLEDGE-BASED (COGNITIVE) TASKS

In addition to analysis that is based on an indexed task list such as that on Worksheet 3–4, the tasks of a job are often identified and analyzed according to the domains of intellect the tasks represent.

Most training tasks fall into either the knowledge or the skills domain of intellect. It is useful when designing the objectives for learners to know the composite intellectual categorization of tasks that make up the training experience. Most courses have portions that are focused on cognitive tasks and portions that are focused on skills (motor) tasks. Techniques of teaching appropriate for learning cognitive tasks are different from techniques of teaching for learning motor tasks. It is helpful for the training designer to have identified and analyzed the cognitive and motor tasks of training before the course is written so that appropriate teaching techniques can be developed and used.

The knowledge-based domain of intellect, often called the cognitive domain, has been identified and explored thoroughly by Benjamin S. Bloom. His pioneering work, *Taxonomy of Educational Objectives, Book 1, Cognitive Domain* (New York: Longman, Inc., 1954), has had wide acceptance in the education and training communities ever since its publication. The cognitive domain, according to Bloom, is characterized by tasks that require the doer to:

- recognize, label, recall
- comprehend, re-state, paraphrase
- use what was learned
- make abstractions of learned concepts
- analyze, figure out
- synthesize, re-combine
- evaluate

The above tasks are listed in hierarchical order, from simple to complex.

Instructions

Group the tasks identified on Worksheet 3–2 into three groups—simple cognitive tasks, mid-range cognitive tasks, and complex cognitive tasks. Use Bloom's seven categories (listed above) to guide your choice of group.

The following verbs will alert you to the possibility that the task is a cognitive task:

calculate	differentiate	reduce
categorize	estimate	represent
choose	formulate	revise
compare	identify	simplify
compute	list	solve
conclude	match	specify
contrast	plan	translate
define	predict	verify

Example

Simple cognitive task: Enter the data on a code sheet ("paraphrase," "re-state")
Mid-range cognitive task: Choose the heaviest item ("use what was learned")
Complex cognitive task: Terminate John's employment ("synthesize," "evaluate")

WORKSHEET 3–5

KNOWLEDGE-BASED (COGNITIVE) TASKS

Name of Job _____

Simple Cognitive Tasks

-
-
-
-
-
-
-
-

-
-
-
-
-
-
-
-

Mid-Range Cognitive Tasks

-
-
-
-
-
-
-
-

-
-
-
-
-
-
-
-

Complex Cognitive Tasks

-
-
-
-
-
-
-

-
-
-
-
-
-
-

(Expand each section if necessary by adding more pages.)

HOW TO IDENTIFY SKILLS-BASED (MOTOR) TASKS

Use Worksheet 3–6 in the same way as you use Worksheet 3–5.

Worksheet 3–6 is used to group the tasks identified on Worksheet 3–2 (composite task list) into three groups of motor tasks—simple motor tasks, mid-range motor tasks, and complex motor tasks. Motor tasks are trained differently than cognitive tasks are. It is important during task analysis to recognize and identify the motor task requirements of a job, so that appropriate training can be designed.

Most jobs involve human interface with equipment, and this requires the use of motor skills. These skills require eye-hand coordination, skillful use of finger, hand, arm, or leg movements, or proper use of large muscles such as those in the back or shoulders. These tasks are motor tasks, sometimes called psychomotor tasks, and have in common the obvious involvement of the trainee's muscle, or motor, system. Technical training often has a motor component that is strong in eye-hand coordination tasks. (Technical training generally also has a cognitive component with strong requirements for computational and analytical tasks.)

Pioneering work in analyzing and categorizing psychomotor tasks was done by Elizabeth J. Simpson in 1966. Her work followed the work of Benjamin S. Bloom. In her book, *The Classification of Objectives, Psychomotor Domain* (Urbana: University of Illinois, 1966), she characterized the psychomotor domain of intellect by tasks that require the doer to:

- perceive a stimulus
- prepare for appropriate action
- respond on command or cue
- establish a pattern of action
- perform consistently over time

The above tasks are listed in hierarchical order, from simple to complex.

Instructions

Group the tasks identified on Worksheet 3–2 into three groups—simple motor tasks, mid-range motor tasks, and complex motor tasks. Use Simpson's five categories (listed above) to guide your choice of group.

The following verbs will alert you to the possibility that the task is a motor task:

build	demonstrate	insert	monitor	set
calibrate	depress	isolate	move	straighten
collect	dissect	lift	open	strike
construct	feed	mark	pick	throw
cut	indicate	modify	pull	

Example

Simple motor task: Feel the vibration ("perceive a stimulus")

Mid-range motor task: Load the disk after the beep ("respond on command")

Complex motor task: Open the valve whenever the temperature reaches 120°F ("establish a pattern of action")

WORKSHEET 3–6

SKILLS-BASED (MOTOR) TASKS

Name of Job _____

Simple Motor Tasks

- •
  - •
- •
  - •
- •
  - •
- •
  - •
- •
  - •
- •
  - •
- •
  - •
- •
  - •

Mid-Range Motor Tasks

- •
  - •
- •
  - •
- •
  - •
- •
  - •
- •
  - •
- •
  - •
- •
  - •

Complex Motor Tasks

- •
  - •
- •
  - •
- •
  - •
- •
  - •
- •
  - •
- •
  - •

(Expand each section if necessary by adding more pages.

HOW TO DO DISCREPANCY ANALYSIS: PERFORMANCE DISCREPANCY OBSERVER'S CHECKLIST

This kind of task analysis is especially helpful when valued employees need extra training to improve performance on a specific task. Observations should be done by at least two observers working independently in order to establish inter-rater reliability.

Instructions

Construct an observer's checklist from Worksheet 3–3. Right away, this exercise will give you an idea of perhaps a whole category of tasks that require extra training emphasis. Discrepancy analysis allows the training department to fulfill one of its major functions, retraining.

Observe only the tasks in categories where improvement is sought. Be sure to verify the task list with the employee to be observed and the employee's supervisor. Remember that your job is to create training; not to engage in promotion/demotion decision-making.

Check the "discrepancy" column only if the doer of the task does not perform the task to criterion level (usually 100 percent). If you can, note a "criterion estimate percent" of the task that you believe was exhibited by the employee when you observed him or her at work. This dichotomous (check or no check) analysis is generally all that's needed at the initial stage of training design. However, a more detailed scale can be constructed on each task if the instructional designer feels this is necessary. At the bottom of each Worksheet 3–7 a space should be left for additional explanation of discrepancy.

Example

Discrepancy	Criterion Estimate Percent Performed	
		Category: *Log-On Tasks*
	100	Task 1 Enter password and User ID
√	75	Task 2 Load new operating system
√	90	Task 3 Bring up the graphics program

In this example, task 1 was performed correctly; tasks 2 and 3 were not. Therefore, training is needed on tasks 2 and 3. The training course does not need to be concerned about task 1, since it is already being performed according to a 100 percent standard.

WORKSHEET 3–7

DISCREPANCY ANALYSIS: PERFORMANCE DISCREPANCY OBSERVER'S CHECKLIST

Observer's Name: _____

Date of Observation: _____

Person Being Observed: _____

Job Title: _____

Discrepancy	Criterion Estimate Percent Performed	
		Category:
		Task 1
		Task 2
		Task 3
		Task 4
		Task 5
		Task 6
		Task 7
		Task 8
		Task 9
		Task 10
		Category:
		Task 1

Additional explanation of discrepancy:

_____

_____

_____

_____

(Expand this worksheet as necessary.)

CHAPTER 4 _____

HOW TO WRITE A _____
TRAINING PROPOSAL _____

The training proposal is the comprehensive planning document that sets the training program in motion. It is based on data gathered from your needs assessment, job analysis, and task analysis; all up-front studies which are completed beforehand.

The training proposal takes this information to the next logical step—that is, it justifies the need for training and lays out a plan for carrying out an appropriate program. This is done through a comprehensive description of:

- Trainee population
- Delivery staff
- Training program and course
- Costs of personnel time, travel, and expenses
- Costs of material resources required
- Program development and monitoring plan
- Learning objectives for trainees.

WHO SHOULD WRITE AND PRESENT TRAINING PROPOSALS

The training proposal is generally written by a training manager, a subject matter specialist, or a consultant. Sometimes, all these people collaborate to write the proposal. It is generally presented to upper management or to those with budget responsibility for the training department as well as other departments (such as personnel or operations) within the company.

KEY POINTS TO KEEP IN MIND WHEN DEVELOPING
A TRAINING PROPOSAL

The following are general concerns that should be addressed when developing a training proposal:

- Get management support for the general idea of the proposed training solution before you write the proposal. Do this formally or informally, depending on the style of your management.

- Focus on the outcomes of your proposed training program: the transfer of technology or information to persons who need it, the improvement of a product, the increase of sales, or the reduction of expense.

- Involve your customers (or internal organization you intend to serve) in the rationale statement, statement of desired outcomes of training, and cost benefit statements.

- Incorporate marketing studies, if possible, so the training program is seen in a broader context within the corporation or agency.

- Indicate flexibility and an ability to be responsive to continued problem identification and needs assessment.

- Write in some risk-taking, but always suggest justification for it. Risks in a proposal can typically be found in these areas:
  1. defining a target population slightly beyond the known target population,
  2. listing learner objectives that are difficult and require the learner and instructor to mentally stretch vigorously during learning,
  3. estimating development time on the short side or in terms of the "first phase only" in order to gain proposal approval, and
  4. expanding the projected benefits of training well beyond the immediate organizations of the students who take the course.

HOW TO USE THE WORKSHEETS IN THIS CHAPTER

The worksheets in this chapter are designed to be used sequentially in step-by-step fashion as follows.

Worksheet 4–1: Corporate Background

Use this worksheet to describe the corporate background in which the training program will take place, including a short description of the company and its customers or the internal organization that will be served by the program.

Worksheet 4–2: The Training Organization and Its Capabilities

Use this worksheet to describe the training organization and its capabilities.

Worksheets 4–3 and 4–4: Introduction to the Proposed Training Program

Use these worksheets to write an introduction to your proposal. The introduction includes a rationale justifying the need for the proposed training solution to the identified business problem. It also outlines broad program or course goals.

Worksheets 4–5 through 4–7: Proposed Training Program

Use these worksheets to write a description of the proposed training program, including:

- The target population to be served by the training
- List of specific learner objectives

- List of subjects/topics in the program or course
- List of required media and other material resources.

Worksheets 4–8 through 4–12: Write in Accountability

Use these worksheets to:

- Estimate cost for development
- Estimate cost for delivery
- Estimate development schedule
- Estimate delivery schedule
- Prepare equal employment opportunity guarantees.

Worksheet 4–13: Projected Benefits

Use this worksheet to write a short description of each specific projected outcome of training. Demonstrate the dollar value of training in terms of increased revenues and/or decreased expenses, estimated for the first year and within three years.

SAMPLE LAYOUT OF TRAINING PROPOSAL

Before writing your training proposal, review the recommended layout in Figure 4–1. This sample illustrates proposal structure and the order in which topics are presented.

Figure 4–1 Layout of Training Proposal

1

Cover

2

Table of Contents

3

Corporate Background

The Company:

Our Customers:

4

The Training Organization:

Our Capabilities:

5

Introduction

Rationale for and Description of Proposed Training:

Program/Course Goals:
-
-
-
-
-

6

Description of Proposed Training

Target Trainee Population:

Learner Objectives:

Unit 1
-
-
-

Unit 2
-
-
-
-

7

Learner Objectives (continued):

Unit 3
-
-
-

Unit 4
-
-
-

Unit 5
-
-
-

Unit 6
-
-
-

8

Major Topics:

Unit 1	Unit 2	Unit 3
•	•	•
•	•	•
•	•	•
•	•	•
•	•	•
•	•	•

Unit 4	Unit 5	Unit 6
•	•	•
•	•	•
•	•	•
•	•	•
•	•	•
•	•	•

9

Media and Hardware Required:
·
·
·
·
·
·
·
·

Other Materials Needed:

·
·
·
·
·
·
·

10

Accountability

Development Cost:
· $ _____
·   _____
·   _____
·   _____

Delivery Cost:
· $ _____
·   _____
·   _____
·   _____

TOTAL COST $ _____

11

Development Schedule:

Step	Month 1	Month 2	Month 3
·			
·			
·			
·			
·			
·			
·			
·			
·			
·			
·			
·			
·			
·			

12

Delivery Schedule:

	Week 1	Week 2	Week 3	Week 4
Jan			X	
Feb			X	
Mar			X	
Apr	X			
May	X			
Jun	X			
Jul				
Aug				
Sep		X		X
Oct		X		X
Nov		X		X
Dec				

13

Equal Employment Opportunity
Guarantees:

___
___
___
___
___
___
___
___
___
___
___

14

Projected Benefits

· Outcome:

Value $_____

· Outcome:

Value $_____

· Outcome:

Value $_____

· Outcome:

Value $_____

TOTAL VALUE,
1st YEAR $_____

TOTAL VALUE
WITHIN THREE
YEARS

$_____

**SAMPLE
COVER**

Training Proposal

Peripheral Interface Unit

Progressive Company

April 10, 19XX

XYZ, Inc.
1 Corporate Plaza
City, State 00010

SAMPLE

TABLE OF CONTENTS

INTRODUCE THE CORPORATION

1. *The Company*

Include the following in your description:

- Brief history of the company
- Leading products and services
- Number of employees
- Financials, including net sales and profits
- Public perception of company.

Example: XYZ Inc., founded in 1979, is a leading producer of office supplies for companies in the Northeast. XYZ employs 327 people at two plants in northern New Jersey. Net sales for 1988 were $15 million. XYZ is widely regarded as a state-of-the art supplier of business supplies for computerized offices.

2. *Our Customers*

- Primary markets, including names and size of leading customers
- Secondary markets
- Major distribution channels.

Example: XYZ is a primary supplier of office products to high-tech manufacturing firms. Our leading customers include Smithchip, a $50 million manufacturer of silicon chips based in Massachusetts; and Progressive Company, a manufacturer of fiber optics equipment located in Delaware, with total net sales of $20 million. XYZ distributes 89 percent of its products directly to clients; the remaining 11 percent are distributed through wholesalers in major cities in the Northeast. Last year, we had 132 client firms.

Our state-of-the-art supplies often have specialized markets within a client organization, requiring product training targeted to various offices at a client site. XYZ has a policy of making training available to our clients in order to create product acceptance and use as early as possible after the product sale.

> *TRAINING TIP*: Tap these sources of data when writing the Corporate Background section: annual reports, marketing studies, corporate public relations, results of last year's successful training.

WORKSHEET 4–1

CORPORATE BACKGROUND

1. *The Company*

2. *Our Customers*

DESCRIBE THE TRAINING ORGANIZATION

1. *Training Organization*

This section covers:

- Size of training staff
- Credentials of training staff
- Specialized expertise of training staff
- Reporting structure of training within the corporation.

Example: The XYZ Training Department has an experienced professional staff of six persons, all holding master's degrees, representing instructional design and delivery expertise in many specialty areas concerned with computer support.

A clerical staff of ten persons, including two computer graphics specialists, handles production of training materials in-house.

The Training Department reports to the Director of Sales and Marketing Support Services at XYZ.

2. *Our Capabilities*

In this section, include the following information as appropriate:

- Recent indicators of growth in the training organization
- Reference to design of this proposed training
- Reference to similar training previously delivered
- Brief description of successful outcomes of previous training
- Expectations for this proposed training.

Within the past six months, the XYZ Training Department has increased our client training base 400 percent, going from services provided to four client companies during second quarter 1989 to sixteen companies during first quarter 1990. More and more clients are finding that our product training provides their employees with essential skills to maximize the benefits of applying the new technology.

Recently, five members of XYZ staff became certified by our leading hardware vendor to provide training under the XYZ logo on all peripheral interfaces. In your training, XYZ proposes to train twelve persons from your Peripheral Interface Unit. This training will benefit from our recently-acquired expertise in peripherals. We would expect you to realize a 15 percent increase in throughput within three months after training, and up to a 40 percent increase within six months after training. These numbers are based on XYZ's experience with three similar training programs and on our trainee evaluations from those programs, which cite our excellent instructional design and delivery techniques.

WORKSHEET 4–2

THE TRAINING ORGANIZATION AND ITS CAPABILITIES

1. *Training Organization*

2. *Our Capabilities*

WRITE AN INTRODUCTION TO THE PROPOSED TRAINING PROGRAM

1. *Rationale and Description*

Begin this section with a concise description of the rationale behind your training program and the justification for it.

- Describe the training problem and show how the proposed training can solve it.

Example: Progressive Company has purchased $8 million of advanced printers and $150,000 of XYZ cables, graphics pads, and mice. The new equipment and supplies are scheduled to be in full use in sixty days to coincide with Progressive Company's commitment to its client. XYZ proposes to train twelve persons in Progressive Company's Peripheral Interface Unit to use our supplies and the printers in an efficient and cost-effective manner so that you can honor your commitment to your client and maximize your profit. Training will be instructor-led in a laboratory setting. It will last for two days.

- Identify other potential solutions to the problem and give reasons for discarding them.

Example: Although the manufacturer offers training in the use of its printers, that training is scheduled for three months from now, a date that is not timely for Progressive Company. The manufacturer's training also is more generic, and classes are filled with trainees from several companies. XYZ's proposed training precisely addresses your training need and your bottom line.

- Use needs assessment data to build your rationale statement.

Example: Preliminary discussions between J. Nelson of our staff and A. Howard of your staff indicated that your unit has had consistent difficulty during the past year with the graphics interface and use of peripheral graphic devices. Also, your Director indicated to our Vice President that . . .

- State a clear business purpose for the proposed training.

Example: With XYZ's proposed training, you will be able to serve your immediate client, increase the productivity of the Peripheral Interface Unit over the next six months, and provide other units at Progressive Company (e.g., Word Processing) with a model for customer service that focuses on your profit margin.

- Show how the proposed training responds to customer needs.

Example: This program is customized to your identified needs in serving your three principal clients over the next year.

- Explain how the proposed training helps accomplish the purchaser's company mission.

Example: Increased productivity resulting from this training will contribute to Progressive Company's corporate mission of increasing productivity in every business unit by 3rd quarter.

WORKSHEET 4—3

INTRODUCTION

1. *Rationale and Description*

WRITE AN INTRODUCTION TO THE PROPOSED TRAINING PROGRAM (continued)

2. *Program/Course Goals*

Two kinds of objectives are specified in a training proposal. The first is a simple statement of goals you have as the designer or instructor for the course. The second is a set of objectives you hope the trainee will have accomplished at the end of each unit or section.

This section addresses the first type of objective: your own goals for the course.

Example: This training program will enable trainees to:

- Operate the new printers efficiently and effectively
- Use XYZ's cable, graphics pad, and mice
- Enhance the capabilities of the new printers through appropriate use of XYZ's cable, graphics pad, and mice.

TRAINING TIP: It is particularly important that your proposal be free of extraneous words and flowery language. Have a colleague review your proposal for clarity before sending it.

WORKSHEET 4–4

INTRODUCTION (continued)

2. *Program/Course Goals*

-
-
-
-
-
-

DESCRIBE THE PROPOSED TRAINING PROGRAM

1. *Target Training Population*

In this section, describe:

- Number of trainees who will attend training
- Job titles of attendees
- Experience level of trainees
- Skill level of trainees.

Example: The target population for the proposed training includes twelve members of the Peripheral Interface Unit: supervisor, six technicians, two graphics engineers, one text processing specialist, and two technical assistants. All personnel have at least two years experience using computer printers. A range of skills is represented, with technicians and graphics engineers at the high end.

2. *Learner Objectives*

Break the content of your training program into separate sections/units built around major concepts or skills. Describe the objectives you hope the trainees will accomplish at the end of each major section/unit of the course. Keep the lists simple, focused on doing something, and specify behaviors or actions that can be observed and measured against some standard.

Example: Upon completion of unit/section 1, the trainee will be able to:

- Identify the five basic parts of the XYZ cable
- Demonstrate a successful connection of the XYZ cable to the new printer
- Describe major similarities and differences between the current printer and the new printer.

TRAINING TIP: A common error made by many trainers is to write learner objectives from an instructor's point of view—e.g. "to cover all the material regarding printer connections." Instead, put yourself in the learner's position and specify precisely the knowledge or skills that will be acquired—e.g., "to connect the printer using the XYZ cable, within 15 minutes."

WORKSHEET 4–5

PROPOSED TRAINING PROGRAM

1. *Target Training Population*

2. *Learner Objectives*

Upon completion of unit/section 1, the trainee will be able to:

-
-
-
-
-

Upon completion of unit/section 2, the trainee will be able to:

-
-
-
-
-

Upon completion of unit/section 3, the trainee will be able to:

-
-
-
-
-

(*Note*: Add extra pages for more units/phases/sections.)

DESCRIBE THE PROPOSED TRAINING PROGRAM (continued)

3. *List Major Topics in the Course/Program*

List program topics in the order in which they are to be learned. List only major topics in the training proposal. Keep detailed topic and subtopic listings in training files.

Example

Unit/Section 1	Unit/Section 2
• Overview of peripherals	• Printer parts
• XYZ service guarantees	• Printer functions
• Cable parts	• Connecting the printer
• Cable functions	• Operating the printer

WORKSHEET 4–6

PROPOSED TRAINING PROGRAM (continued)

3. *List of Major Topics in the Course/Program*

Unit/Section 1   Unit/Section 2

-
-
-
-
-
-
-
-

Unit/Section 3   Unit/Section 4

-
-
-
-
-
-
-

(*Note*: Add extra pages for more units/sections.)

DESCRIBE THE PROPOSED TRAINING PROGRAM (continued)

4. *List Media and Hardware Required*

Include here a listing of all media and hardware that will be required during the training program, including numbers of each. Media and hardware include, for example, projectors, screen, computer terminals, videotape recorders, audio tape recorders, blank tapes, transparency film, flip chart, and so on.

Example

The following media and hardware will be used during the course of the training program:

- Computer terminals (2)
- New printers, XYZ cables, graphics pads, mice (12 each)
- Videotape recorder
- Flipcharts (2)
- Blank videotapes (2 six-hour).

5. *List Other Materials Needed*

Other materials include stationery and miscellaneous supplies, for example, course manual workbook, calculators, textbooks, pencils, T-squares, grid paper, 3-ring binders, 3-hole punch, and so on.

WORKSHEET 4–7

PROPOSED TRAINING PROGRAM (continued)

4. *List of Media and Hardware Required*

   The following media and hardware will be required during the training program:

   -
   -
   -
   -
   -
   -
   -
   -
   -

   -
   -
   -
   -
   -
   -
   -
   -
   -

5. *Other Materials Needed*

   -
   -
   -
   -
   -
   -
   -

   -
   -
   -
   -
   -
   -
   -

WRITE IN ACCOUNTABILITY

Note: In the proposal, keep the accountability section spare and uncomplicated. Back it up with detailed worksheets in your training department files. The three major parts of accountability are cost, schedule, and equal employment opportunity guarantees.

1. *Development Cost*

- *Professional Salary*

  Guidelines: 20:1 and 40:1

  It takes 20 person-days of professional development time for one day of class time for major revision of an existing course.

  It takes 40 person-days of professional development time for one day of class time to write a new course.

  That is, it takes 120 person-days to develop a new three-day course.

- *Fringe Benefits*

  Cost for development includes the pro-rated cost of fringe benefits for salaried employees, typically calculated at 35 percent of gross salary.

- *Support*

  Cost for development includes a standard percentage of professional salary for support functions (secretarial, editing, text processing, clerical); for example, 15 percent of professional salary equals support salary. Add 35 percent for fringe benefits on the 15 percent figure.

- *Expense*

  Cost for development includes expenses such as research, consulting, computer time, printing and binding instructor materials, travel, telephone, postage, and office supplies.

- *Overhead*

  Cost for development generally includes an overhead cost (to cover heat, light, power, room rental, security, insurance, and maintance) typically calculated at 20 percent of the total cost of development.

WORKSHEET 4—8

COST SUMMARY

1. *Development Cost*

   • Professional salary and fringe benefits . . . . $_____

   _____ person-days @ $_____

   • Support salary and fringe benefits . . . . $_____

   _____ person-days @ $_____

   or

   15 percent of professional salary and fringe benefits

   • Expense . . . . $_____

research	$_____	telephone	$_____
consulting	_____	postage	_____
computer	_____	supplies	_____
printing	_____	travel	_____

   • Overhead . . . . $_____

   (Transpose to Cost Summary Worksheet 4–10.)

WRITE IN ACCOUNTABILITY (continued)

2. *Delivery Cost*

- *Student Cost*

  The biggest part of the cost of a training program/course comes during delivery with lost productivity because trainees are away from their jobs while they are in training.

  This cost is typically referred to as *student salary*, and is derived by multiplying the average per diem salary and benefits rate of a typical trainee by the number of trainees enrolled in the course/program (or the projected total target population).

  Add to this an average travel and lodging cost multiplied by the number of students enrolled in the course/program (or the projected total target population).

  The rule of thumb is that delivery costs make up $\frac{2}{3}$ of total costs; development costs make up $\frac{1}{3}$ of total costs.

- *Expense*

  Delivery costs include expenses for equipment purchase or rental, trainee supplies, trainee manuals, trainee textbooks, hospitality, evaluation, testing, and scoring.

- *Instructor Salary*

  Delivery cost also includes instructor time in class, instructor time setting up and taking down the training session, instructor travel and lodging, and an overhead cost of 20 percent of the instructor salary plus benefits figure.

WORKSHEET 4–9

COST SUMMARY (continued)

2. *Delivery Cost*

- Student salary and fringe benefits . . . . $ _____

    _____ students × _____ course days × $ _____

- Student travel and lodging . . . . $ _____

    _____ students × $ _____ per diem

- Expense . . . . $ _____

    equipment $ _____   hospitality $ _____
    supplies   _____   evaluation   _____
    manuals   _____   testing
    textbooks   _____   scoring

- Instructor salary, benefits, overhead . . . . $ _____

    _____ days @ $ _____ plus overhead

    (Transpose to Cost Summary Worksheet 4–10.)

WORKSHEET 4–10

COST SUMMARY

Development Cost

- Professional salary and fringe benefits . . . . $ _____
  _____ person-days @ $ _____

- Support salary and fringe benefits . . . . $ _____
  _____ person-days @ $ _____
       or
  15% of professional salary and fringe benefits

- Expense . . . . $ _____

  research $ _____   telephone $ _____
  consulting   _____   postage   _____
  computer   _____   supplies   _____
  printing   _____
  travel   _____

- Overhead . . . . $ _____

Delivery Cost

- Student salary and fringe benefits . . . . $ _____
  _____ students; _____ course days × $ _____

- Student travel and lodging . . . . $ _____
  _____ students × $ _____ per diem

- Expense . . . . $ _____

  equipment $ _____   hospitality $ _____
  supplies   _____   evaluation   _____
  manuals   _____   testing
  textbooks   _____   scoring

- Instructor salary, benefits . . . . $ _____
  _____ days @ $ _____

- Overhead . . . . $ _____

TOTAL COST $ _____

COST SUMMARY

Development Cost

- Professional salary and fringe benefits .... $ 12,000
  ___40___ person-days @ $ ___300___

- Support salary and fringe benefits .... $ 2,160
  ___20___ person-days @ $ ___108___
  or
  15% of professional salary and fringe benefits

- Expense .... $ 1,200

research	$ 0	telephone	$ 200
consulting	0	postage	100
computer	0	supplies*	400
printing	300		
travel	200		

  * does not include calculators to be provided by Progressive Company

- Overhead .... $ 3,072

Delivery Cost

- Student salary and fringe benefits .... $ 4,560
  ___12___ students; ___24___ course days × $ ___190___

- Student travel and lodging .... $ 0
  _____ students × $ _____ per diem

- Expense .... $ 275

equipment	$ 0	hospitality	$ 85
supplies	70	evaluation	0
manuals	120	testing	
textbooks	0	scoring	

- Instructor salary, benefits .... $ 405
  ___2___ days @ $ ___202.50___

- Overhead .... $ 648

                                              TOTAL COST $ 24,320

WRITE IN ACCOUNTABILITY (continued)

3. *Development Schedule*

Plan a timeline in quarters that follows the fiscal year, so that adjustments can be made based on financials. Indicate with a horizontal line when each step is projected to be completed. Divide each monthly column into two parts, indicating the 15th and 30th of the month.

Example

Development Step	Month 1	Month 2	Month 3
1. Interview A. Howard (Progressive)			
2. Order 15 printer manuals from vendor			
3. Verify skill levels of trainees			
4. Get parts diagrams from XYZ graphics lab			
5. Design visuals for functions and operations			
6. Specify learner objectives and topics per unit			
7. Verify objectives and topics with Progressive unit supervisor			
8. Prepare instructor guide			

WORKSHEET 4–11

DEVELOPMENT SCHEDULE

Development Step	Month 1	Month 2	Month 3
1.			
2.			
3.			
4.			
5.			
6.			
7.			
8.			
9.			
10.			
11.			
12.			
13.			
14.			
15.			

(*Note*: Add additional schedule sheets for development plans of longer duration.)

WRITE IN ACCOUNTABILITY (continued)

4. *Delivery Schedule*

Indicate with an X the weeks in which this training program/course is expected to run.

Example

	Week 1	Week 2	Week 3	Week 4	
January					
February					
March					
April					
May					
June					
July					
August	Pilot X				
September			X		
October					
November					
December					

WORKSHEET 4—12

DELIVERY SCHEDULE

Note: Indicate with an X the weeks in which this training program/course is expected to run.

	Week 1	Week 2	Week 3	Week 4	
January					
February					
March					
April					
May					
June					
July					
August					
September					
October					
November					
December					

5. *Equal Employment Opportunity (EEO) Guarantees*

Training is considered an employment opportunity. Adhere to principles of equal access and equal opportunity during training development and delivery. In your proposal, include a list of all EEO guarantees that you will assure during this training.

Use the following checklist in your planning. Transfer all appropriate items, without dates, to the proposal under the heading, "Equal Employment Opportunity (EEO) Guarantees."

Checklist for EEO Guarantees

Date This Item Was Accomplished/ Guaranteed	EEO Guarantees
_____	Trainee manuals have been cleared of sexist, racist, ethnic, or any discriminatory language.
_____	Textbooks have been approved for absence of sexist, racist, ethnic, or any discriminatory language and artwork.
_____	Handouts have been cleared of sexist, racist, ethnic, or any discriminatory language and artwork.
_____	Visuals/slides/films have been approved for absence of sexist, racist, ethnic, or any discriminatory artwork and text.
_____	Classrooms, laboratories, and training areas are accessible to handicapped persons.
_____	Restrooms are accessible to handicapped persons.
_____	Eating rooms are accessible to handicapped persons.
_____	Course registration form contains an equal opportunity/ non-discrimination statement.
_____	Course has been fairly and equally advertised to men, women, and persons in all job classifications who could benefit from taking the course/program.
_____	Course evaluations are solicited, received, and processed equally from all trainees, giving each an equal voice in feedback to improve training.
_____	Corporate procedures exist to report and discipline violators of equal employment opportunity guarantees.

> *TRAINING TIP*: Assign one of your training staff members to be responsible for checking these items. The course author, instructor, or manager is too busy to do this, and EEO details can easily "slip through the cracks." A responsible assistant (clerical or professional), focusing only on this checklist until it is completed, is your best choice for help with this important task.

WORKSHEET 4–13

EQUAL EMPLOYMENT OPPORTUNITY (EEO) GUARANTEES

It is our intent and practice to accomplish the following EEO guarantees in our training development and delivery:

-

-

-

-

-

-

-

-

-

-

DESCRIBE PROJECTED BENEFITS

Because training is expensive, it must be designed and delivered in response to clearly identified needs. Benefits of training can have a dollar value placed on them by considering the savings to the company because of the outcomes of training. Look for value in both increased revenues and decreased expenses.

Typical areas in which to find training-related savings include reductions in the following costs:

- Equipment downtime
- Incorrect use of equipment
- Equipment repair
- Personnel turnover
- Recruiting
- Arbitration
- Grievances
- Strikes

- Accidents
- Production errors
- Rewrite
- Duplicated efforts
- Unskilled employees
- Obsolete skills
- Customer complaints

In this section of the proposal, briefly describe each projected outcome of the proposed training, attaching a dollar value to it.

Total the dollar values of all training outcomes to be realized by the end of the first year in the program/course. Project this one-year total out to the end of three years, to indicate short-term and longer-term value to the corporation.

Example

- Outcome:

  2 minutes per printed page saved by using XYZ cable on new printer
  estimate 60,000 pages printed
  × 2 minutes = 120,000 minutes =
  2,000 hrs. @ $25 = $50,000

  Value $50,000

WORKSHEET 4–14

PROJECTED BENEFITS

- Outcome:

Value $_____

- Outcome:

Value $_____

- Outcome:

Value $_____

- Outcome:

Value $_____

TOTAL VALUE, 1st YEAR _____

TOTAL VALUE WITHIN 3 YEARS _____

CHAPTER 5 _____

HOW TO DESIGN _____
YOUR OWN COURSES _____

WHY DOING IT YOURSELF OFTEN PRODUCES THE BEST RESULTS

In order to solve a training problem, the training manager has three options:

- Write your own course/program,
- Purchase a course/program "off the shelf," or
- Hire a consultant to write a course/program for you.

Each of these options has merit. This chapter provides guidelines for the first option, write your own course/program. If a thorough needs asessment and job and task analyses have been done, designing your own course/program has greater potential than the other two options for providing the highest quality solution to your training problem.

Because you know your problems, your staff, your target audience, and your management better than any outside consultant, you have the best chance of designing a results-oriented training program in the shortest time.

When you design your own course, you monitor and check each part as it is being created. Insiders always have a better chance of designing relevant courses.

If you buy programs off the shelf, you risk having to design your own solutions into the generic structure of a purchased product targeted at a mass audience. If you hire a consultant, you run the risk of that person's having to "learn the ropes" regarding your company before he or she can get to work on your project—and there's always the danger that nuances of your corporate culture and working relationships will be missed by the outsider.

WHAT'S INVOLVED IN THE COURSE DEVELOPMENT PROCESS

For simplicity, the rest of this chapter will use the term *course* instead of course/program. Understand that courses can be put together in a program, or parts of courses can be packaged together and called a program. Guidelines are discussed in relationship to a course, and you can expand these guidelines to cover training program development.

The Training System

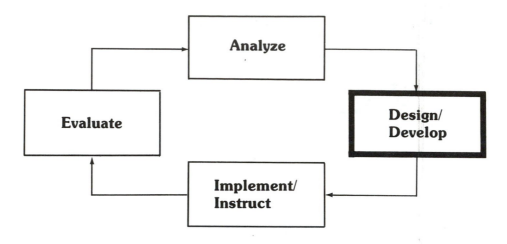

Figure 5–1

A System Focus on Design/Develop

The four essential functions in training development are:

- Analyze,
- Design/develop,
- Implement/instruct, and
- Evaluate.

These various functions are tied together in a training system. The focus of this chapter is the design/develop function highlighted in Figure 5-1.

How Instructional System Design (ISD) Evolved

This systematic approach to training was initiated by the United States government in the 1940s when tremendous training demands were created by wartime and defense requirements for new knowledge and skills. It was codified and developed largely by vocational-technical educators in the 1950s, and was expanded and widely promoted by Robert F. Mager in the 1960s and 1970s. Mager wrote prolifically on the subject of objectives and course development standards. The American Society for Training and Development (ASTD) and the National Society for Performance and Instruction (NSPI) throughout those decades, and currently, have featured programs and articles based on instructional system design at their national conferences and in their publications. Many graduate degree programs in Instructional Technology incorporate this approach to training design.

How to Structure a Course[1]

The two basic building blocks of a course are objectives and content outline. These work together and are expanded into units of instruction, comprised of lessons, which often include practice exercises and lab sessions; and tests, which are also sometimes created and formally administered as part of a course. How to design tests is covered in Chapter 6.

HOW TO USE THE WORKSHEETS IN THIS CHAPTER

Worksheets in this chapter are of two basic types—fill-in-the blank forms and guidelines. The guidelines are designed to help you create objectives, content outlines, and lessons, and expand these into units of instruction. You will also find guidelines for designing practice exercises and lesson plans.

The worksheets will assist you at various stages of the course design process and facilitate design reviews by peers or managers at each stage.

Worksheet 5–1: Writing Course Objectives

Use these guidelines to write objectives spelling out what trainees will accomplish during training.

Worksheet 5–2: Writing a Content Outline

Use these guidelines to outline the information you will include in the course to enable the trainee to accomplish each objective.

Worksheet 5–3: Developing a Lesson

Based on your content outline, develop lessons spelling out what you expect trainees to accomplish during each training session. The guidelines presented here will help you write lessons that include all key components.

Worksheet 5–4: Writing Behavioral Objectives

Behavioral objectives are an integral part of each lesson. Use this worksheet to develop behavioral objectives that are specific and measurable.

Worksheet 5–5: Developing a Unit

Refer to your objectives, course outline, and lessons to organize material into logical sets of content. These sets become units of instruction. Consult the guidelines presented here as you write units and arrange them in proper sequence.

Worksheet 5–6: Developing Practice Exercises and Laboratory (Lab) Sessions

Use these guidelines to design exercises/lab sessions to teach trainees a specific

[1] For further reading regarding course structure, see Banathy, B.H. *Instructional Systems* (Belmont, CA: Fearon, 1968); Finch, C.R. and Crunkilton, J.R. *Curriculum Development in Vocational and Technical Education* (Boston: Allyn & Bacon, 1979); and Mager, R.F. and Beach, K.M. *Developing Vocational Instruction* (Belmont, CA: Lear Siegler/Fearon, 1967).

task or group of tasks. Exercises/lab sessions are integral parts of units, lessons, and the content of a course.

Worksheet 5–7 and 5–8: Design Review Accountability Forms

Use design review to make sure you're on the right track as you develop your course. Depending on your organization, you can choose Peer Review or Management Chain Review to validate your ideas and your decisions.

Worksheet 5–9: Curriculum Chart

Use this worksheet to graphically display the courses in the curriculum in the order that trainees should take them.

Worksheet 5–10: Materials and Facilities Planning

Use this worksheet to list the specific training materials and physical facilities you will need to carry out the training.

WORKSHEET 5–1

WRITING COURSE OBJECTIVES

A good way to think about an objective is to think about a 15-minute segment of a course. During this time, the learner focuses on learning something or doing something. Chances are, that small segment of the course is designed around an objective. When you design a course, try to define an objective for each 15-minute segment of that course. Think about what you want the trainee to be able to do at the end of that 15-minute segment and about how that trainee can demonstrate to you that he or she has "gotten the point" of that small segment of the course.

What to Cover When Writing an Objective

A good objective:

- Tells what the trainee will do.
- Can be taught.
- Can be learned.
- Can be measured.
- Has a business purpose.
- Follows a task analysis.
- Relates to other objectives of the course.

DON'Ts for Writing Objectives

When you write an objective:

- Don't intimidate or insult an adult learner.
- Don't write it in instructor jargon (i.e., objectives are written from the learner's point of view, not the instructor's).
- Don't create learning for learning's sake. Training in the business world always has a business or "bottom line" purpose.

Here's an example of a well-written objective: Access the Employment History screen of the System for Personnel Administration (SPA) within two minutes of logon.

WORKSHEET 5–2

WRITING A CONTENT OUTLINE

Because a course is not just information—it is behavioral change—objectives are written before the content outline is developed. Shortly thereafter, however, the content outline is developed. Probably the easiest way to develop a viable outline of the content of a course is to write each objective at the top of a piece of paper, and list all the topics and subtopics of content related to that objective. It's a good idea in this topic listing to have only three levels of content—topic, subtopic, and sub-subtopic, or outline form I, A, and 1. Remember that you are creating an outline here, not the whole course. It is from this outline that lessons are then built.

What to Include in a Content Outline

A good content outline:

- Provides information to enable the learner to accomplish the objective.
- Contains only necessary information.
- Is presented in logical groupings of information.
- Includes "branches" to specialized information that is necessary to learn new concepts or skills (e.g., cross-reference to vendor manuals, conceptual information regarding handouts, equipment operating procedures, etc.).

DON'Ts for Writing Content Outlines

When you write a content outline:

- Don't get topics out of sequence with each other
- Don't aim topics too high or too low for your target audience
- Don't become too theoretical. Training content should be 90 percent practical.

Example

Following is an example of a content outline for one objective of a course in Electronic Graphics.

Objective: Construct pie, bar, and line graphs using "Graphatronic" software.

Content outline for this objective:

I. Definitions, examples, and uses of graphs
   A. Pie graph
   B. Bar graph
      1. Vertical bars
      2. Horizontal bars
   C. Line graph
II. The structure of graphics files
   A. Naming conventions
   B. Relationships with directories
   C. Limitations
III. Graphics menus
   A. Help menu
   B. Main menu
   C. Varietal menus
   D. Point sizes and space measurements
IV. Building techniques
   A. Using up, down, across arrows
   B. Positioning
      1. Enlarging
      2. Reducing
      3. Creating negative space

WORKSHEET 5–3

DEVELOPING A LESSON

A lesson puts down in specific terms what you expect trainees to accomplish during each class or meeting, the desired changes in trainee behavior, and the steps you will take to facilitate those changes. Lessons can be put together to form units.

What to Include in a Lesson.

A good lesson:

- Includes a statement outlining the basic purpose of the training session. State the purpose from the trainee's point of view.
- Contains a general plan, which is simply a brief statement of how the purpose will be carried out.
- Contains behavioral objectives that tell what desired changes in employee behavior will result from the training.
- Outlines the steps or sequence of topics to be covered.
- Allows enough time to adequately cover each step or topic.

DON'Ts for Writing Lessons.

When writing a lesson:

- Don't cram too many topics into a single lesson. Think in terms of 15-minute lessons.
- Don't write overly general behavioral objectives. Focus on highly specific changes in behavior.
- Don't present steps or topics out of sequence with each other.

Example

Following is a lesson plan for the procedure of bagging groceries.

Lesson Title: Bagging groceries

Purpose: To place grocery items correctly into the paper bag.

General Plan: Use lecture and demonstration to show trainees how to bag groceries correctly. Trainees will then practice bagging a variety of grocery items.

Behavioral Objectives: Trainees will be able to place 10–12 items in a paper bag without crushing any items.

Content Outline:
1. Open the bag.
2. Place the bag on the shelf.
3. Begin bagging as soon as about half of the order is rung up.
4. Put large cans and bottles on the bottom.
5. Put meats, fish, and poultry in plastic bags.
6. Put frozen foods in freezer bags.
7. Place produce where it won't be crushed.
8. Put breads on top.
9. Put a "paid" sticker on items too big for bags.

TRAINING TIP: Express each step in the content outline of a procedure-type instruction as an active verb.

WRITING BEHAVIORAL OBJECTIVES

A fundamental purpose of training is to foster a change in trainee behavior. Accordingly, it is important to spell out precisely what changes you expect to occur as the result of training. Behavioral objectives are an integral part of lesson plans and should be identified before you write the actual content of a lesson.

A good behavioral objective spells out the behavior to be achieved, the condition under which this behavior is to occur, and the criteria for measuring actual achievement of the behavior.

1. Identify the behavior desired.

   Example: ● Input six lines of data.
   ● Pack 12 grocery items in the paper bag.

2. Explain under what condition the change in behavior will be accomplished.

   Example: ● Sitting at computer terminal.
   ● With the bag open.

3. Explain the criteria for measuring achievement.

   Example ● With no more than two errors.
   ● So that none of the items is crushed.

WORKSHEET 5–4

WRITING BEHAVIORAL OBJECTIVES

Behavior Desired: _____

_____

_____

_____

Conditions: _____

_____

_____

_____

Criteria: _____

_____

_____

_____

WORKSHEET 5–5

DEVELOPING A UNIT

Lay out all the objectives, content outlines, and lessons in front of you on a big table. Organize the pages into sets that make sense, e.g., from general to specific, familiar to new, low-level skill mastery to high-level skill mastery, and so on. The logical sets of content become units of instruction, sequenced for motivated and efficient learning, and are doable within a specific time frame.

What to Include When Developing a Unit.

A good unit:

- Has a name.
- Has an apparent developmental design, constructed to help the learner through content.
- Presents concepts and skills in a way to accommodate various learning styles.
- Contains transitions between topics.

DON'Ts for Writing Units

When you write a unit:

- Don't put the most difficult content first—let the learner ease into the tough stuff.
- Don't assume that everyone learns best by listening and taking notes—that old model of learning seldom works in training because it is boring, it wastes time, it treats adults as if they were children, and it seldom can be justified as job-specific. Adults want more action when they go to classes at work.
- Don't use coffee breaks to conclude a unit. Always design unit beginnings that relate to the end of the previous unit, and unit endings that lead into the next unit. Use ideas and tasks, not artificial "housekeeping" breaks, to motivate trainees to keep going. (Otherwise they will find more interesting things to do, and extend their coffee breaks and lunch hours to make phone calls, answer their mail, go sightseeing, or snoop around the hotel.)

Example

Incorporating the content example from Worksheet 5–2, a unit of that course in Electronic Graphics might include the following objectives:

Unit 3–Building Graphs Using Graphatronics Software

- Decide which data belongs on the x axis and on y axis.
- Construct pie, bar, and line graphs (see previous Content Outline).
- Integrate graphs into text.

This unit might take four hours, or roughly one afternoon. It might be taught with each trainee in front of a terminal and a roving instructor helping out, and by using flip charts, software user guides, and class discussion.

Other units of this course in Electronic Graphics might be:

Unit 1–Overview of Electronic Publishing

Unit 2–Graphics Applications Workshop

Unit 3–Building Graphs Using Graphatronics Software (see above)

Unit 4–Building Graphs Using Designmate Software

Unit 5–Standard and State-of-the-Art Hardware Options

There is not room in this book to write a complete unit. Put lessons together to form units, are put units together to form a course.

WORKSHEET 5–6

DEVELOPING PRACTICE EXERCISES AND LABORATORY (LAB) SESSIONS

A practice exercise is a specific, observable, measurable task associated with a learning objective. Practice exercises come in many varieties, and are meant to allow the student to learn something new through repetition and supervised problem-solving.

A lab session is an integrated group of practice exercises requiring the student to come to conclusions regarding use of course information, often employing trial and error as a way of learning.

Practice exercises and lab sessions usually require interaction with equipment or specific materials used on the job. They are integral parts of units, lessons, and the content outline of a course.

What to Include in a Practice Exercise/Lab Session

A good practice exercise/lab session:

- Presents motor tasks in the context of cognitive tasks first (i.e., helps the student discover why this needs to be done).
- Allows enough time.

DON'Ts for Writing Practice Exercises/Lab Sessions

When you write a practice exercise/lab session:

- Don't assume that all equipment works.
- Don't assume that all students are equally dexterous, knowledgeable, or energetic.
- Don't assume that all students love to be "put on the spot" by having to "perform" exercises and labs. Adults do not like to do things wrong, and this kind of learning often exposes mistakes. Support risk takers. People do learn effectively this way. Realize that some students will be preoccupied with other concerns, will be tired or hassled, or just won't be as "up" as other students.

Examples

1. Practice exercise: Translate the next three paragraphs into Russian.

   Lab session: Choose a partner and two persons as an audience. For the next hour, your partner will read the first section (2 pages) of the paper, "Quality-based Strageties for Marketing R&D Services." Your task is to translate this section into Russian as he or she speaks for your audience of two persons. You may refer to your dictionary and grammar manual, but must keep going until the end of the section. Work with your partner to establish a pace that will allow you to keep going. If you finish early, that's fine!

2. Practice exercise: Your task in tomorrow's lab session will be to install a tapedeck in one of the cars in the Accessories Lab. This afternoon before you leave, practice removing only the necessary front (dashboard) panels of each car in the lab (Cadillac, Ford LTD, Saab, Mercedes-Benz and Honda).

   Lab session: You are assigned this car for today's lab session: _____. Install the tapedeck. The lab closes at 6:00 P.M.

HOW TO CONDUCT DESIGN REVIEWS

Check your work as you do it. Don't wait until your course is done to verify that you're on the right track. Heading off in the wrong direction will cost you more if it goes undetected until the end of course development.

Call upon your peers or manager early in the development process to check your ideas and decisions. Think of the results of course design as individual documents and review each one against its own design guidelines.[2]

How you do this depends on the nature of your corporate culture. Choose either a Peer Review or a Management Chain Review. Using either option, seek comments from all constituencies with a stake in the outcomes of the course. These constituencies might be content experts, researchers in related areas of content, potential trainees, potential instructors, or managers and supervisors of the course author or of the potential trainees. Make adjustments to your work immediately, before going on to the next part of your course. This process of reviewing documents in progress is an example of formative evaluation.[3] It is the only way to ensure that the course being created will, in fact, serve the company that's paying for its development. A design review is essential when you choose to design your own course.

It is up to the training manager to call for a design review as each part of the course is complete. It is a good idea to review all objectives of the course together at one time. All lessons in a unit should be reviewed together. In a course lasting more than two days, the content outlines should be reviewed as groups of content. Lab sessions should be reviewed in the context of the unit in which they are placed. No more than two units should be reviewed at one design review meeting. Limit design review meetings to no more than two hours. Limit the number of reviewers to no more than 8 people. Be sure someone takes notes.

Option 1: Peer Review

A bottom-up, grass-roots, collegial, team-centered, participatory organization uses Peer Review with good results.

Option 2: Management Chain Review

A top-down, bureaucratic organization uses Management Chain Review with good results.

Accountability forms for each option are included on the following pages. Enlarge them to make them more useful.

---

[2] Design reviews have been successfully used in software inspection for many years. The work of M.E. Fagan at IBM's System Science Institute in the 1970s is classic. Design review in course development evaluation is similar.

[3] For more information on formative evaluation, see Stufflebeam's presentation of the CIPP model for improvement-oriented evaluation in Chapter 6, and the discussion of process evaluation on pp. 174ff in Stufflebeam, D.L. and Shinkfield, A.J., *Systematic Evaluation* (Boston: Kluwer-Nijhoff Publishing, 1985). See also the Instructional Design Model using Feedback and Modification in Birnbrauer, H. (ed.), *Handbook for Technical and Skills Training* (Alexandria, VA: The American Society for Training and Development, 1985).

WORKSHEET 5–7

PEER REVIEW ACCOUNTABILITY FORM FOR DESIGN REVIEW

Item	Review Date	Reviewer's Initials	Item Reference or Comment
Objectives			
Content Outline			
Unit/Lesson			
Exercise/Lab			

SAMPLE

PEER REVIEW ACCOUNTABILITY FORM FOR DESIGN REVIEW

Item	Review Date	Reviewer's Initials	Item Reference or Comment
Objectives			
for Unit 1	7/12	NN, RCD, KN	excellent as is
for Unit 2	7/14	NN, RCD	change obj. 3 to include higher criteria
for Units 3 & 5	7/15	NN, KN, CPD	ok as is
for Unit 4	7/18	NN, RCD, CPD	problems—too advanced— rewrite and review by 7/20
Content Outline			
for entire course	7/18	NN, RCD, CPD, KN	content or target with exception of middle of Unit 4—modify
Unit/Lesson			
lessons 4, 5, 6 of Unit 4	7/22	NN, RCD, KN	omit section on assessment skills and measurement methods—ask Lisa to sit in on rewrite of this section
Unit 4 (rewrite)	7/26	NN, RCD, LND	ok now—but verify cross references because of new page numbers
Exercise/Lab			
Unit 3 lab	7/15	NN, KN, CPD	add 20-minute stress management practice
Unit 4 exercises	7/26	NN, RCD, LND	delete all but the first two exercises (too advanced)

WORKSHEET 5–8

MANAGEMENT CHAIN REVIEW ACCOUNTABILITY FORM FOR DESIGN REVIEW

	Objectives		Content Outline		Units/Lesson		Exercises/Lab	
	Initials	Date	Initials	Date	Initials	Date	Initials	Date
*Management Chain**								
Training Manager								
1st Level Manager								
2nd Level Manager								
3rd Level Manager								
Client Sponsor								

* Each item of course development requires sign-off at the appropriate level. This worksheet may be expanded to include more managers at lower levels for courses with broad applications across many departments.

CREATING A CURRICULUM CHART

A curriculum is a group of courses arranged in a sequence to make learning a subject easier. In schools, a curriculum spans several grades, for example, the mathematics curriculum or the health education curriculum. In business, a curriculum spans several months or years. Trainees enter it at various points depending on their job experience and the needs of the business.

Curriculum building addresses these issues:

- arranging courses in a hierarchy for optimum learning
- increasing complexity in level of skill
- increasing sophistication of course materials
- increasing sophistication of teaching methods.

Since the goal of most training is more effective business practices, training has to be put into a curriculum that helps produce better decision makers, more skilled workers, and more effective problem solvers.

A curriculum chart graphically displays the courses in a curriculum in the order in which they should be taken. Read the chart from top to bottom. Some mid-level courses will have no advanced courses following them; others will be followed by several advanced courses. A sample curriculum chart format is on the next page.

Example

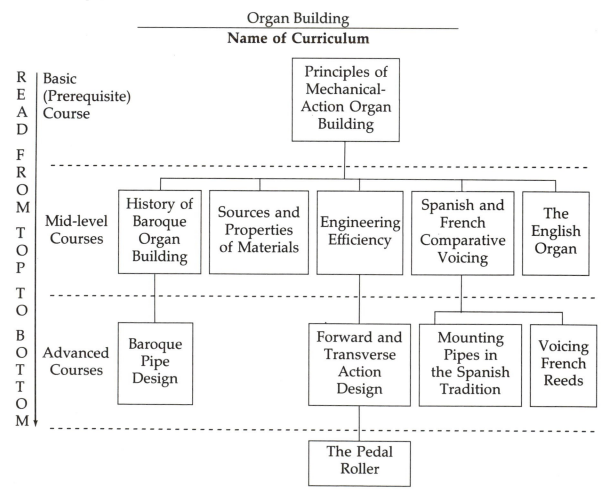

WORKSHEET 5–9

CURRICULUM CHART

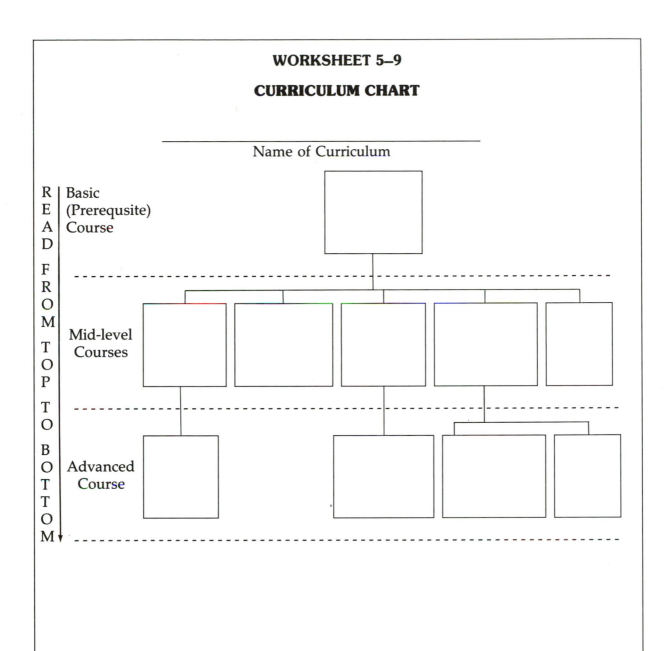

Name of Curriculum

R
E
A
D

F
R
O
M

T
O
P

T
O

B
O
T
T
O
M

Basic
(Prerequsite)
Course

Mid-level
Courses

Advanced
Course

Note: Add vertical connecting lines among boxes to indicate hierarchical relationships among the courses in your curriculum. Add or delete boxes in this configuration to customize the curriculum chart to your training situation.

PLANNING MATERIALS AND FACILITIES

As part of your course planning, list the types of materials and physical facilities you will require in order to carry out the training. Add this planning document to the instructional design documents that you have created for your course.

1. *List training materials* including:
   - Books
   - Handouts
   - Tests
   - Training manuals
   - Lab exercises
   - Answer keys
   - Evaluation forms
   - Job aids

2. *List audiovisual materials* you will require, including:
   - Slide projector
   - Film projector
   - Video cassette recorder
   - Cameras
   - Television
   - Overhead projector
   - LCD projection pad
   - Audio tape recorder
   - Headphones
   - Stereo/record player
   - Speakers
   - Screen
   - Microphone

3. *List training equipment*, including machinery, simulators, and computers. Specify type of computer and peripherals.

4. *List facilities* required, including room size and location, and number of desks, chairs, and tables needed. It is helpful to draw a diagram illustrating your preferred training room layout.

WORKSHEET 5–10

MATERIALS AND FACILITIES PLANNING

Course Title: _____

Training Materials Required:

_____
_____
_____
_____

Audio-visual Materials Required:

_____
_____
_____
_____

Training Equipment Required:

_____
_____
_____
_____

Facilities Required:

_____
_____

Diagram:

TRAINING TIP: Before you specify in writing your materials, equipment, and facilities needs, be sure you've gotten input from enough students—that is, not from only one instructor.

Before you add a materials and facilities list (page 134) to your course documentation, read the relevant sections of student evaluation forms from at least three previous offerings of the course. The students' comments will verify the instructor's lists, and will frequently suggest improvements that can be made in training materials, equipment, and facilities.

If this is a new course not previously offered, be sure that the instructor has verified the list of requirements with one or two other instructors with similar interests.

SAMPLE

MATERIALS AND FACILITIES PLANNING

Course Title: Editing Electronic Manuscripts

Training Materials Required:

1. PUBLISHER'S HANDBOOK FOR ELECTRONIC MANUSCRIPTS, Schlosser

2. List of keyboarding codes (handout)

3. Simulated editing exercises (on disk)

4. Transparencies accompanying PUBLISHER'S HANDBOOK

Audio-visual Materials Required:

1. Overhead projector

2. Screen

Training Equipment Required:

1. PCs with printers (6)

Facilities Required:

6 workstations with suitable chairs in computer lab;

one lectern; one table with instructor PC

Diagram: Standard arrangement of workstations in computer lab is satisfactory.

CHAPTER 6

HOW TO DESIGN
TESTS

Employee testing serves several business purposes.

- It helps determine level of competency for a specific job.
- It is useful when an employee wants to enter a job.
- It is useful when an employee has to leave a job.
- It measures the direct effects of training.

Differences Between Testing and Evaluation

Testing usually involves quantification of results—a number that represents an ability or characteristic of the person being tested. A test is presented as a set of items, often in the form of questions. Each item of a test is directly related to the tasks of a job or training program. (See Chapters 2 and 3).

Evaluation is the process of gathering information in order to make good decisions. It is broader than testing, and includes both subjective (opinion) input and objective (fact) input.

An example of evaluation is inspecting and rejecting a week's production of advertising designs based on the 1950s for a new product, and deciding to send the artist to a half-day seminar on *Psychology of Color in the 1950s* before the artist revises the designs. Something seems wrong with the colors.

An example of a test is to examine the drawings and determine that of 10 acceptable colors, the artist used only three. His "color savvy" on this assignment was only 30 percent. The artist is told his score is 30 percent.

Never Play "I Gotcha"

The quality of performance on the job should be determined by how well the employee does all the various tasks that make up the job—or the training for the job. While the employee might be deficient in some other skills, these deficiencies should not be held against an employee if they are not relevant to the specific tasks that he or she is expected to perform.

For example, an employee might not be able to drive a fork lift truck, but if his only job is to update the inventory control charts in the warehouse, his inability to drive a fork lift truck should never be a factor in anyone's making a judgment about his job *performance*. (However, his flexibility, promotability, and usefulness to the warehouse operation might be affected by this skill deficiency.)

The issue in testing is how well a person performs a specific job or training task. The best way to find out is to design each test item around a specific objective of the job. This kind of testing is fair.

Resist the temptation to design tests too broadly; when you fall into this trap, you play "I gotcha" with the employee and testing is not fair. Legal action can be initiated against unfair testing. If good performance objectives are written for the job, good test design can follow.

TWO BASIC OPTIONS IN TESTING

The two basic options in testing are:

- Testing at many points *during* training (formative), and
- Testing *at the end of* training (summative).

Five Important Advantages of Formative Testing in a Business Setting

Formative testing is generally preferred in business because it is:

- Clearly and directly related to training tasks.
- Easier to administer and score.
- More likely to reflect the mission, goals, or standards of your specific company, rather than those of a general business population across the country.
- Conducive to more informal options in test design.
- Easier on the trainee than a summative test at the end of training.

This chapter will focus on formative testing during training. This testing is often done at the end of lessons or units, and is often of short (5 minutes–30 minutes) duration.

Note: Readers should consult references on personnel practices to learn about psychological tests used for entry into jobs such as bank tellers, morticians, financial advisors, stockbrokers, car salespersons, real estate salespersons, or child care workers. This book will not address this kind of testing.

Key Terms Used in Testing During Training

Test designers often have to explain the following terms during the development and application of testing.

Valididty: Testing that fairly and accurately represents the content (skills and knowledge) covered by training.

Reliability: Testing that is repeatable over time with similar types of trainees; testing designed to measure the same thing with different groups of trainees.

Competency: Qualities of a person that make him or her fit for a job; competency can be acquired through talent, experience, or training.

Achievement: A measurement of what a person knows or can do after training.

Sensorimotor Skills: Skills that require auditory, visual, and tactile acuity; skills that require small muscle or large muscle training such as finger dexterity, eye-hand coordination, or strength in legs, arms, or back; skills that are tested typically through one-to-one observation of performance. (Related to motor tasks; see Chapter 3.)

Norm-referenced Test: A test of an employee's rank in reference to a selected group of people, often expressed as a percentile. An example is: The average score on the accounting test was 60 out of 100. Your score was 80, 20 points above the norm for all persons at your salary-grade level throughout the state.

Criterion-referenced Test: A test of an employee's accomplishment in relation to a standard; often expressed as "performing according to standard" or "not performing according to standard," that is, in yes or no terms. An example is: The mechanic who fixed your flat tire only tightened three or four screws that attach the hubcap. He performed to only 75 percent of the standard. He did not meet the criterion for this task.

Pre-Test: Examination of knowledge and skills a trainee already has in the content area of the training course/program.

Post-Test: Examination of knowledge and skills a trainee can demonstrate directly after a training course/program; often a summative test, administered at the end of a course.

Certification: Guarantee of competency in a specific job because entry criteria or continuation criteria have been met; assured through testing, often controlled by a professional association (e.g., accountants, beauticians, American Guild of Organists) or legal body (State Department of Education, Department of Motor Vehicles); often sought by trainees at the end of a training program.

How to Make Up a Scale

There are many occasions in training evaluation and testing in which using a scale is desirable. The most common use of a scale is to record employee opinion—used widely by groups of trainees after a course or conference, or to record job satisfaction.

Scales also can be used in performance testing by a test administrator or instructor to rate a trainee's performance on a specific task. Grading scales are frequently based on a "failing" grade of 50 on a scale from 1 to 100.

Training designers pay attention to the logic and specific wording of scales for evaluation and testing purposes. The following are some guidelines for creating good scales.

1. *Logic.* Present respondents with a scale that is logically differentiated. Some examples are:

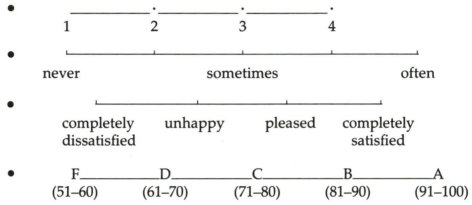

In the same measurement session, present scales that "read" in the same direction, that is, low to high, left to right. Be careful not to unwittingly affect results by a confusing or illogical way of asking a question or presenting a scale. Check your form for consistency.

2. *Choices.* Present no fewer than four choices and no more than seven choices on a scale. Don't invite respondents to always choose the midpoint.

3. *Weighting.* Be sure each item on a test or questionnaire is equally and accurately weighted, so that responses on a scale have equivalent meaning during data analysis.

4. *Freedom.* Always include a space for free response, elaboration, or explanation with any scale. People sometimes cannot fit their responses into your mold. Allow them the freedom to add narrative comments.

Additional comments: _____

_____

HOW TO USE THE WORKSHEETS IN THIS CHAPTER

The worksheets in this chapter are designed to be used sequentially in step-by-step fashion as follows.

Worksheet 6–1: Checklist for Determining Whether Testing Is Practical

Use this checklist to ask yourself some key questions before you decide to test employees. Training and testing must serve a clear business purpose. This checklist will help you focus on that purpose.

Worksheet 6–2: Types of Tests Related to Scoring

Use this matrix to see the relationship of 10 common types of tests to scoring characteristics. Use this worksheet before you begin test design.

Worksheet 6–3: Checklist for Designing Test Questions (Test Items)

Use this checklist as a quality control guide for the test items themselves. Use it as you are writing test items and as a review guide after all items have been completed.

Worksheet 6–4: Test Spec

Use this form to assure that the content of the test items and the behaviors you intend to test are well balanced and represented adequately.

Worksheet 6–5: Checklist for Legal Compliance

Use this checklist to satisfy federal legislation regarding your test design. This checklist is derived from procedures for developing, administering, and using the results of tests as outlined in the *Federal Register*.

Worksheet 6–6: Checklist of Steps for Administering Tests

Use this checklist to assure that you are following acceptable practices in administering your test. As a training manager, be sure that your test designer communicates with your test administrator. A good test administrator will know where the test taker might have difficulty understanding content or procedures, and will anticipate these areas of difficulty by giving clear instructions at the beginning of the test.

HOW TO DETERMINE WHETHER TESTING IS PRACTICAL

This checklist can help you focus on various good reasons why your company might need to test employees. Use each question as a discussion question among your training staff or across managerial levels in various departments of the company.

If you answer "yes" to any of these questions, then a training program probably is indicated, and a testing program related to that training program will yield useful results related to a clear business purpose.

Examples

- *Testing is practical*

YES	NO
√	

Are turnover rates high?

Discussion: Over the last year, data entry operators have lasted, on average, four months. Possible reasons seem to be too much new equipment, lack of system experience, and a confusing help wanted ad. We should probably test skills and seek their opinions about their work situation.

- *Testing is not practical*

YES	NO
	√

Do we need to classify employees?

Discussion: Not really. The Mountaineering Association certifies and classifies all instructors. When they get assigned to us, we know what their competencies and skills are. They are paid on a separate salary scale established by the Mountaineering Assn. and agreed to by the consortium of companies using their services.

WORKSHEET 6–1

CHECKLIST FOR DETERMINING WHETHER TESTING IS PRACTICAL

YES	NO	
		Do we have safety problems?
		Do we need to hire large numbers of people for entry-level jobs?
		Do we have an unusually large number of persons in a specific job category?
		Do we need to select, classify, or rank employees?
		Are our employees under-developed from a technological point of view? Do we need to slot them into career development opportunities?
		Do trainees in similar jobs have widely dissimilar experience or competency levels?
		Are turnover rates high?
		Is training costing too much? Can some employees "test out" of training?
		Are unqualified people being placed in jobs they can't handle?
		Do we have an intense need for quick profit in manufacturing or sales?
		Do we need to deploy our "fast track" employees to solve a burning problem?

HOW TO SELECT THE RIGHT TYPE OF TEST

Often the usefulness of a test depends on the kind of information about a trainee that the score represents. While it is obvious that scoring is related to the content of a test, it is not so obvious that scoring is also related to the form of the test questions—that is, the type of test.

It does no good, for example, to test a trainee's knowledge of overseas markets by having him or her write an essay about why the company should enter an overseas market, if there's no one on your staff with the expertise to grade the essay.

About Scores

Norm-referenced scores show that the test taker has a certain degree of skill/ knowledge in relation to a range of persons in a specific reference group. A norm-referenced score does not necessarily indicate whether or not the test taker is competent. It could tell only that the person earning the score is better than everyone else.

Criterion-referenced scores show that the test taker has a certain degree of approximation toward a standard. A criterion-referenced score indicates level of proficiency or competency regarding a skill or body of knowledge.

Trainers seldom need to know how a trainee scores in relation to others. What trainers really want to know is how well the trainee can do a certain task. Therefore, the preferred choice of test for most training purposes is a criterion-referenced test. This kind of test yields a score that tells how the trainee performed relative to a standard, or criterion.

Examples

- What type of test should I choose to design?
- What do I have to do to make the results of testing as useful as possible?

Situation 1: Top management believes in the value of case study, and has urged us to use case study analysis in all of our management training courses. We know that case studies are hard to score, so we will assign an instructional technologist to the case study author to assist her with developing objectives for the learner and criteria for testing. This will help ensure that case study analysis can be used as a test of the trainee's analysis skills.

Situation 2: When the new diagnostic panel becomes operational, we will have to have 10 trained technicians on the job. We can rent a diagnostic panel simulator, into which we can program up to 20 additional applications that are unique to us. Or, we could wait until the panel arrives and schedule actual hands-on practice after normal working hours. We favor the simulator choice for these reasons: (1) we can't be sure we'll get enough practice time in while the installers are finishing up their work, (2) error read-out is built into the simulator so trainees can see immediately what they did right or wrong, (3) we need fewer instructor hours per trainees at the simulator than we would need in one-to-one practice, and (4) instruction will probably be haphazard if we opt for after-hours practice—testing certainly will be haphazard. By choosing simulation, we can constantly test the trainee, and the program itself can help the trainee correct his or her errors. It will cost us a rental fee, but better learning can be expected to occur.

WORKSHEET 6–2

TYPES OF TESTS RELATED TO SCORING

	Scoring			
Types of Tests	**Easy to Score**	**Hard to Score**	**Tends to Be Criterion-referenced**	**Tend to Be Norm-referenced**
Direct, oral question and answer	√		√	
Short answer, fill-in-the-blank	√			√
Multiple-choice	√			√
Narrative, essay		√		√
Case study analysis		√	√	
Drill, practice	√		√	
Simulation	√		√	
Sorting, prioritizing	√			√
Performing	√		√	
Problem solving		√	√	

Use this matrix before you begin designing your test.

CHECKLIST FOR DESIGNING TEST QUESTIONS (TEST ITEMS)

Use this checklist as you write test items to design quality into your items. The checklist can also be used as a review tool after all items have been written.

When a course includes written testing, it is a good idea to have someone other than the course author or test writer review all of the test questions. Worksheet 6–3 can provide the reviewer with some things to look for during test analysis.

Examples

In a course on *Customer Relations Techniques for Fine Furniture Salespersons*:

- This is a good test item:

  You will be observed on the job by four experienced salespersons for a period of 45 minutes each, any time between 7:00 and 9:00 P.M. Each observer will rate you using the Customer Relations Checklist presented on page 61 of your training manual. The observers will identify themselves at 9:00 P.M.

  During the hours between 7:00 and 9:00 P.M., exhibit at least eight out of ten "Behaviors Leading to the Close" with two or more customers, and demonstrate knowledge of at least three types of furniture.

  This is a good test item because it is relevant to the person's job, it is important to the job and nontrivial, the language and procedures are clear, the item difficulty is appropriate for the trainees, and the criteria seem fair.

- This is a bad test item:

  List the locations of all our other stores in the tri-state region. There are 97 stores; strive for a score of 75 or better.

  This is a poorly designed test item because it is an irrelevant skill for a course in Customer Relations Techniques, and it is unnecessarily difficult. Such a list is posted above every cash register and is readily available as a handout in open bins around the store.

  A more appropriate test item for this content would be:

  At your on-site practice session, direct at least 80 percent of your customers to the "Store Locations" poster or handout bin.

WORKSHEET 6–3

CHECKLIST FOR DESIGNING TEST QUESTIONS (TEST ITEMS)

_____ The difficulty of a test question is based on the difficulty of the problem involved, not the difficulty of the language used in the question.

_____ The test item is relevant and significant.

_____ Avoid knowledge and skills that can be demonstrated by general intelligence. Avoid the trivial and unimportant.

_____ The test question uses the language of the job or business problem.

_____ Words used to ask test questions have only one meaning and are used in a clear context.

_____ Each test question is independent of every other test question.

_____ The difficulty of the test is appropriate for the intended use of the scores.

_____ Testing has been designed into each lesson if possible, or at least into each unit (group of lessons).

_____ Where possible, test questions are direct and informal, with immediate feedback given to the person being tested.

HOW TO DESIGN A TEST SPECIFICATION (TEST SPEC)

The test spec is a chart that cross-references the content of the test with the behaviors/skills that are being tested. The purpose of the test spec is to provide a graphic representation of the structure of the test.[1]

Using a test spec before you write test items helps keep your test balanced. It helps you test the content knowledge and behavioral skills in the correct proportion to your instruction. Remember that testing can be a very important reinforcer of instruction. Using a test spec provides a test designer with the framework of the course upon which to construct the test. The test spec helps you make sure that you have enough items in each training area that you consider important.

A test spec can be used effectively by a task force or group of designers as well as by an individual. The best way to develop a test spec is to focus on one unit at a time, limiting each unit's spec to no more than 20 test items. The test spec is useful in creating all types of tests (short answer, case study, practice exercise, multiple choice, sorting, simulation, and so on).

To create a test spec, unit by unit:

1. Identify major chunks of content across the top of the matrix.

2. Identify major skills down the side of the side of the matrix.

3. Decide how many total test items you want for this unit. (Be sure you allocate enough time for the testing you design.) Enter the total number in the "total" box, outlined at lower right of the matrix.

4. Determine how many items you want in each content/behavior area and fill in the matrix with numbers of test items in each appropriate box.

5. Check your work to be sure the total is correct.

Example

This is a test spec of unit 5, "Place Service in the Dining Room," from a course in *Quality in Restaurant Service*. This test is structured as a performance test in which the trainee is required to demonstrate skills to a test administrator on a one-to-one basis.

		CONTENT				
		Philosophy & Psychology of Service	Meats, Fish, Fowl	Beverages	Serving Techniques	TOTAL ITEMS
B E H A V I O R	establish rapport with seated customer	2 items			1 item	3
	relay information about the restaurant, the menu, the wine list, service policy	3 items	2 items	2 items		7
	serve food and beverages	2 items	1 item	1 item	4 items	8
	remove empty dishes				2 items	2
TOTAL ITEMS		7	3	3	7	**20**

[1] For a thorough discussion of planning a test, including elaboration on the test spec, see Chapter 7 in *Measurement and Evaluation in Psychology and Education*, by R.L. Thorndike and E.P. Hagen (New York: John Wiley and Sons, 1977).

WORKSHEET 6–4

TEST SPEC

		CONTENT			TOTAL ITEMS
B E H A V I O R					
TOTAL ITEMS					

(Add more rows of behavior and columns of content if needed.)

CHECKLIST FOR LEGAL COMPLIANCE

Good test administration practices will keep you out of court. This is especially true in testing for personnel selection or for promotion or demotion. Trainers are often called upon to administer tests whose results are used in other departments related to the training department.

Worksheet 6–5 presents a summary of testing considerations detailed by U.S. government agencies. This checklist helps you to ask the right questions about testing before you embark upon any kind of employee testing.

The *Federal Register* contains rules and regulations governing the broad personnel function, "Employee Selection." Four agencies cooperated in defining these procedures; the Equal Employment Opportunity Commission, the Civil Service Commission, the Department of Justice, and the Department of Labor. Concern for compliance with the law in testing of employees began with adoption of the Civil Rights Act of 1964, Title VII. In 1972, the issues were broadened by the EEO. The *Federal Register* of August 25, 1978 specifies the procedures to follow in developing, administering, and using the results of employee tests. Refer to these documents for details, or check your Congressman's office for updates.

Key Rules of Thumb for Developing Tests

One rule of thumb to follow is: Don't test large groups of people with a pencil-and-paper test. The law comes down hard on invasion of privacy, inequality, and unfairness. Testing is a highly specialized field, and should not be espoused by novices. Stay away from norm-referenced tests. Test frequently during training, and keep test questions directly related to the training being conducted. Be clear about objectives. Give each trainee an equal opportunity to succeed or fail in testing. Never play "I gotcha."

WORKSHEET 6–5

CHECKLIST FOR LEGAL COMPLIANCE
(derived from *The Federal Register*, 8/25/78)

_____ Is the person to be tested in a Title VII protected class (race, color, religion, sex, national origin)? The test will be legally judged by its fairness with regard to protected classes.

_____ Is test performance a necessary factor in personnel decision-making?

_____ Is test performance an important factor in entry to or exclusion from training or career development?

_____ Are test items clearly based on job and task analysis?

_____ Have all alternatives to testing been considered and dismissed?

_____ Is there opportunity to re-test, tutor, or coach persons who might perform poorly on the test?

_____ Have good test design practices been followed, e.g., creation of a test spec, content validation by a panel of experts or peer review, agreement on mastery levels and competency standards, use of experienced or trained item-writers and test administrators, pilot or field testing with a sample population?

_____ Have troublesome items on the pilot test been revised prior to testing the target group?

WORKSHEET 6–6

CHECKLIST OF STEPS FOR ADMINISTERING TESTS

Most people get nervous before a test. Never administer a test in a haphazard or casual way. Be sure everyone understands testing instructions. Use this checklist as you prepare to administer any kind of the test. A rule of thumb as you face your trainees is "Equal and All"—that is, equal instructions are given to all persons taking a test; all persons have an equal opportunity to succeed or fail during testing.

☐ Review the test and its scoring key for accuracy (typographical errors, clarity of language, correspondence between each item and the correct answer). Make corrections if necessary.

☐ Regulate the test environment for access, light, heat, chairs, tables, and space. Be sure each person to be tested has an equivalent test environment.

☐ Be sure the test site is near a clock, drinking water, and rest rooms.

☐ Post no smoking signs and don't allow smoking during testing.

☐ Get a list of persons to be tested. Prior to the test, notify each person on the list at the same time that testing will be done, when it will be done, and where it will be done.

☐ Prior to the test, tell persons to be tested how test results will be used.

☐ Prepare testing instructions. Ask several colleagues to check the instructions for clarity and usefulness.

☐ Assemble all testing materials at the test site: e.g., videotapes, terminals, disks, audio tapes, cameras, pencils, paper, simulation props, job-related equipment, and so on. Secure the test site if materials have to be left overnight.

☐ Administer the test equally to all test takers.

☐ Be sure each test has a place on it for identification of the test taker. Be sure test instructions include instruction to fill in the identification information. (Test takers often forget this in their haste to get on with the test.)

☐ Collect all testing materials and answer sheets (disks, etc.) from test takers immediately after the test.

☐ Formally solicit, document, and report feedback on the test design, environment, and administration from test takers to those who designed the test.

☐ Keep testing materials and scores in a locked storage place.

CHAPTER 7 _____

HOW TO CHOOSE _____
THE RIGHT _____
TRAINING MEDIA _____

A key element in training design is the design of the training media and materials—the videotapes, audio segments, slides, transparencies, and printed pages that enhance instruction. It is important for trainers to choose materials that combine good communication ideas with good instructional ideas. Information in this chapter will help you plan for and choose appropriate training materials.

Good Materials Enhance Good Instruction

Training materials are sometimes called media, or audio-visual (A/V) aids to training. These materials are a powerful part of the instructional message: They need to be designed carefully and used appropriately. Retention by trainees improves tremendously when lessons are presented both orally and visually. Learning can be enhanced by a multi-sensory learning environment.

A Word or Two of Caution

Two items to remember are:

- Training materials reinforce instruction; they don't replace it.
- Be choosey. Never do a media blitz just because you have all the equipment available. The medium should not become the message.

Realities of the training world dictate that the number of probable trainees times the tuition revenue they generate over the life of the course has to be greater than the combined costs of developing or purchasing instructional materials and running the course. Before you begin designing or planning for the use of expensive materials, be sure to verify that there will be trainees to use these materials. Zealous training managers and designers sometimes lose sight of the economic analysis that has to precede the use of training materials. The question is, "Is enough value added?"

155

Choose Wisely for Maximum Learning Value

This chapter discusses considerations in choosing training materials. Worksheets are included to help you—through your choice of media—to assess your training situation, to reinforce your instructional goals, and to accomplish the objectives you've set for your trainees.

Guidelines and forms presented here focus on what you need to do to make the delivery of your training message have impact. This chapter is helpful only if you have already done the up-front analysis, objectives, and content design of the training that's needed. This chapter focuses on the sensory and graphic design of training delivery and its learning environment.

These media are considered: teletraining, videotape, audio tape, slides, transparencies, and print. Appropriate applications of these are suggested:

Teletraining

Teletraining is training delivered by using telephone lines to carry the training program. Telephone lines can carry both voice and data over long distances, making it possible to link many remote classrooms with a central instructor. Speech, video pictures, and computer-generated information can all be transmitted via teletraining either by ground telecommunications or by satelite. Trainees on the receiving end can interact with messages being transmitted.

Training delivered this way requires an "instructor" at the receiving sites who is a combination technician and facilitator of discussion. This kind of instructional specialist is hard to find. Before choosing teletraining, be sure you have the right kind of staff available.

Videotape

Videotape is produced by taking a picture with a video camera of people in action or of processes at work, or by creative video artwork using animation and computer-generated graphics. Videotapes can also be purchased already made from training supply companies. The primary advantage of videotape is that it is active—it realistically represents its subject. It can be edited, interrupted, or "frozen" during instruction in order to clarify its message.

The most common type of videotape format is ½ inch VHS. Be sure you know which tape format your camera and VCR will accept. The recording system (camera, blank tape size) and playback system (VCR, monitor) have to be compatible. Videotape comes in various sizes: 1 inch, ¾ inch, and ½ inch. Mini-cassettes, which are even smaller than these, are also available, and the technology is changing fast. Be sure to investigate the latest advances in video before you purchase any video equipment or tapes. It is wise to use the same size tape in all your courses to make storage and cataloging easier, to make the instructor's job easier, and to save money on equipment by avoiding incompatible materials.

Audio Tape

Audio tapes are useful in independent study at one's desk, on the road in car tape decks, and at home. Audio tapes are especially helpful for the study of music and languages. Audio tapes are also the training medium of choice for jobs that are voice-intensive such as telemarketing, fund raising, and sales through 800 numbers. Audio tape recorders and players can be inexpensive, and require very little space to store or to use.

One drawback of audio tape is that trainees often expect a printed manual or guide to accompany it. Lessons delivered via audio tape often require the intervention of an instructor at some point during the tape. Establishing an "Instructional Hot Line" is one way of providing an instructor on call for trainees using audio tapes without having to provide a full-time instructor.

Slides

Slides are effectively used in training large or small groups of people arranged in theater-style seating in a classroom or auditorium. They are useful when visual emphasis is desired or expansion of concepts is required. Slides are especially good at enlarging the mechanical details or special features of manufactured products. They are good at visually describing tangible goods for purposes of sales training and new product introduction. Slides capitalize on the camera's ability to use a close-up lens and the projector's ability to greatly enlarge an image on a screen. Slides are inexpensive to make and easy to use. They can be accompanied by sound.

One disadvantage of slides is that the classroom generally has to be darkened during instruction. This often causes trainees to "turn off," especially right after lunch. Another problem can arise because the information on slides cannot be changed during presentation: Although the instructor controls the speed of viewing, the information cannot be controlled. Slides must be carefully previewed for accuracy and relevance prior to using them for instruction. Having to turn lights on and off again during instruction can negate the positive impact of slides.

Transparencies

Transparencies, sometimes called "overheads" or "view-graphs," are generally 8½ x 11 inch pieces of acetate with letters or graphics on them designed to be projected on a screen in front of a group of trainees. Transparencies are most frequently made by a graphic artist on a drawing board or on a personal computer using graphics software. A paper master can be turned into an acetate transparency by a thermal printer or an office copier. Trainers can make quick transparencies by using rub-on letters and felt-tip markers either on paper masters or on "write-on" pieces of acetate themselves. Designed and used correctly, transparencies can be a highly effective, interactive, and inexpensive medium supporting the instructional message. Because a transparency is much larger than a slide to begin with, the room does not have to be darkened during projection.

A major disadvantage of transparencies is that they are often created by persons with no graphic sense. Wise trainers will always preview an instructor's handmade transparencies. Often, well-meaning presenters make transparencies that are not readable when projected because the type is too small, the letter or graphic strokes are too light, and information is too crowded on the page. The "Rule of 7" applies: no more than seven items of information per transparency. Be sure margins are adequate and graphics are surrounded by "white space."

Print and Flip Charts

The most common types of print materials are 8½ by 11 inch papers, instructor-made handouts, paper copies of transparencies or slides, and reprints of journal articles and business documents. Posters and flip charts are also commonly used print media to facilitate instruction.

When choosing print as your major medium for instruction, consider the style of lettering and the size of letters. Use color judiciously, to differentiate and highlight. Choose type that is easily readable and free of decorative lines. Use sans-serif type; avoid script styles. When letters and numbers have to be read in the back row of a classroom, write or project them large enough—a letter has to be at least 1¼ inches high to be read 35 feet away. When using a flip chart, be sure that your markers don't "bleed" through to the next page. If you have plenty of paper on your flip chart pad, it's a good idea to print on every other page. If you post blank pages on walls, to write on later, be sure that your markers don't bleed through to the walls.

HOW TO OBTAIN PERMISSIONS IF YOU MAKE YOUR OWN SLIDES, VIDEOS, AUDIO TAPES, OR COMPUTER-GENERATED IMAGES

Get permission from any employee you photograph for use in training media. Employees have a habit of leaving the company long before you finish using their pictures in training materials. Protect against legal action by getting signed and witnessed permission from anyone whom you photograph. Pay that person one dollar if necessary. Of course, check with your corporate attorney regarding the wording of the permission form. A generic form is suggested below.

A/V PERMISSION FORM

Instructions: Please complete this form in ink. Witness must be of legal age.

I, _____ , grant to
(Print Name)

_____
(Legal Name of Corporation)

the right to use and continue to use for educational, scientific, or public information purposes, recordings of my voice, photographs, videotapes, motion pictures, and computer-generated images of me, with or without my name, made on this date, _____ . I grant this use in consideration of my employment or payment of one dollar ($1) which I have received.

_____   _____
(Signature)   (Date)

_____   _____
(Witness)   (Date)

HOW TO USE THE WORKSHEETS IN THIS CHAPTER

The worksheets in this chapter can be used sequentially in step-by-step fashion as follows.

Worksheet 7–1: Training Media Cost Analysis

Use this worksheet to document the key cost variables of training materials for each course.

Worksheet 7–2: Delivery Needs Analysis

Use this worksheet to focus on the presentation of the course as it pertains to media needs for delivery.

Worksheet 7–3: Recommended Choice of Training Material and Percent Usage During the Course

Use this worksheet to specify the media recommended for a specific course.

Worksheet 7–4: Use and Cost Matrix for A/V Materials

Use this worksheet to see at a glance which media have certain use and cost characteristics. Essential checkpoints for each type of A/V medium are outlined on a "Use and Cost Considerations" page opposite the worksheet.

HOW TO ZERO IN ON KEY COST VARIABLES
OF TRAINING MEDIA

Use this worksheet to isolate and estimate the cost of variables which affect your choice of A/V media.

Six common variables are suggested in Worksheet 7–1. They are:

1. Number of trainees →

2. Length of course →

3. Travel expense of trainees →

4. Loaded salary of trainees →

5. Lead time— possible development or installation costs →

6. Support— possible need to purchase more services or supplies →

Course Title: _____ Date: _____

1. **Number of Trainees:** _____

2. **Desired Length of Course:** _____ Hours: _____

3.

Job Locations of Trainees		
How Many?	**Where?**	**Contact Person**

4. Average cost per day to attend the training $ ___
(Include loaded salary, travel, lodging, productivity loss estimate.)

(calculation space)

5. Is there enough lead time for chosen materials? __ yes __ no
If no, what's the problem? _____
_____

6. Does the training environment support the choice of materials? e.g., telephone lines and bridging charges, equipment purchases and rentals, film developing, supplies, tapes, 3-ring binders, editing, printing and duplicating services, graphic artists? __ yes __ no

Estimated, itemized costs for materials support:
1. _____ $ _____
2. _____ _____
3. _____ _____
4. _____ _____

WORKSHEET 7–1

TRAINING MEDIA COST ANALYSIS
(To be completed by training manager or instructional designer.)

Course Title: _____ Date: _____

Number of Trainees: _____

Desired Length of Course: _____ Hours: _____

Job Locations of Trainees		
How Many?	Where?	Contact Person

- Average cost per day to attend the training $ _____
  (Include loaded salary, travel, lodging, productivity loss estimate.)

  (calculation space)

- Is there enough lead time for chosen materials? __ yes __ no

  If no, what's the problem? _____

  _____

- Does the training environment support the choice of materials? e.g., telephone lines and bridging charges, equipment purchases and rentals, film developing, supplies, tapes, 3-ring binders, editing, printing and duplicating services, graphic artists? __ yes __ no

  Estimated, itemized costs for materials support:

  1. _____ $ _____
  2. _____ _____
  3. _____ _____
  4. _____ _____

SOURCES OF HIDDEN MEDIA COSTS

Look for hidden media costs here:

- sufficient electrical wiring
- adequate and convenient placement of outlets (table or wall)
- expiration date of transparency acetates
- compatibility of transparency acetates with your thermal or office copy machine
- supply of blank audio or video tapes
- supply of VCRs/competing users of VCRs
- need for professional writers, editors, camera crew, graphic artists, film developing and printing
- extra telephone charges
- printing manuals
- binders for manuals
- revising manuals and reprinting them
- supply of flip chart pads and markers
- supply of projector bulbs
- average number of students per course times number of times course will be given before revision

SAMPLE

TRAINING MEDIA COST ANALYSIS

Course Title: Uses and Abuses of MemoryRenew Tablets   **Date:** 7/29/XX

Number of Trainees: 100 salespersons

Desired Length of Course: 2   **Hours:**

Job Locations of Trainees

How Many?	Where?	Contact Person	
40	Northeastern Region	John	x 7362
30	Southeastern Region	Herb	x 4456
10	Central Region	Miriam	x 4395
20	Western/Southwestern Region	Zia	x 0086

- Average cost per day to attend the training $ 5,000
  Include loaded salary, travel, lodging, productivity loss estimate. (If training is held in Ohio at the Corporate Sales Center (CSC), maximum travel is required. Better choice is teletraining originating at SCS. Minimal losses of time, salary, productivity. No travel or lodging needed.) Estimate ¼ day delivery time—100 at $50 = $5,000.

- Is there enough lead time for chosen materials? _X_ yes   __ no

  If no, what's the problem? _____

  _____

- Does the training environment support the choice of materials? e.g., telephone lines and bridging charges, equipment purchases and rentals, film developing, supplies, tapes, 3-ring binders, editing, printing and duplicating services, graphic artists? _X_ yes   __ no

Estimated, itemized costs for materials support:

1. 4 instructor/technicians, 1 day each @ $400	$	1,600
2. videotape production		1,000
3. telephone and transmission charges		5,000
4. _____		_____

DELIVERY NEEDS ANALYSIS

Use this booklet to analyze the delivery requirements of a course. Follow these steps:

1. Check the main purpose of the course.
2. Check the area of the business supported by this course.
3. Check the preferred delivery mode for this training.
4. Select and record probable media for this course.
5. Note the advantages of the media you selected.

Several examples of analysis variables are:

Purpose ☐	_Area_ ☐	_Mode_ ☐	_Best Medium_ ☐
skills	management	team problem solving	video class exercises
skills	manufacturing	one-to-one	print
concepts	personal productivity	small group	transparencies
concepts	maintenance	large group	slides
information	product sales	role play	print
information	career planning	large group	videotape

WORKSHEET 7–2

DELIVERY NEEDS ANALYSIS

Course Title _____

Main Purpose of Training:

learn skills ☐   learn concepts ☐   receive information ☐

Primary Area that Training Supports:

product sales	☐	career planning	☐
customer service	☐	quality control	☐
maintenance	☐	manufacturing	☐
safety	☐	policy information	☐
management	☐	procedures	☐
personal productivity	☐	clerical	☐
		other _____	

Preferred Delivery Mode for this Training:

large group presentation	☐
small group lecture/discussion	☐
small group interactive (role-play, simulation, team problem solving, etc.)	☐
individual instruction	☐

Best Medium:

Advantages to this Chosen Delivery Mode:

_____

_____

_____

_____

_____

_____

RECOMMENDED CHOICE OF TRAINING MATERIAL AND PERCENT USAGE DURING THE COURSE

After you have gone through all the delivery needs and cost analyses, use Worksheet 7–3 to specify the percentages of media usage within the course. (Remember, they don't have to add up to 100 percent—some of the instructional time will be taken up with verbal interactions among the instructor and the trainees, lab exercises, drill and practice, observation, and tests, with no media being used.)

Worksheet 7–3 is probably most effectively filled out by the instructor of the course (or an instructional technologist) right after he or she has delivered the course. Such forms can be useful at annual budget request time for new equipment, especially in large training centers where hundreds of courses are offered. If you have a Media Manager, turn over responsibility for this worksheet to this person.

Examples of comments that training managers should look for might include:

- Audio tapes were on call during 90 percent of this course, but were badly labelled, thereby causing a lot of wasted time and confusion.

- This course would benefit from two duplicate videotapes to be used in small group sessions where discussion is more frank and open.

- Type styles vary too much on this set of 30 overheads—can we have them re-done so they're consistent?

- Although teletraining has been shown to save money in training regarding the new line of tractors, it really is not the best medium for dealers to experience the feel of the new transmission systems. One hundred percent teletraining is too much—they also need to see and drive the new machines. Maybe we could afford to bring in the top producing dealers to the factory for a four-hour demo and test drive.

WORKSHEET 7–3

RECOMMENDED CHOICE OF TRAINING MATERIAL AND PERCENT USAGE DURING THE COURSE

Course Title: _____ **Date:** _____

Teletraining   ☐   _____ percent usage

Videotape   ☐   _____ percent usage

Audio Tape   ☐   _____ percent usage

Slides   ☐   _____ percent usage

Transparencies   ☐   _____ percent usage

Print   ☐   _____ percent usage

Comments: (contigencies, constraints, potential problems, other requirements, and so on)

_____

_____

_____

_____

_____

_____

_____

USE AND COST CONSIDERATIONS FOR A/V MATERIALS

Worksheet 7–4 is a matrix of usage and cost considerations of the six types of media discussed in this chapter. Refer to it as you choose the best medium or combination of media for your courses. Use this matrix on a course by course basis.

Worksheet 7–4 is supplemented by this summary of essential checkpoints for each basic type of A/V medium.

Teletraining

- Quality of transmission
- Competence of instructor/technician
- Trainee access for feedback
- Design of remote sites for learning

Videotape

- Equipment compatibility
- Voice and visual quality
- Placement of monitors

Audio Tape

- Clarity
- Pace
- Steadiness, waver
- Volume
- Batteries, electrical outlets

Slides

- Image size, readability
- Focus
- Sequence
- Synchronization with sound
- Variable lighting
- Extra bulb

Transparencies

- Readability
- Focus
- Clutter
- Erasable markers
- Cord taped to floor
- Extra bulb

Print

- Clean lines
- Paper/marker strength
- Clear message
- Duplication quality
- Copyright and attribution

WORKSHEET 7–4

USE AND COST MATRIX FOR A/V MATERIALS

	Teletraining	Videotape	Audio Tape	Slides	Transparencies	Print	
Useful in self instruction		x	x	x		x	
Useful in computer-based instruction	x		x		x	x	
Useful in laboratories		x	x			x	
Useful in workshop course		x	x		x	x	
Useful in lecture course	x	x	x	x	x	x	
Visual concerns	x	x		x	x	x	
Audio concerns	x	x	x	x			
Overall presentation concerns	x			x			
Up-front/development costs	x	x	x	x	x	x	
Installation costs	x	x		x			
Presentation costs	x						
Maintenance costs						x	
High overall expense	x	x					
Moderate overall expense				x		x	
Low overall expense			x		x		

CHAPTER 8

HOW TO PACKAGE TRAINING: MANUALS AND JOB AIDS

What Makes Manuals and Job Aids Successful

Success in packaging training depends on your ability as a training designer to get to the heart of the matter. Adult learners typically don't do homework, and they don't spend hours poring over pages of explanation or description. They often learn "on the fly," and instructors of adults at work seldom stand in front of a lectern and read from their notes. Trainees and instructors move during training.

Manuals and job aids must be direct and to the point, designed and printed so that trainees and instructors can read them easily and quickly. These basics will help you:

- Avoid long sentences.
- Outline information.
- List steps and procedures.
- Leave "white space" around new ideas and logical groupings of information.
- Don't overload pages with words.
- In manuals, use plenty of divider pages to help readers organize information.
- In job aids, simplify, and simplify again.
- Choose a type style that is plain, comes in different sizes, and prints well.

Key Elements of a Good Trainee Manual

To a trainee, the first "engagement" in learning generally occurs when the trainee picks up the training manual for the first time. The manual has to look and feel right—graphically attractive, substantial, and easy to use. A manual can be thought of as a tool that needs to fit the job of learning and fit the hand of the learner.

The trainee manual must be packaged in a way that makes learning happen easily. It is more than a visual aid; it is the pathway to acquire new skills and knowledge.

Options: The Secret of Success in an Instructor Manual

The instructor manual has to be designed and packaged so that a variety of instructors can teach from it. Helpful hints, options in delivery methods, and information about administrative support should be clearly presented. Like the trainee manual, it must look attractive and be easy to follow. It also must be grounded in solid instructional delivery theory and practice as they apply to adult learners. Instructors need some flexibility in the way training courses are delivered. Good instructors will adapt their styles to the particular students in their classes, using the concerns and current problems of each class of trainees. A good instructor manual allows for flexibility in instructional presentation.

How Job Aids Can Replace Training and Save You Money

Job aids, too, are more than simply audio/visual aids that supplement course units. They often are used in place of a course or training activity. They are a great boost to self instruction. Because they often are used by individuals with no instructional or peer support (as in a classroom situation), job aids especially have to be packaged to motivate students and to facilitate learning. A job aid is a more direct training tool than a manual.

Job aids can save you money. Well-designed job aids can reduce the time a learner has to spend away from the job in class, thus doubly saving money—the trainee's salary while attending class, and the cost of designing and delivering a course.

Job aids also present information more succinctly and with greater motivation than course manuals, thereby cutting down on the time required to develop and use a manual. Job aids make good sense in situations where self-instruction is chosen, or where there is little time for learners to attend class.

A Word About Adult Learners and Going to Class at Work

Most people at work are there to do a good job and to make money for themselves and their employers. When they stop working to go to class at work, chances are they bring with them to class a work-related problem that needs to be solved.

They bring with them an expectation that the training they chose or agreed to attend will help them solve that particular problem. Adult learners at work focus on learning only what they need to do or need to know in order to perform their jobs better. They seldom learn for learning's sake—and employers seldom send a person for training that is unrelated to the company's growth.

Adult learners are experienced learners—they probably have several decades of schooling experiences behind them and they know the ways in which they learn best. Adult learners generally enjoy learning from other students in classes at work. Adult learners are opinionated, hard to "level" or "group," and they require flexible learning approaches and tools. In many cases, adults in class at work are older and more experienced in the business than the instructor.

Manuals and job aids must reflect a respect for the practicality, expertise, and independence of the adult learner.

HOW TO USE THE WORKSHEETS IN THIS CHAPTER

Three worksheets in this chapter can be used independently of one another. They provide checklists to use when designing a manual or job aid. Simple graphics illustrate options in design. These worksheets are:

Worksheet 8–1: Trainee Manual Checklist

All trainees receive this manual at the start of class, and they take it back to the job with them to use later as a reference. Use this checklist to help you write with clarity and relevance as you design the trainee manual.

Worksheet 8–2: Instructor Manual Checklist

The instructor uses this manual as a guidebook from which to teach the course. It is often written as a set of lessons and always includes the same information found in the trainee manual. This manual generally is returned to the training library at the end of class, so that the next instructor can use it the next time this particular course is offered. Use this checklist as a guide to the extras that should be included in an instructor manual to make teaching the course easier and more effective.

Worksheet 8–3: Job Aid Checklist

This checklist presents some key characteristics of job aids. Use it to focus your design decisions on the elements that make the job aid the best tool for delivering instruction.

THE TRAINEE MANUAL

The trainee manual documents the course and often is a reference book for trainees back on the job. First and foremost, it is a learning tool.

The trainee manual has to be carefully put together, using principles of good written communication and principles of how adults learn. The trainee manual has to meet the "necessary and sufficient" test—that is, only the necessary information and all of the sufficient information to do its job of helping trainees to learn is included in the trainee manual. A trainee manual sometimes includes appendices and bibliographies of related information for the trainee to use outside of class or back on the job. (Unbound handouts of reports, articles, and so on often supplement the material in the trainee manual.)

The trainee manual—and the instruction—should never be an information "dump." The manual should be written to encourage the trainee to think analytically—to compare, to explain, to break a problem down into small parts. The trainee manual often includes reprints of slides or other visuals used in the course, to remind the trainee of class discussions around these visual items. Reprinted visuals give the trainee plenty of space around the central message to make notes in order to refresh his or her memory later. Trainees should be encouraged to personalize their manuals.

The writing in the trainee manual should spark the imagination of the trainee, especially where new management or technical concepts have to be learned. The manual should help trainees to imagine how their own problems could be solved by using the new skills or knowledge earned in this course. The manual should be written to achieve an application of learning or a transfer of learning from the classroom to the job in as short a time as possible.

Writing in the trainee manual that links new information to previously learned information helps the trainee to build upon the familiar. Such writing gives the trainee a frame of reference and a big picture in order to fit the new into the old order of things.

Training managers who check the packaging of a trainee manual can use Worksheet 8–1 as a checklist.

WORKSHEET 8–1

TRAINEE MANUAL CHECKLIST

A good trainee manual has the following characteristics:

- It defines terms

- It describes and elaborates concepts

- It explains by example (case study, sample, illustration)

- It describes procedures

- It teaches procedures step by step

- It encourages the reader to think

- It encourages the reader to apply new knowledge and skills to a variety of situations

- It contains clear labels to allow scanning and previewing

- It has a consistent format

- It uses simple and direct words

- It uses simple and direct sentences.

THE INSTRUCTOR MANUAL

Everything in the trainee manual goes into the instructor manual. In addition, other kinds of information are suggested for inclusion in the instructor manual. This other information helps the instructor to elaborate on specific points, provides answers to tests or exercises, and helps the instructor to make the trainee's stay in class easier and more productive. Worksheet 8–2 is a checklist for these other items.

When writing or evaluating an instructor manual, be sure to avoid a "spoon-feeding" mentality. Scripted manuals are cumbersome, too wordy, and often demeaning. Strive for clarity and simplicity, not a word-by-word account of what to say and how to say it.

Instructors generally move around the class during training, so they need a manual that is easy to catch a glimpse of from a slight distance. Instructor manuals should highlight text that will be helpful during delivery of instruction. This can be done in a variety of ways: putting that text in a box, printing that text in a bolder type, double spacing that text, putting that text on a page by itself (for example, reserving the left page of a manual for the instructor text), or dividing a page into columns, one of which always contains the instructor text. The illustrations below are options for packaging the instructor manual.

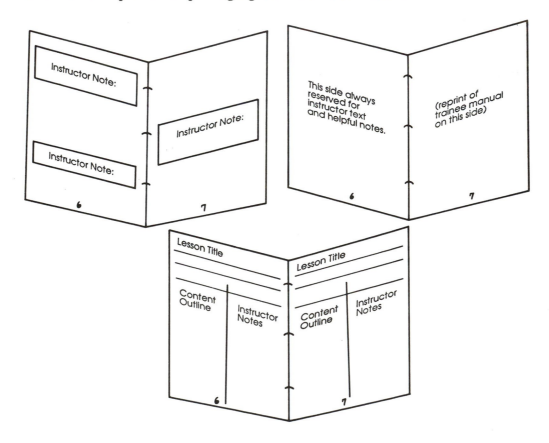

WORKSHEET 8–2

INSTRUCTOR MANUAL CHECKLIST

A good instructor manual contains these items in addition to what's in the trainee manual:

- Descriptions of the course and target audience

- Time schedule for the course, broken down by lessons/units each morning and afternoon; indication of break times; indication of time for any evening seminars and group activity

- Classroom layout

- Building services—rest rooms, cafeteria, gym, library, bank

- Description of required equipment

- List of books, handouts, materials used in the course

- Glossary of terms

- Tests, lab exercises, and answer keys

- Options in training delivery strategies

- Helpful hints on how adults learn, classroom management, instructor preparation

- Elaboration on points of content in trainee manual.

JOB AIDS

Job aids are training materials used on the job. The most common and most useful functions of job aids are to help employees to remember information that is critical to doing a job and to learn procedures required to perform a job.

Since job aids often replace training, they must be carefully designed to promote learning in an efficient and cost-effective way.

The illustrations below indicate some typical formats for job aids. Worksheet 8–3 is a checklist of characteristics of job aids. The training manager or designer can use these illustrations and this checklist for ideas about applications of job aids in his or her situation.

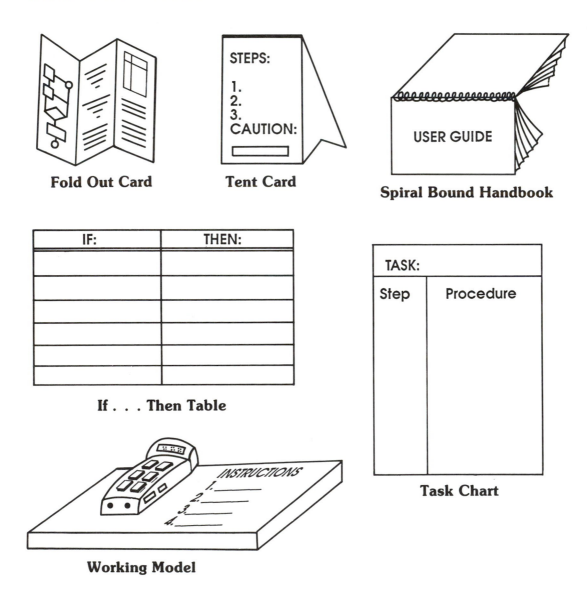

Fold Out Card   **Tent Card**   **Spiral Bound Handbook**

If . . . Then Table   **Task Chart**

Working Model

WORKSHEET 8–3

JOB AID CHECKLIST

Job aids have the following characteristics:

- They tell or show what to do

- They indicate when and in what order to do certain tasks

- They define specific terms and use them in job-specific contex

- They are graphic rather than narrative

- They represent generic or standardized information

- They are separate from other materials, and are often compact, sturdy, and easy to use

- They are posted or distributed for broad use

- They have simple instructions printed clearly on the job aid.

CHAPTER 9 _____

HOW TO CONDUCT A_____
FIELD TEST _____

In training design and delivery, the term *field testing* generally means trying out a newly-written course before a sample trainee group. Field testing is best administered by a training designer who is not the course author. It can also be done by a training manager. As in all testing, field testing should strive to be as objective as possible. It is helpful for the course author to observe during the field testing, but objectivity can be best assured if the administration and feedback session are conducted by someone else.

WHY FIELD TESTING IS CRUCIAL

The reason for field testing is to see if a course "hangs together" as a course—not as a document. The field test is analogous to the dress rehearsal of a play, and includes the props, the lighting, the sets, and the timing of events. It is presentation of the whole course, completely designed and delivered as it is meant to be for paying customers.

Field testing is important because it is the only way to validate the creation of the course as the thing it was designed to be. A course has unique parts—objectives, materials, lessons, lab exercises, measurements, an instructor, and an intended audience. These are the elements that distinguish it as a course, and differentiate it from a talk, a report, minutes of a meeting, a sales presentation, or some other structure crafted from words and ideas.

KEY TESTING TERMINOLOGY

Field testing borrows some terminology from testing and measurement theory and from the practice of technical design reviews. These terms are defined and listed in order of desirability and in order of how closely each approximates the actual presentation of the course to customers. From walkthrough to field test, remember that the purpose of testing and reviewing is to improve the product. Testing activities are processes aimed at measuring quality. In all testing activities, strive for consistency in instructions to those participating; strive for clarity and conciseness in your choice of words. The two essentials of testing are validity and reliability: Your care as a testing administrator can help ensure good results from the field test process.[1]

- *Field Test*: Presentation of the entire course to a full-size and typical sample audience in an environment like the one in which the course will be presented. Field tests include exercises and tests, so that timing of the course can be verified. The purpose of field testing is to see if the course is teachable and learnable.

- *Pilot Test*: A review of the course as soon as a first draft of the major parts of the course is complete. A pilot generally is a partial presentation of some sections of a course to a small audience. No attempt is made to randomly sample the trainee population. Friends or colleagues often are the audience; they function simply as "live bodies" to respond to instruction. The purpose of a pilot is to give reviewers a chance to see the general direction of the course, and to give the course author an early indication of reviewers' perceived appropriateness of the content, objectives, and instructional techniques of the course.

- *Dry Run*: A small group meeting at which a course draft is studied in manuscript form. A dry run generally does not include presentation of the course by an instructor, although it might include some simulated instructional elements. It is essentially a review of all of the course documents.

- *Walkthrough*: The course author's presentation of his or her work to management for approval. A walkthrough occurs at the first milestone in the management of the course development process. Its purpose is to get management approval to continue.

This chapter focuses on the field test—its administration, and the collection and use of feedback for training improvement. This chapter includes a worksheet to assist the training manager or course designer to identify a group of sample trainees to be the audience for the field test, and a checklist of topics for discussion in order to obtain reliable feedback at the conclusion of the field test.

THE TRAINING MANAGER'S ROLE IN FIELD TESTING

In a large training department, a course is typically created by an author (course designer), and field tested by another course designer who is a peer and colleague of the author. These two designers typically report to a training manager or supervisor who is responsible for directing and supporting both the design efforts and the delivery efforts associated with the course. Your primary responsibil-

[1] For a more complete discussion of field testing and evaluating instruction, see Chapter 2, "Designing Instructional Systems" and Chapter 15, "Evaluating Instruction" in Gagne, R.M. and Briggs, L. J. *Principles of Instructional Design*, NY: Holt, Rinehart & Winston, 1979.

ity as a manager regarding field testing is to show by your actions that you are committed to the field test process. It takes time and resources to conduct a field test. Setting aside this time and providing these resources is the first test of a manager's commitment. The following are other specific things the manager can do:

- Help out with physical arrangements (e.g., rooms, projectors, computers, lunch).
- Pay to transport sample students in order to get a good representation of the target audience.
- Show by your actions that you highly regard feedback from the field test.
- Listen to and act upon feedback from the sample students, even if you think you know better. They have the only valid student point of view.
- Reward field tests that are conducted well.
- Punish field tests that are conducted poorly.
- Support those who have to revise a course after a field test; allow them the time and resources to incorporate the feedback suggestions.

HOW TO USE THE WORKSHEETS IN THIS CHAPTER

The following worksheets can be used together or independently to facilitate field testing.

Worksheet 9–1: Guidelines for Indentifying Sample Trainees for the Field Test

This worksheet is designed to help you select a representative cross-section of trainees who will be invited to try out the course.

Worksheet 9–2: Four Areas for Training Improvement

Use this worksheet to get feedback from the sample training group following the field test of the course.

HOW TO IDENTIFY SAMPLE TRAINEES FOR THE FIELD TEST

Identifying sample trainees for a field test requires teamwork and coordination between the training manager and training designers. Each might have access to sources of information the other does not have.

1. *Identify the total population for the course.* Use valid sources of data such as the original proposal for the course, the customer's budget allocation for the course, a state certification or safety requirement, a corporate prerequisite of a certain course, and so on. Don't be tempted to do your identification based on casual conversation around the microwave or water-cooler.

2. *Specify the ideal number of trainees for each session of the course.* Knowing this number will enable you to determine how many times the course will probably be offered.

3. *Identify similar organizations.* Filling in this section of Worksheet 9–1 is an attempt to collect some preliminary marketing data. In discussions during steps 1 and 2, you probably will generate ideas about who else could benefit from this course. This is the place to seriously consider "microwave and water-cooler" conversations. Get names of contact persons if possible, and specify a general number of trainees from these similar organizations who might need to take the course too. You might need to draw upon these organizations for sample trainees for the field test.

4. *State a total number of trainees needed for the field test.* The sample class should represent the range of probable organizations named in step 1 and could include the most likely organizations named in step 3. The size of the sample is controlled by the limitations of the classroom, instructor, and equipment (e.g., can't be any larger than 20 since we will only have lab stations for 20 during actual training, and we have to limit the field test to one occasion since we have only one free instructor).

5. *Draw a sample.* Choose a sample class from among the persons in the organizations named in step 1, and in step 3 if appropriate. List the names drawn on the back side of Worksheet 9–1 or on a separate attached page. Draw 20 percent more than you need.

   In a sample random sampling, all persons have an equal and independent chance of being selected as a member of the sample. Putting all names in a box, mixing them up, and drawing the required number of names is one sampling method.

   Random sampling can be done by using a table of random numbers or a computer-generated list of random numbers. If a random sampling cannot be used, sample as systematically as possible (e.g., choose every third person).

TRAINING TIP: Field testing is serious business. Make it clear at the start of the field test that the sample trainees are chosen for their potential contribution to the evaluation of the new course. This means that they will have to stay about 45 minutes longer after the course material has been presented to provide you with feedback. Make it worth their while to stay—have a wine and cheese party, take them to dinner, arrange limo pickup, or do whatever it takes to let them know their comments are valued.

WORKSHEET 9–1

GUIDELINES FOR IDENTIFYING SAMPLE TRAINEES FOR THE FIELD TEST

Title of Course to Be Field Tested _____

Date of Field Test _____

Location of Field Test _____

1. Identify the total population for the course:

Organization Name	Estimated Number of Persons
_____	_____
_____	_____
_____	_____
_____	_____
_____	_____
_____	_____

2. What is the ideal number of trainees for the course?   [_____]*

3. Identify similar organizations:

Organization Name	Contact Person	Number of Trainees Needed
_____	_____	_____
_____	_____	_____
_____	_____	_____
_____	_____	_____
_____	_____	_____

4. TOTAL NEEDED FOR FIELD TEST: [_____]*

5. Sample:

The sample was drawn by the following method: _____

_____

_____

_____

Names of sample trainees for the field test are listed on the following page.

* The numbers in these boxes should be equal.

WORKSHEET 9–1 (continued)

Sample trainees for the field test:

	Organization Name	Sample Trainee's Name	Phone Number
1.			
2.			
3.			
4.			
5.			
6.			
7.			
8.			
9.			
10.			
11.			
12.			
13.			
14.			
15.			
16.			
17.			
18.			
19.			
20.			
21.			
22.			
23.			
24.			

(Add more pages if necessary.)

GUIDELINES FOR GATHERING DATA FROM FIELD TESTING

Good useful data will reward your careful efforts to conduct a valid and reliable field test of your new course. The process of field testing is the final formative evaluation of the course before it is given to customer trainees. It is, therefore, very important that data about both the form and the dynamics of the course is collected from the sample trainee audience.

Four Areas for Training Improvement

The person who conducts the field test feedback session has a choice of collecting data on written forms or through an oral feedback session (or some combination of written and oral methods). Items for consideration during the feedback session fall into four areas for training improvement. These are:

1. Instructional design
2. Teaching techniques
3. Course environment
4. Pre-course and post-course considerations.

Accurate analysis of data depends on the characteristics of the sample, the completeness of the evaluation questions, the quality of the data-gathering session at the end of the field test, and the skill of the analyst.

The purpose for formal data-gathering is to improve the course. The skillful data analyst sets a serious tone during the feedback session, and thanks the sample trainees for their important part in training improvement. During feedback, sample trainees are encouraged to respond in a narrative way to allow more variation in expression.

How Much Time to Allow for Responses

If forms are developed around each of the four areas for training improvement, allow at least 30 minutes for sample trainees to complete the forms. Add 15 minutes for oral feedback discussion at the end of written feedback, to give people a chance to express themselves in the give and take of oral communication.

If only oral feedback is chosen as the feedback forum, allow 45 minutes for open discussion structured around the four areas for training improvement.

How to Encourage Reluctant Participants

About 10 percent of your trainees will not be interested in giving you thorough feedback. Don't embarrass them into participating; some folks just don't like to participate in evaluation tasks. Your goal, of course, is to get as much useful feedback as possible so that you can expeditiously fix any problems with the course before it goes to paying customers. Sometimes a reluctant minority can be encouraged by your thanking them in advance for their help at the end of the course, and by reminding them that the intent is not to focus on what's wrong with the person who wrote or is delivering the course. The evaluation process is strictly for the purpose of course improvement. It's also comforting to evaluation participants to tell them that you'd appreciate having their names, but that giving their names is not required.

TRAINING TIP: Use an independent "third-party" evaluator to conduct a feedback session. Invite the course author to listen to the feedback from sample trainees, but not to talk (i.e., not to defend his or her course) during the feedback session. Provide the course author with the list of sample trainees (Worksheet 9–1) and the feedback guideline, four areas for training improvement (Worksheet 9–2) for reference during feedback discussion.

WORKSHEET 9–2

FOUR AREAS FOR TRAINING IMPROVEMENT

Instructions: The items and questions in these four areas can be designed into a written feedback form or used in checklist fashion by a feedback session leader during oral feedback at the end of the field test of the course. Choose a method for data-gathering that will yield the best results, given your corporate culture and management style. Whatever style you choose, strive for feedback in at least these four areas:

1. *Instructional Design*
   - ☐ Objectives
   - ☐ Content
   - ☐ Organization
   - ☐ Tests
   - ☐ Exercises, labs
   - ☐ Handout materials
   - ☐ Manuals
   - ☐ Timing

2. *Teaching Techniques*
   - ☐ Established and kept rapport
   - ☐ Explained goals/objectives
   - ☐ Taught with clarity
   - ☐ Encouraged interactions
   - ☐ Knew content
   - ☐ Respected students

3. *Course Environment*
   - ☐ Choice of media
   - ☐ Choice and Performance of software
   - ☐ Hardware, equipment
   - ☐ Arrangement of learning space
   - ☐ Involvement level of trainees
   - ☐ Light, heat, noise, air
   - ☐ Refreshments, social time

4. *Pre-course and Post-course Considerations*
   - ☐ Is the course description accurate?
   - ☐ Did we correctly identify the target audience?
   - ☐ What conditions make this course necessary?
   - ☐ How will you use this course on your job?
   - ☐ In what time period will you use this course?
   - ☐ Will you recommend this course to others?
   - ☐ What courses, talks, or workshops on related topics should be offered?

TRAINING TIP: If you choose to expand these four areas into four forms for written feedback, include the personal information section at the *end* of the last form. The reason for this is to encourage the sample trainees to concentrate on course improvement before identifying him or herself. Some trainees will not want to identify themselves. Asking them to provide personal information up front sometimes discourages participation. The personal information section of a form should look like this:

Your Current Job: _____
Years With the Company: _____ Work Location: _____
Your Name (optional): _____ Telephone (optional): _____

Thank you very much for your help.

CHAPTER 10

HOW TO DELIVER TRAINING

Delivery of training is both a management problem to be solved and a skill to be mastered. This chapter presents training delivery in both these contexts, suggesting tried and true techniques for successfully accomplishing this special training function. This chapter focuses on the instructor and his or her role in helping learning to occur.

OPTIONS AMONG DELIVERY METHODS

The training manager always faces a decision about how to deliver training at the moment a training need is clarified. There are many choices for cost-effective delivery. These delivery methods vary according to the amount of participation by the instructor. Among these methods are:

High Instructor Participation	Low Instructor Participation
● lecture	● role playing
● team teaching	● case study
● demonstration	● simulation game
● tutoring	● field trip
● on-the-job training	● computer-based instruction
● teletraining	● independent study

Many business factors affect the choice of delivery method. The training manager has to balance development costs against delivery costs, weigh the advantages and disadvantages of hiring an outside vendor to deliver a course, figure out if the training need can be addressed by the current staff or possibly by quickly training someone with a special subject matter expertise in another department in the company to become an instructor, and has to consider all of these economic issues within a framework of learning.

Definitions and Examples of Training Delivery methods

The following six training delivery methods require a high level of instructor participation in the delivery:

—*Lecture*: Delivery of a course by a single instructor, generally from a prepared outline, script, or notes. A lecture generally lasts one to two hours and requires little trainee participation. The instructor is often behind a lectern or podium during delivery.

Examples

- Reorganization of the FDA and Its Projected Effects on Over-the-Counter Drug Sales
- Trends and Procedures in Commercial Truck Leasing

—*Team Teaching*: Delivery of instruction by two or more instructors who share the presentation of a body of content. Team teaching is a method which apportions content of a long course (more than three days) among instructors with specialized expertise or particularly dynamic delivery styles. This is often done to keep trainees interested in the content and motivated to keep coming back to class.

Examples

- An Exploration of Modern Korean Art, Language, and Engineering
- Export Practices Among Nations in the European Common Market

—*Demonstration*: Delivery of instruction by a single instructor who shows the trainee how to do something or how something works—that is, step by step how to perform a procedure or how a piece of equipment operates.

Examples

- Techniques of Jungle Gym II Assembly
- 50 Ways of Do-It-Yourself Typewriter Repair

—*Tutoring*: Delivery of instruction by a single instructor to a single trainee. Tutoring is very intense, specific instruction, often remedial in nature, and is often tied to equal employment opportunity. Tutoring often is provided after regular working hours.

Examples

- English Grammar, Usage, and Business Writing for Asian-born Managers
- Refresher Course in Shop Math: Proportions and Percents, Liters and Meters

—*On-the-Job Training*: Delivery of instruction by a master worker to a novice worker while both are on the job doing productive work. On-the-job training (OJT) is often used in a situation where complex procedures or skills need to be learned and where the experience of a master worker or craftsperson is the best body of content to pass along to a trainee. OJT is especially useful where complex processes for doing a job have evolved over several years, and where the trainee can benefit from supervised practice as his or her skills are developed.

Examples

- Bindery Crafts
- Fall Pruning of Deciduous Trees

—*Teletraining*: Teletraining is training delivered by means of telephone lines from a central transmitting studio or classroom to remote locations. Because telephone lines can transmit data as well as voice, teletraining has an enormous possibility for delivery of information of all sorts, and can incorporate some interaction between trainee and instructor. It, of course, lacks the immediacy of human interaction, and therefore has limitations. It is instructor-driven at the point of transmission. Facilitators, or instructional aides, are required at the remote locations. However, because of its capacity to reach large audiences, teletraining can save instructional time and personnel in the long run.

Examples

- Case Study of Homecare Products, Inc.'s Market Share of Door-to-Door Sales
- Policy Issues and Administrative Priorities Regarding Cable Networking

The following six training delivery methods require a considerably lower level of instructor participation than the previous six delivery methods. In the following delivery methods, the instructional designer plays perhaps a more significant role. (Delivery methods which are high in instructor participation are usually also high in the instructor's contribution to the design of the course.) In many of these delivery methods, the instruction is designed to enable trainees to learn from each other.

Methods of delivery featuring low instructor participation often cast the instructor as a facilitator, monitor, organizer, or feedback expert. When the instructor functions in any of these roles, it is especially important that the course be carefully crafted so that content can be completely delivered and so that the varied processes of delivery stay focused on instruction.

Trainee interactions with each other or with technology characterize these delivery methods:

—*Role Playing*: Delivery of instruction through trainees' acting out a prescribed character faced with a business problem. In role playing, the instructor provides trainees with a statement of the problem to be addressed, and a description of the character and the character's role in the problem solving process. The instructor also provides directions for listening and observing to trainees who are not engaged in playing the roles. The instructor coordinates and manages the role playing, and generally summarizes what was learned. Role playing adds interest, liveliness, and elements of reality to instruction for problem solving and decision-making skills.

Examples

- Interviewing Techniques for Selection of Middle Managers
- Retirement Planning Seminar

—*Case Study*: Delivery of instruction through trainees' analysis of an actual business situation defined and described as a "case." The instructor's function is to present the case to the trainees, to encourage thorough analysis and expression by all trainees, and to define the kinds of outcomes desired as a result of the analysis. In case study, the instructor often sets the parameters of analysis and group structure, and then functions in a more passive role as a facilitator or manager of the process. A course often is comprised of a series of case studies, each illustrating a different approach to a defined problem.

Examples

- Metamorphosis of a Profit Center: How CBT Services Inc. Outgrew the Cost Center
- Terminate with Care: How Supervisors Protect the Corporation and Preserve the Individual's Self Worth

—*Simulation Game*: Delivery of instruction through a game that all trainees play. Winning is secondary to strategizing. A game used in training is designed around actual business operations and processes—that is, a game simulates work. Sometimes a game can be played against a computer, thereby minimizing the human interfaces of traditional board games. Games are often used to foster better communication, to figure out best use of human or material resources, and to model complex systems like battles or a city's mass transit network.

Examples

- The Radon Race: Find It, Fix It, Follow It
- Meltdown Madness: Overcoming Human Error

—*Field Trip*: Delivery of instruction through direct experience of a new situation or new content at a site away from the trainee's work location—that is, a "field" site. On a field trip, the instructor functions as a trip coordinator and generally as the facilitator of a follow-up discussion synthesizing the field trip experience.

Examples

- How to Manage the Computerized Search from Query to Delivery: Three

Views of Industrial Libraries
- Better Delivery of Apprentice "Related" Instruction: A Visit to Six Classrooms in the Steamfitter's Consortium

—Computer-Based Instruction (CBI): Delivery of instruction by a computer. In CBI, there is generally no instructor. A technician is often responsible for managing the instruction, keeping track of the schedule of use of a particular course and of time spent by each trainee at the computer, and for troubleshooting technical problems the trainee might have in using the computer during learning. Sometimes a CBI course designer is available for consultation via a telephone "Hot Line." CBI trainees can be networked together in a kind of electronic classroom.

Examples

- Programming in BASIC
- Exercises in Dispersion and Central Tendency: Module 2, Standard Deviation

—Independent Study: Delivery of instruction designed to be learned by a trainee studying alone, with no interactions among classmates. Interactions with an instructor might occur if a periodic reporting or testing requirement is built into the course. Books and manuals used in independent study are often supplemented by motivational media such as videotapes, slides, audio tapes, and job aids.

Examples

- State Legislative Positions Impacting Light Industrial Pollution Control Practices
- Human Factors in CRT Display Design and Use

U.S. GOVERNMENT-FUNDED TRAINING

The following nationwide training programs are funded by federal legislation administered by the U.S. Department of Labor and the U.S. Department of Education through various cooperative relationships among and within the levels of government (federal, state, and local). More information on these programs is available from the office of your elected representatives, your State Department of Education (Vocational Education Division), or your State Department of Labor.

Among the major pieces of job training legislation are:

MDTA (1962)—Manpower Development and Training Act
CETA (1973)—Comprehensive Employment and Training Act
JTPA (1982)—Job Training Partnership Act.

Job training, as funded by federal legislation over the last three decades, has been seen as an economic policy tool to develop a national pool of stable and productive workers. Such programs have been targeted to specific groups who are defined by the legislation as disadvantaged in the workplace. These programs generally consist of training to encourage general maturation among young disadvantaged workers, training to become socialized to and motivated for work, education for literacy and basic employability, and skills training for occupations in a variety of industries.

A primary goal of much of this training is to enable workers to be mobile within the workforce and to have greater freedom to choose satisfying work. Income level is generally the major criterion for participation in job training.

Apprenticeship

In addition, Apprenticeship Training has been administered largely through the Department of Labor, with substantial funding costs assumed by industries and local employers who employ apprentices. Apprentices earn licenses and certifications by fulfilling Department of Labor and industry standards of training while they are active wage earners.

Apprenticeship Training generally takes about four years of study, broken down historically into 2000 hours of on-the-job training and 144 hours per year of related classroom instruction. This "related" instruction is usually funded by federal legislation, complementing the costs borne by the industry itself.

Although training managers in corporations generally do not design job training programs, you might find yourself helping to administer such a program in your company in cooperation with your State Department of Labor or State Department of Education (Vocational Education Division).

It is the intent of this brief definition and description to introduce simply the concept of government-sponsored job training and apprenticeship. For additional reading, several commentaries on job training can be found in the 1982 Yearbook of the American Vocational Association, *Contemporary Challenges for Vocational Education*.

HOW TO TEACH ADULTS

Teaching adults is different from teaching children primarily for two reasons: (1) Adults are experienced learners, and (2) they want useable results from learning.

Adults who sign up for training courses or programs, engage in computer-based instruction, or go to conferences, expect to find a solution to a work-related problem that faces them today.

Instructors of adults begin with these premises:

- Trainees are equal to, not subordinate to, the instructor.

- Trainees are in class voluntarily, and they can leave any time they want to.

- Trainees are often experts in their fields; they need to be recognized as such.

- Trainees expect to learn from each other during training, and they need the opportunity to do so.

- Trainees prefer to be active, not passive, learners.

- "Life" always intervenes—trainees have very real pressures and responsibilities during the time they are in class; training has to be flexible, direct, and clear.

- Trainees want practical, useful information and skills to do their jobs better.

- Trainees are willing to pay for good instruction; they are not willing to pay for poor instruction.

Instructors who recognize the nature of the adult learning situation can design, deliver, and evaluate instruction so that it is fun, effective, and contributes to productivity and profit.

TRAINING THE TRAINER

One of the most difficult jobs in training is to be the instructor of future trainers. A "Train-the-Trainer" course is an important addition in most companies to the courses in various work-related subject areas. It must be taught by an experienced and skillful instructor who can model the good techniques he or she is teaching this special group of trainees. Generally, the ideal instructor for adult learners is one who is first an expert in the subject being taught, and second, one who can demonstrate that he or she can teach adults. Training the trainer well can lead directly to a better bottom line.

The Train-the-Trainer Course

The course in instructional techniques focuses on delivery of instruction. In many training organizations the reality of staffing, however, is that the subject matter expert who is learning to become a trainer to teach his or her subject very often also has the job of designing the course. Instructional designers, also called instructional technologists and educational technologists, can be extremely helpful to a subject matter expert who is writing a course. Often, however, training organizations do not have instructional designers, and the Train-the-Trainer course has to do the whole job—that is, teach the subject matter expert to both write a course and teach a course.

Other chapters in this book detail various topics in course design, evaluation, and delivery. These chapters will be helpful to instructors who have to write their own courses. They are:

The professional literature in the field of training has many books on the subjects of training the trainer and instructional techniques. The purpose of this book is to simply introduce the subject, in order to provide the training manager with some insights into the dimensions of the topic.

Major Areas of Content in the Train-the-Trainer Course

- How adults learn
- How to stay focused on business goals and useful outcomes of training
- How to design a course: objectives for the learner, and units of content
- How to write and use lesson plans
- How to select and use media
- How to perform the many functions of a trainer: leader, expert, coordinator, facilitator
- How to judge timing of various sections of the course
- How to choose the right method to deliver instruction
- How to set up the classroom
- How to design and conduct a laboratory session
- How to present information
- How to manage a group
- How to test and evaluate.

HOW TO USE THE WORKSHEETS IN THIS CHAPTER

It is beyond the scope of this book to present specifics of a Train-the-Trainer course. The worksheets that follow are divided into two major groups of guidelines and worksheets that can be useful to veteran instructors as well as trainers in training. The two groupings are: the more generic "Techniques to Guarantee Active Learning," and the more specific "Training Delivery Tool Kit."

TECHNIQUES TO GUARANTEE ACTIVE LEARNING
(four worksheets)

Worksheet 10–1: How to Define Instructional Groups

Use this worksheet to plan the most appropriate seating arrangements for your group of trainees.

Worksheet 10–2: How to Get a Stalled Group Moving Again

Use this "If . . . then" table to find the right strategy for handling a tough group.

Worksheet 10–3: Presentations for Real People

Use this checklist to remind yourself that good instructors teach people first and content second. All four areas of the presentation deserve attention during each 15-minute segment of instruction: interaction, content, materials, and media.

Worksheet 10–4: Instructor Preparation Checklist

Use this checklist to prepare to teach—one month ahead, one week ahead, and one hour ahead of your scheduled course.

TRAINING DELIVERY TOOL KIT (seven worksheets)

Worksheet 10–5: Lecture Notes Planner

Use these guidelines to plan a lecture.

Worksheet 10–6: How to Teach by Demonstration

Use these guidelines to guide your delivery of training by demonstrating a procedure.

Worksheet 10–7: What It Takes to Be a Tutor

Use this worksheet to determine if tutoring is appropriate for you and if it is a delivery method you can handle.

Worksheet 10–8: Performance Feedback Form for Skills Training

Use this form to give feedback to a trainee regarding skills performance.

Worksheet 10–9: Role Play Guidelines

Use these guidelines to facilitate role playing.

Worksheet 10–10: Case Study Planner

Use these guidelines to structure a case study.

Worksheet 10–11: Field Trip Planner

Use this worksheet to plan a field trip.

WORKSHEET 10–1

HOW TO DEFINE INSTRUCTIONAL GROUPS

The instructor always has the option of organizing the seating in a classroom so that the design of the course supports the delivery of it. Active learning occurs when the factors of delivery and design are congruent. Below are three standard ways of defining instructional groups. A single course could have all three kinds of groups.

ⓘ =Instructor ☐ = Group	Appropriate Situations for This Group
Instructor as lecturer	• When you have large amounts of information to convey • When the trainee population is large (more than 50 people) • When the instructor is an expert on the subject • When the instructor is an excellent speaker • When high quality media support the lecture
Instructor as facilitator	• When trainees break into small groups for discussion or problem solving • When the level of trainee expertise is high • When the level of trainee experience is high • When you want trainees to interact with and learn from each other
Instructor as leader	• When directions or procedural steps are required • When a problem needs to be clarified • When new content needs to be defined • When the whole group is treated as one group and moves forward through the course together

WORKSHEET 10–2

HOW TO GET A STALLED GROUP MOVING AGAIN

The perceived quality of training delivery often rests on the trainer's skill in managing the group. In most groups, people will try to avoid conflict, and when a group runs into trouble, group members withdraw and lose focus. An effective trainer will recognize that when conflict occurs, it needs to be skillfully managed, because most people have not learned strategies to deal with conflict. (An effective instructor will support those few group members who take the risk to resolve the conflict.)

The following techniques can be useful in groups in which energy is low, dominance by a clique or individual is obvious, tempers are too hot, and in many other situations where "process" is important to accomplishing "task."

IF:	THEN:
1. The group is bored,	1. **Introduce a new piece of data.** *Example*: "You might be interested to know that at the Iowa Conference they found out that. . . ."
2. The group is dull and passive,	2. **Change places.** *Example*: Move from in front of the lectern to the back or side of the room.
3. Small groups aren't working,	3. **Regroup into smaller or different sets.** *Example*: Break into pairs instead of fours or fives; organize a "fishbowl" in which half the class is active and the other half functions as observers around the perimeter of the active group.
4. The group is argumentative,	4. **Present feedback to the group.** *Example*: "I observe at this very moment that we seem to be. . . ."
5. The group is out of control and noisy,	5. **Make an assignment.** *Example*: "STOP—shift gears, find a pencil and piece of paper. List three things that. . . ."
6. The group "can't see the forest for the trees"—nitpicks, and has lost focus,	6. **Focus on the uses of the report or decision.** *Example*: "Let me remind you that the state of New Mexico has agreed to fund this study as soon as we get the functional specifications finished."
7. A group member behaves badly,	7. **Give immediate behavioral feedback, but refrain from judgmental remarks.** *Example*: "Manny, you are smoking in a 'no smoking' area; please extinguish your cigar."

WORKSHEET 10–3

PRESENTATIONS FOR REAL PEOPLE

There is both art and craft in delivering training. Delivery requires style, grace, and an intuitive and anticipatory sense of what individual trainees need to know during the next 15 minutes.

Good delivery is more than looking good, sounding good, and handling flip charts with ease. Good presentations are carefully designed so that the roomful of knowledgeable, experienced, responsible, real people with real problems will be able to get something from the course and give something to it.

The following checklist is organized in four categories: interactions, content, materials, and media. Good presentors demonstrate their presentation skills in each of these four areas during every 15-minute segment of presentation.

This checklist can be used as a quick reminder to the instructor immediately before class, and can be used as an evaluation checklist during a field test or train-the-trainer course exercise. It can also be used effectively to evaluate a videotaped presentation by an instructor.

Interactions	Content	Materials	Media
☐ Makes trainees feel at ease	☐ States objectives	☐ Provides all trainees with equal materials	☐ Chooses and uses media to support, not replace instruction
☐ Handles administrative details quickly and thoroughly	☐ Defines terms	☐ Provides reading lists or additional handouts for more advanced or more eager trainees	☐ Uses media effortlessly (practices prior to class)
☐ Answers questions	☐ Is orderly and logical	☐ Refers to manuals at appropriate times	☐ Places media so that all trainees can see and hear
☐ Pauses and reviews	☐ Makes transitions	☐ Engages trainees in using materials	☐ Keeps media organized during the presentation
☐ Creates expectations for learning	☐ Enhances descriptive language by using: · analogies · examples · nonexamples · stories · humor · questions · drawings · graphs	☐ Keeps materials organized during the presentation	☐ Manages media "on the fly"— skips over or discards outdated or inappropriate items
☐ Motivates individual trainees			☐ Encourages trainees to interact with media (e.g., flip charts, slides, videos)
☐ Paces the presentation correctly			
☐ Establishes personal rapport with each trainee	☐ Exercises and tests trainees often on their understanding and application of course content		
☐ Creates opportunity for trainees to establish their own credibility	☐ Reorganizes and summarizes content if necessary		
☐ Gives and receives feedback			
☐ Moves around the classroom			

WORKSHEET 10–4

INSTRUCTOR PREPARATION CHECKLIST

Use this checklist as you prepare to teach a course. Active learning occurs when the instructional environment is properly set up and instructional supports don't get in the way during delivery of instruction.

One month before the course:	• Confirm your reservation for the facility • Verify the content of the trainee manual and handouts • Check with another instructor to be sure your time schedule for each lesson is realistic • Practice all lab exercises and demonstrations to be sure they can be done in the time you planned.
One week before the course:	• Order food and beverages for breaks and lunch • Assemble and inspect all course materials • Assemble all supplies for yourself and for trainees • Practice using all media and equipment • Get names and registration information of your trainees • Get the name and phone number of the nearest media support person in case bulbs burn out or fuses blow • Be sure flip chart sheets can be posted on the classroom wall and markers don't bleed through—order more paper if they do.
One hour before the course:	• Check computer hookups and electrical connections • Be sure projectors work • Adjust classroom heating, lighting, and ventilation • Arrange handouts and attendance sheet on a table near the entry door • Lay out all supplies and materials you need to use in a place where they are easily accessible and won't interfere with your use of the instructor manual • Practice the first five minutes of your presentation.

WORKSHEET 10–5

LECTURE NOTES PLANNER

Title: _____ Audience: _____

Length of Lecture: _____ Date of Delivery: _____

A. Define a succinct framework

    1. List objectives for the learner
    2. Define key terms alphabetically for your quick reference during the lecture
    3. List media and equipment required

B. Structure the body of the lecture

    1. List key points in the order in which you will present them
       · Allow plenty of space between them
       · Write out key phrases; practice saying them aloud
    2. Define positive and negative instances of each conceptual point (examples of what it is and what it is not)
    3. Make notes in the margin correlating media with content
    4. Underscore or highlight transitions between topics

C. Structure the end of the lecture

    1. Synthesize important information
    2. Re-emphasize or re-cast key points
    3. Suggest job-related action based on the key points
    4. Send them home challenged and smiling!

Situation Analysis for Using This Training Delivery Tool: Lecture

You are the regional manager of 80 auto dealers. Recently, new procedures for commercial truck leasing have come down from industry management. It is your responsibility to be sure your dealers know what's involved, why the changes occurred, the tie-in with the company's new marketing thrust, and how they can estimate their own potential lease customer volume.

You decide to structure this lecture as a luncheon speech. You rent a private dining room in the hotel nearest the largest dealership and bring all the dealers in for a noon to 2 P.M. luncheon.

You choose to deliver this training by the lecture method, using a set of company-prepared 3-color overhead transparencies. You plan a 10-minute question and answer period after the lecture, which you estimate will take 20 minutes. You also will hand out a packet of information, including new forms, to each dealer at the end of the lecture.

HOW TO TEACH BY DEMONSTRATION

Subject: _____ Audience: _____

Estimated Time: _____ Date of Delivery: _____

A. List objectives for the learner

B. List steps in the demonstration

    1. Prepare a "Step-by-Step" handout for each trainee

    2. Use a job aid wall chart

C. Make the delivery personal

    1. Be sure each trainee can see all steps being demonstrated

    2. Maintain eye contact with each trainee during the demonstration

    3. Relate the demonstration to personal applications

    4. Relate the outcomes of training to a personal business goal

D. Make the delivery active

    1. Involve each trainee; encourage each to handle equipment prior to or during the demonstration

    2. Supervise each trainee's demonstration of competence individually

    3. Provide feedback regarding success rate to each trainee immediately

    4. Involve each observer trainee in commentary, questioning, or assisting

---

Situation Analysis for Using This Training Delivery Tool: Demonstration

You are the floor manager of a "Terrific Toys" retail franchise. The lull after the holidays affords you the time to train your floor clerks to assemble the new line of spring outdoor climbing toys for young children.

You decide to take the time during January to demonstrate how "Jungle Gym II" goes together, and let each of the 20 floor clerks practice doing it. You believe that this training will pay off in terms of customer satisfaction and repeat business. You offer prizes for outstanding performance. You plan to use your clerks' training success in spring advertisements in local newspapers.

The demonstrations will be done twice a week all month with two or three trainees per session. You plan to hire a photographer and to use employees' photos in your ads.

WORKSHEET 10–7

WHAT IT TAKES TO BE A TUTOR

Program/Course: _____

Employee(s) to Be Served: _____

Duration and Dates of Delivery: _____

A. Do a self-assessment (answer YES to each item, or do not choose tutoring as a delivery method)
   1. Do you value the contribution of each individual you will be tutoring?
   2. Have you repeatedly in the past demonstrated your flexibility in presentation of content?
   3. Do you consider yourself an excellent instructional designer?
   4. Are you patient?
   5. Will you facilitate each trainee's push to his or her limits of learning in order to achieve high performance?

B. Be creative in your design of the tutoring program/course
   1. Choose the appropriate tutorial method: On-the-Job Training, Individual Remedial Sessions, Individual Advanced Sessions, Tutorial for Credentialling and Testing, Resource Room Tutorial Services
   2. Schedule tutoring sessions at a time when trainees are fresh and alert
   3. Get background information on your trainees' specific problems on the job; design the tutoring to address these problems
   4. Teach content that is uniquely relevant to each individual

C. Focus on the individual
   1. Clarify the individual's objectives and expectations
   2. Set realistic goals for each trainee
   3. Give positive and negative feedack often during each tutoring session
   4. Report to each trainee the progress towards reaching his or her goals in a formal way at regular intervals

Situation Analysis for Using this Training Delivery Tool: Tutoring

You are the lead engineer for a work team of five mechanical engineers who all happen to be foreign-born. Each needs help in English pronunciation and writing in order to accurately and assertively represent the work of the team throughout the company.

Native languages represented by this group are Russian, German, French, and Spanish. You hire an English tutor who has a good reputation as an instructor of adults and who has experience working with engineers.

You considered the idea of running an On-the-Job Training program, paying the tutor to be present in the work group for six weeks, but decided against that because it wasn't focused enough. Instead, you chose an Individual Remedial Sessions program. You allow the tutor the freedom to develop a specialized program of language learning on a one-to-one basis for each of your five employees. Tutoring sessions are set for 10 A.M. to noon once per week for each trainee, in the Engineering Conference Room.

WORKSHEET 10–8

PERFORMANCE FEEDBACK FORM FOR SKILLS TRAINING

Use this form to provide feedback to a trainee after a skills training course/lesson. This form is appropriate after tutoring, demonstrations, laboratory sessions, simulation games, or any training where achievement of skill proficiency is closely monitored by the trainer.

Performance Feedback

Name: _____

Course/Unit/Lesson: _____

Date of Performance Observation: _____

Instructor: _____

Performance Rating Key:

1 = Proficient at this task

2 = Needs practice

3 = Unsuccessful try; repeat after more training

Skill/Task List	Performance Rating (Check one)			Comments Regarding Specific Behaviors Observed by Instructor
	1	2	3	
1.				
2.				
3.				
4.				
5.				

Situation Analysis for Using This Training Delivery Tool: Performance Feedback Form

Three data entry clerks, all just hired, have recently completed an On-the-Job Training program. Each clerk was paired with an experienced data entry clerk who functioned as an instructor.

Each instructor was given a Performance Feedback Form on which a task list for the job was already typed. These tasks included:

1. Translate appropriate groups of data into correct code
2. Input coded data
3. Move data among all files in the system
4. Use data to generate reports
5. Access archived data.

Each instructor received 12 hours of train-the-trainer instruction in using the task list for trainee observation, rating, reporting, and giving feedback.

Performance Feedback Forms were submitted within 24 hours after the conclusion of training to each new clerk's supervisor.

Role: _____

Trainee Performing This Role: _____

Observer's Name: _____ Date: _____

A. Present the role with great clarity

1. Present facts
2. Present descriptors of the fictitious person in the role
3. State the problem simply: Challenge the role player to solve it
4. Prepare a written briefing sheet containing these first three items for each trainee who is performing the role
5. Choose a role player who identifies with some part of the character

B. Structure the observation

1. Give each trainee a chance to be both role player and observer
2. Instruct observers to look and listen for specific things during the role play, and to write down their observations. These are the basics:
   · body language
   · attitudes; tone of voice
   · bad behavior
   · assertiveness
   · turning point in problem solving

C. Have fun

1. Make the situation believable and the problem real, but interject the exercise with humor
2. Do several "warm up" exercises to set trainees' minds for role play. Choose exercises that will make trainees smile or put them at ease. This can be done through simple questions and statements like these:
   "Did you ever notice that Lynn always looks in the left corner of the room when she's doing a presentation?"
   "I'll bet you didn't know that I always have to remove my loose change from my pockets before work so I don't rattle it at meetings!"
   "Do you remember that TV commerical about the guy who makes the donuts—does he remind you of anyone around here?!"
   "Can you think of a time when your teenage daughter willingly cleaned her room?"

Situation Analysis for Using This Training Delivery Tool: Role Play

You are a staff psychologist in a major corporation that has just embarked on a forced early retirement program as part of a downsizing strategy. Already you are swamped with visits from fifty-year-olds who are filled with fear about their benefits, their mortgages, their kids' college expenses, and their future daily existence as a potential retiree.

You decide to offer a voluntary Retirement Planning Seminar to all employees age 50 and above. You choose role play as the best delivery method to get all the facts and feelings out, to provide a forum for discussion of all retirement issues, and to initiate a support group for early retirees.

WORKSHEET 10–10

CASE STUDY PLANNER

Case Title: _____

Audience: _____

Instructor: _____ Date: _____

A. Prepare or choose a case to fit your need, your trainee audience, and the time allotted for training
   1. Be sure it is not overly complex
   2. Be sure it illustrates precisely the problems you face
   3. Be sure to allow enough time for problem analysis: the current situation, the desired situation, and the actions necessary to reach resolution
   4. Tell trainees why you chose this case; state learner objectives
B. Provide each trainee with the narrative of the case
   1. Lead trainees into the case with a brief description of your own
   2. Give them time to read and analyze the narrative—overnight, if necessary
C. Provide each trainee with case analysis guidelines
   1. Be sure all trainees know what problem has to be discussed; if there is more than one obvious problem, be sure each one is differentiated from the others
   2. Provide character descriptions
   3. List major events in the case
   4. Point out how this case relates to their work
   5. Provide study guidelines such as "look at relationships; uncover motivations; define feeelings. . . ."
D. Lead the discussion of the case in a "brainstorming" fashion, setting an informal, non-judgmental, accepting, and creative tone
   1. Accept all comments as valid
   2. Involve all trainees in discussion
   3. Steer discussion toward conclusions only after all trainees have contributed ideas several times—new ideas grow from old ideas
   4. Close the training session by asking trainers to relate what they learned from case analysis to their own jobs

Situation Analysis for Using This Training Delivery Tool: Case Study

You are the entrepreneur initiator of a CBT Services consulting group within a fledgling management consulting firm. Your boss and you seem to be the only ones who believe that you can operate CBT Services as a profit center within the company.

You and your boss decide that if you team up, maybe you can help the other consultants sort out the facts, see avenues toward profit, make more informed and realistic judgments about the hurdles you face, and become more adept at respecting each other's point of view. You choose Case Study as the delivery method for this "self-development" training need.

WORKSHEET 10–11

FIELD TRIP PLANNER

Date of Field Trip: _____

Destination of Field Trip: _____

_____

Site Contact Person: _____ Telephone: _____

Date of Pre-trip Orientation: _____

Location of Pre-trip Orientation: _____

Names of Trainees Who Are Going on the Field Trip:

Objectives for the Learner:

Situation Analysis for Using This Training Delivery Tool: Field Trip

You are the director of a small corporate R&D library which has just received a bequest from a wealthy former company officer to increase your computerized information services through on-line searching.

You decide to use some of the money to take three of your key staff members to visit libraries that have outstanding computerized search services. You choose Field Trip as the best delivery method to begin to address your training need regarding on-line searching.

CHAPTER 11 _____

GUIDELNES FOR _____
SELECTING AND _____
USING COMPUTER- _____
BASED INSTRUCTION (CBI) _____

Computer-based instruction is the broad term that refers to using a computer to deliver teaching on a one-to-one basis of interaction with a student. It is learning by means of a computer.

FOUR MAJOR CBI APPLICATIONS

Major applications of computer-based instruction include tutorials, drills, simulations, and games.

Tutorials: Do-It-Yourself Instruction

Tutorials are very common applications of CBI. An example is learning how to use a piece of software on your computer. Word processing, financial spreadsheets, and data base management programs often have this kind of do-it-yourself instruction built into a diskette.

In a tutorial, the computer asks the student to type in short answer responses (verbal and numerical) and to perform analysis tasks in response to a problem set up by the computer. The student generally progresses at his or her own pace. The computer is programmed with a limited number of feedback responses to the student to encourage the student to keep going through the lesson. At the end of the lesson, the student will have been tutored by the computer.

Drills: Repetitive Exercises

Drills are exercises of a repetitive nature. They use the speed feature of a computer to advantage. An example of a drill is learning to spell words with "ei" in them. In this case, the computer has been programmed to present the student with many sentences containing blank spaces for the student to insert an appropriate "ei" word. For example, "Give the customer a (*receipt*) after handing her or him the package." If the computer has been programmed with hundreds of "ei" sentences, it can feed them to the student for hours without tiring or making an error. At the end of the lesson, the student will have been drilled by the computer, and hopefully will have learned how to spell "ei" words. The pace of "feeding" can usually be varied.

Simulations: Complex Trial-and-Error Decision Making

In a simulation, the computer has been programmed to behave the same way as some kind of process. This can be a physical process such as drawing a jet engine or water flowing through a pipe, or a mental process such as managing a warehouse or purchasing a product. The student's task is to observe the simulated process as it unfolds and interrupt it to make additions, deletions, and modifications to make the process continue in a different way. Simulations use the ability of the computer to access and rearrange huge amounts of data. At the end of a simulation lesson, the student will have participated in complex trial-and-error decision making regarding the simulated process, and will have experienced the nature of relationships that interact to make the process work.

Games: Making Learning Interesting

Games are often a good way to learn because motivation (winning, figuring out the mystery) is built into the interaction between computer and learner. Generally the computer is set up as the partner in the game, and the learner actually plays the game against the computer. Games also frequently employ humor in their design, which also sometimes acts as a motivator for students.

Any lesson that is highly mathematical (e.g., chess, bridge) or that requires diagnostic skills (e.g., find the best route from Ashford, CT to Sheffield, OH) could be taught and learned through a game. Early applications of CBI got a bad reputation because they were boring—turning a lesson into a game generally solves the problem of being boring.

HOW CBI WORKS

Computer-based instruction is based on stimulus-response educational psychology. An essential element of this approach to learning is a belief that positive and immediate reinforcement of the student's correct response facilitates learning.

In a computer-based lesson, the computer screen might instruct the student to choose the correct answer in a multiple-choice question. If "B" is the correct response, and the student typed in "B" at the computer's prompt, the computer would send a message back to the student immediately congratulating him or her on choosing the correct answer. (This is very different from the same test given in a classroom, taken home and graded by a teacher, and returned several days later.)

In the case of CBI, the computer provided a specific stimulus, the student made a discreet response, and the computer fed back an affirmation (or instructions for further action if the answer was wrong), completing the learning loop.

Computer-based instruction is presented in small steps designed to allow the student to master the content and to minimize the incidence of error. Well-designed computer-based instruction provides alternate paths through complex lessons to accommodate individual differences among learners.[1]

KEY CBI TERMINOLOGY

- *Authoring System*: A high-level language used without programming commands to create a computer-based course. It is generally in dialogue format, asking questions of the course designer and requiring a response. A good authoring system builds in adequate and flexible formats for both course structure and course content.

- *Branching*: Instruction that allows the student to bypass or return to some elements of content. Branching is based on either student choice or student performance. Branching treats errors diagnostically.

- *Computer-Assisted Instruction (CAI)*: Instruction is focused on the computer as a machine or tool; the use of which helps a student to learn.

- *Computer-Based Training (CBT)*: Computer-based instruction that is focused on skills training and modeled on behavioral objectives. It is skill-based, rather than knowledge-based, instruction. It is usually directly applicable to one's job.

- *Expert System*: A computer program designed to imitate the intuitive and logical thinking of an expert. It is often focused on diagnosis, interpretation of error, and problem solving. An expert system is often built into a training program to help the student correct mistakes.

- *Linear Programming*: Taking the student through the course in a straight line; course logic that presents content in stepwise fashion from point to point. Linear programming aims to have students make no errors.

- *Menu*: A list of choices for the student, generally focusing on student control of the learning situation. The menu offers a sequence of learning options, allowing the student to begin and restart wherever he or she chooses. The menu is an important tool for building variety, interest, and quality into the computer-based course design. The menu for a tutorial could include directions; sections of what, how, why, where; graphic sections; video sections; and tests. A menu has options to exit from it and to return to it.

[1] For more information about design of CBI, see Alessi, S. M. and Trollip, S. R., *Computer-Based Instruction Methods and Development*, Englewood Cliffs, NJ: Prentice Hall, 1985.

Good menu design increases the student's sense of control over and responsibility for his or her own learning.

- *Screen*: A unit of instruction with a purpose (objective), instructional content, and a prompt for student action/response. Also called a frame.
- *Videodisc*: Computer-based instruction made more graphic and pictorial by combining video images with the computer's speed, interactivity, and control features. A videodisc is a piece of hardware.

CHECKLIST OF KEY CONSIDERATIONS FOR CBI INVOLVEMENT

When planning a CBI involvement, it is critical to identify and analyze potential problems of CBI development and implementation, and to clearly focus on paths of solution to these problems. One of the first issues is whether or not your computer system is large enough to run CBI as a priority business function. CBI can take up a lot of space inside your computer's memory. Be sure top management is committed (i.e., gives you adequate budget and hardware support) before you begin planning computer-based instruction.

Choosing CBI as a mode of instructional delivery requires up-front analysis of hardware, software, time, personnel, and cost demands. This is a specialized kind of needs analysis, requiring management, instructional design, and programming expertise.

These are some of the major considerations:

☐ *Hardware interface*: Be sure all of your pieces of hardware are compatible with each other and with the CBI program you choose. Ask these questions:

- Do I need a printer? Does the one I have work with the CBI software?
- Do I need a mouse, graphics pad, or light pen?
- Will my system accept these peripheral devices?
- Should several terminals be networked together and all feed back to an instructor station for monitoring students' progress? Should I provide CBI to many students at once or to selected students individually?
- Do I need any internal modifications to my computer for it to be able to accept CBI software? (e.g., additional memory chips, a graphics board, and so on.)
- Do I have a training situation that is supportive to CBI? (i.e., convenient, private, comfortable, accessible.)
- Can I tie up computer processing time and space during prime working hours? Does our system have adequate capacity to run CBI during prime time? What kind of scheduling problems are probable?

☐ *Software adequacy*: Try to determine if the software does what you want it to do. Ask for a demonstration of the software on your computer with your own staff present (including a programmer, graphic artist, and instructional designer). Look for evidence on the instructional screens that tutorials or simulations are complex enough to make students think—beware of "glitz and glitter" that can mask the instructional quality of the lesson. Be sure that drills or games are adequate, appropriate, and not demeaning.

Be sure that screens are not so full of clutter that the student is distracted from the learning task. It is tempting to fill up a screen with colors, graphics, digitized images, animation, and varieties of text just because the technology is available to do so. It is easy to overload a student's brain. Always keep in mind that teaching and learning are the purpose of the endeavor. Be sure your software also has that goal in mind.

☐ *Time commitment of development personnel*: CBI requires a large time commitment. If you have purchased an authoring system and intend to create your own lessons, allow 9 to 12 months of development time for one course. Be sure that the training need will still be there at the end of the development period. Be sure that an experienced instructional designer with computer expertise is in charge of development.

If you are purchasing a ready-made CBI course, be sure to allow adequate time for testing all parts of it on your own computer system with a team of your best reviewers.

☐ *Management commitment*: Implementing CBI requires management commitment in the following ways:

- Large budget up front for purchase of software and possibly hardware
- Experienced instructional designer as project manager
- Graphic support (personnel and dollars)
- Programming support (personnel and dollars)
- Time and scheduling considerations
- Commitment to use the developed CBI course many times.

☐ *Communication needs*: CBI is not for everyone or for every situation. Training managers need to make it very clear to potential students exactly what the objectives of the CBI course are, how and when they are expected to take the course, how progress will be monitored, and how the results will be used. It is important for CBI students to have a human contact—an instructor or counselor readily available. It is management's responsibility to communicate very carefully with potential students regarding CBI.

HOW TO USE THE WORKSHEETS IN THIS CHAPTER

Information in this chapter is presented to help guide the trainer's decision-making processes regarding design and delivery of computer-based instruction.

This chapter is not a guide to designing your own computer-based instruction. Format and design guidelines are included to provide the trainer/manager with technologically sound points to be considered as he or she makes judgments regarding the use of computer-based instruction.

Worksheet 11–1: Decision Checklist for Weighing Advantages and Disadvantages of CBI

Use this checklist to help you decide if the advantages of CBI outweigh the disadvantages.

Worksheet 11–2: CBI Up-front Analysis: How to Know When to Choose CBI

Use this worksheet to evaluate key influences before you choose CBI. These include packaging, target audience, need, measures, and the development team.

Worksheet 11–3: CBI Major Problems

Use this worksheet to identify and analyze the major problems to overcome before embarking on a CBI involvement. Problems can be expected in these areas: hardware, software, personnel, management, and communication.

Worksheet 11–4: Form for Evaluating CBI Programs

Use this form to record your observation of the quality of a CBI program as you view it for the first time. Twenty factors are listed in the areas of human factors, instructional design, and presentation.

Worksheet 11–5: Checklist for Evaluating Authoring Systems

Use this checklist to help you decide the quality of an authoring system.

Worksheet 11–6: Elements of a CBI Lesson

Use this worksheet either to evaluate the learning design of a purchased CBI program or as a guideline for writing your own CBI lessons if you have purchased an authoring system.

Worksheet 11–7: Checklist for Evaluating CBI Tests

Use this checklist to evaluate the quality of a CBI test given on-line.

Worksheet 11–8: Storyboard Template

Use this template for pencil-and-paper design of your CBI course. Storyboards include all content options, questions, cues, feedback messages, tests and exercises, remedial problems and exercises, enhancements or advanced supplemental exercises, and directions/instructions.

Worksheet 11–9: Storyboard Quality Review Form

Use this form for team review of the storyboarded course.

Worksheet 11–10: CBI Graphics Checklist

Use this checklist to evaluate the graphic layout of the screens in your course.

HOW TO WEIGH ADVANTAGES AND DISADVANTAGES OF CBI

Use this Decision Checklist to assist you in weighing the advantages and disadvantages of CBI. Above all, go slowly during the initial decision stages.
To use this worksheet:

- for the Advantages checklist, ask yourself the question:
  "Do I need this for my students?"
- for the Disadvantages checklist, ask yourself the question:
  "Can I absolutely not tolerate this for my students?"

Check any item in either column to which you answer "yes." Add up the check marks in each column. Do the advantages outweigh the disadvantages? Can you afford the advantages? Can you compensate for the disadvantages you can live with?

> *TRAINING TIP*: Even the most preliminary discussions of whether or not to choose CBI should have an instructional technologist/designer present, as well as a computer programmer who is a good communicator in the English language. A team of analysts can use this Decision Checklist and discuss their assessments. A group consensus is probably a good idea, even at the earliest stages of decision-making regarding CBI.

WORKSHEET 11–1

DECISION CHECKLIST FOR WEIGHING ADVANTAGES AND DISADVANTAGES OF CBI

<u>Instructions to the trainer/manager</u>: Check any item that is especially important to your training situation. Do the advantages outweigh the disadvantages?

Advantages	Disadvantages
___ Individualization	___ Isolation from other students
___ High degree of interaction	___ Screen space is limited (typically 24 lines, 40 characters wide)
___ High levels of mastery	___ Time-consuming search through linear programs
___ Learner control	___ Explanatory nature of feedback often limited
___ Immediate feedback	___ Hard to stay focused on objectives for the learner; easy to focus on the features of the computer instead of design for learning
___ Accurate simulation	___ Hard to balance need for uncluttered screen with need for complete content
___ Availability	___ Too easy to design for "wow" rather than for learning
___ Easy to change programs	___ Eye fatigue
___ Easy to maintain course materials	___ Body position fatigue
___ Easy to administer and score tests	___ Cost of development is high: Good CBI requires both excellent programmers and instructional designers
___ Cost savings in instructor time, facility use, course length	___ Use of computer time and memory is often limited for training applications

CBI UP-FRONT ANALYSIS: HOW TO KNOW WHEN TO CHOOSE CBI

Use this worksheet to evaluate key influences on your trainees and your training needs well before you are faced with a decision to buy. Decision making regarding the value of CBI has to be based primarily on the instructional design of lessons. Evaluate whether or not your learning objectives can be met through CBI. Insist that the medium supports the plan for learning.

When filling out Worksheet 11–2, "yes" responses influence the decision to choose CBI. This is a useful worksheet for several instructional designers to use as a means to focus their discussion prior to a decision meeting with training management.

Case Example of "Yes" Responses

We have just purchased "Create-a-form" software with a CBI tutorial built into the diskette. Our word processing operators currently number 157, with a range of service months and experience levels. All need to be trained in "Create-a-form" within five days. We have no classroom facilities.

	Yes	No	Comment
Need			
• Can the content be learned in a week or less?	✓		
• Is variability in current skill levels or job performance of primary consideration?	✓		
• Are adequate learning options related to the training problem built into the CBI?	✓		Cathy, Doug, and Tom reviewed the tutorial 7/1 and confirmed that branching and feedback are excellent

Strong "yes" responses here will influence a strong "yes" decision to choose CBI.

Case Example of "No" Responses

We are about to introduce our new product line. Three hundred sales reps throughout the country need to be trained to accurately present and demonstrate the new line.

	Yes	No	Comment
Packaging			
• Is CBI the most appropriate delivery system?		✓	—They need to *handle* the new products during training
• Is CBI the most attractive training?		✓	—Our sales reps get bored easily—they're too antsy to step through CBI lessons—videotape with music and hands-on demo would be better
• Is CBI accessible to those who need training?		✓	—Most local offices have no hardware for CBI—only headquarters building has an adequately equipped training center

Strong "no" responses here will influence a strong "no" decision on CBI.

WORKSHEET 11–2

CBI UP-FRONT ANALYSIS: HOW TO KNOW WHEN TO CHOOSE CBI

<u>Note:</u> "Yes" answers influence the decision to choose CBI.

	Yes	No	Comment
Packaging			
• Is CBI the most appropriate delivery system?			
• Is CBI the most attractive training?			
• Is CBI accessible to those who need training?			
Target Audience/Trainees			
• Is our target audience motivated by using computers?			
• Do they know enough about computers to be able to go right into the lessons?			
• Can trainees type or easily use input devices required in the course?			
• Do they have a strong interest in the course content?			
• Can we realize cost savings by training about 500 people over three years using this CBI program?			
Need			
• Can the content be learned in a week or less?			
• Is variability in current skill levels or job performance of primary consideration?			
• Are adequate learning options related to the training problem built into the CBI?			
Measures			
• Are performance criteria clear?			
• Is diagnosis of error useful or necessary?			
• Will pretests make training easier and more effective?			
• Is there a policy and procedure in place for using results of mastery tests and performance feedback?			
Training Development Team			
• Is the CBI development team in place? · subject matter expert, instructional designer · programmer, screen designer · artist, writer, editor · project leader.			

MAJOR PROBLEMS TO OVERCOME BEFORE STARTING
A CBI PROGRAM

Use this worksheet to specify problems that need to be solved before starting or during early stages of implementing a CBI program. This worksheet is useful immediately after you have chosen CBI as the training medium.

Example

CBI MAJOR PROBLEMS WORKSHEET	
<table><tr><td>Bob</td></tr><tr><td>**Training Designer**</td></tr><tr><td>6/30</td></tr><tr><td>**Date**</td></tr></table>	
	Action Required
Problem: _____ Hardware _____ Description: 1. We need 4-color monitors. 2. Time-sharing might mean we have to train after 4 P.M. 3. Training room might be too small if we get video capability and printer.	1. See Sonja by 12/10. 2. Check user list for mainframe; see Joyce by 10/2. 3. Look around for more space. See Jim 11/6.
Problem: _____ Software _____ Description: 4. ACE Software package doesn't have adequate error diagnosis feedback.	4. Call sales rep and set up meeting with programmer before Labor Day.
Problem: _____ Personnel _____ Description: 5. We need an instructional designer assigned to this project ASAP.	5. Talk to Nathan, Peter, Kris, and Eric by end of next week 8/10.
Problem: _____ Management _____ Description: 6. Can we borrow Jeff or Beth as project manager for three months to get started? We need to advertise now for replacement on long-term basis.	6. Get input from Lisa after vacation. If money for personnel isn't there, cancel the project. Go or no go decision by Thanksgiving.
Problem: _____ Communication _____ Description: 7. We need internal PR soon.	7. Talk to newsletter people in time for next issue—slant article to feasibility study.

WORKSHEET 11–3

CBI MAJOR PROBLEMS

Training Designer _____

Date _____

	Action Required
Problem: _____ Description:	
Problem: _____ Description:	
Problem: _____ Description:	
Problem: _____ Description:	
Problem: _____ Description:	

TAKING A CLOSER LOOK AT A SPECIFIC CBI COURSE: FORM FOR EVALUATING CBI PROGRAMS

Use Worksheet 11–4 to evaluate three major unique areas of a CBI course or program of learning. Twenty factors are listed in the areas of human factors (human-machine interface), instructional design, and presentation.

It is a good idea to have this evaluation done by several experienced instructional designers prior to purchase of a CBI program. Worksheet 11–4 can also be used immediately after purchase of a CBI program to provide a profile of strengths and weaknesses of the program. Knowing weaknesses before students begin using the program can guide trainers in developing ways to compensate for weaknesses.

On the worksheet, any point to the left of the heavy center line requires special explanation, intervention, or help. Especially in CBI—because CBI learning is a lonely endeavor—trainers must communicate with students prior to their beginning CBI lessons. Having such a profile will help the trainer to target this communication, thus saving valuable time and facilitating learning. In the example below, the help command requires further explanation prior to beginning the course.

Example

FORM FOR EVALUATING CBI PROGRAMS

QOS Design	Noelle Erikson	7/12/XX
Program Being Reviewed	**Reviewer's Name**	**Date**

Instructions: Place an X on the continuum line indicating your evaluation of the quality of each item.

Design Quality Guidelines	No						Yes

Human Factors/Human-Machine Interface

1. Help command is always available. — **X (No, far left)**
2. There is a high rate of relevant trainee response options. — **X (Yes)**
3. Formats are consistent (prompts, instructions, error messages, command inputs, and so on). — **X (Yes)**
4. No scrolling is evident. — **X (Yes)**
5. Highlighting is consistent in its purpose. — **X (Yes)**
6. Restart is easy and fast. — **X (Yes)**
7. Response time is appropriately controlled. — **X (Yes)**
8. Readability is good (text, labels, numbers). — **X (Yes)**

Instructional Design

9. The program is designed to accomplish learner objectives. — **X (center-right)**
10. Interactive lessons exercise trainees on the appropriate skill. — **X (Yes)**
11. Feedback is designed into the correct places. — **X (Yes)**
12. Test results are continuously accessible to trainees. — **X (Yes)**
13. Instructions are clear. — **X (Yes)**
14. Higher-level skills are taught whenever possible. — **X (Yes)**
15. Linkages are made to prior knowledge. — **X (Yes)**
16. Learning options are plentiful in each lesson. — **X (center-right)**

Presentation

17. Branching is evident to encourage problem solving. — **X (Yes)**
18. Text is broken into appropriate steps/segments. — **X (Yes)**
19. Screens have enough "white space." — **X (center-right)**
20. Trainee controls most of the introductory sections of each lesson. — **X (center-right)**

WORKSHEET 11–4

FORM FOR EVALUATING CBI PROGRAMS

_____   Reviewer's Name   Date
Program Being Reviewed

<u>Instructions</u>: Place an X on the continuum line indicating your evaluation of the quality of each item.

Design Quality Guidelines	No							Yes

Human Factors/Human-Machine Interface

1. Help command is always available. _____
2. There is a high rate of relevant trainee response options. _____
3. Formats are consistent (prompts, instructions, error messages, command inputs, and so on). _____
4. No scrolling is evident. _____
5. Highlighting is consistent in its purpose. _____
6. Restart is easy and fast. _____
7. Response time is appropriately controlled. _____
8. Readability is good (text, labels, numbers). _____

Instructional Design

9. The program is designed to accomplish learner objectives. _____
10. Interactive lessons exercise trainees on the appropriate skill. _____
11. Feedback is designed into the correct places. _____
12. Test results are continuously accessible to trainees. _____
13. Instructions are clear. _____
14. Higher-level skills are taught whenever possible. _____
15. Linkages are made to prior knowledge. _____
16. Learning options are plentiful in each lesson. _____

Presentation

17. Branching is evident to encourage problem solving. _____
18. Text is broken into appropriate steps/segments. _____
19. Screens have enough "white space." _____
20. Trainee controls most of the introductory sections of each lesson. _____

CHECKLIST FOR EVALUATING AUTHORING SYSTEMS

An authoring system allows an author/training designer to create CBI without needing to know a programming language. The authoring system generally prompts the course author to respond with training design elements (instructions, test questions, error messages, and so on) to structured questions. If you create your own CBI, consider purchasing an authoring system. Only companies with a strong financial commitment to both instructional design and research and development can create their own authoring systems and their own CBI courses.

Shop carefully for an authoring system. Educational software houses market software of varying quality. The most expensive is not necessarily the best.

If you can't bring along your own instructional technologist, insist on talking with the instructional technologist who helped design the authoring system you are considering for purchase. Check his or her credentials to be sure the person has the competence to design the system for learning.

Often, in one's zeal to "show off the computer," the designer ignores how people learn. Exercises can show off the system, but can be very meager in meeting your objectives for learning.

Do these things as you evaluate an authoring system:

1. Allow a full day to evaluate the authoring system and plan to engage in "hands-on" analysis.

2. Plan ahead. Bring with you two or three days of written lesson plans for two kinds of courses with which you are familiar—courses that you teach regularly. One course should be primarily conceptual (knowledge-based); the other should be one that requires some technical or psychomotor skills (skills-based). Examples are:

   - knowledge-based: Overview of Airline Passenger Service
   - skills-based: Using the Reservation Tracking System

3. Actually attempt to redesign your existing written lesson plans as CBI lessons using the authoring system you are considering for purchase. Sit down in a quiet place to do the work, without a sales person present but with an instructional technologist on call in case you need help.

4. Use Worksheet 11–5 to guide you during your "hands-on" analysis and as a summary checklist at the end of the day.

WORKSHEET 11–5

CHECKLIST FOR EVALUATING AUTHORING SYSTEMS

_____ 1. It allows full screen editing.

_____ 2. A graphics editor is an integral part of the system.

_____ 3. A help feature is included.

_____ 4. The author interacts easily, as through a menu.

_____ 5. Templates exist for standard screens.

_____ 6. New content (subject matter expertise) can be independently added and easily integrated with entries to course structure.

_____ 7. Course logic is apparent.

_____ 8. A choice of software tools exists for structuring the course.

_____ 9. The authoring language is available to clarify and troubleshoot problems encountered in using the authoring system.

_____10. Trainee responses are judged by nontrivial standards.

_____11. The system has scoring and reporting capabilities.

_____12. The system is expandable; new software can be added (AI, expert system, videodisc, and so on).

_____13. Minimal training of the author/training designer is needed.

_____14. The authoring system will work with the kinds of terminals and software we have.

ELEMENTS OF A CBI LESSON

Because CBI is self-study, the trainee does not have the benefit of an instructor standing by to clarify, explain, discuss, illustrate, demonstrate, or digress in order to facilitate learning. Each CBI lesson depends heavily on the strength of its structure and the design of its interactivity for its value. The eight elements listed on Worksheet 11–6 should be present in each CBI lesson.

Use this worksheet to take notes regarding each element during an evaluation of a CBI lesson, or use it as a guideline for designing your own CBI lesson. Evaluate or design lesson elements in the order in which they are sequenced on the worksheet. This lesson plan worksheet helps you to include key elements of instructional structure so that learning can occur more effectively.

Example 1

The example below shows how Worksheet 11–6 can be used to evaluate one of the lessons in a simulation course in boiler startup in a factory.

> **TRAINING TIP:** Fifteen screens were required to complete this lesson. As you evaluate CBI, be alert to a similar situation. A lesson often is not completed in only one screen. It is usually helpful to the student if the CBI lesson has a message to the student at its conclusion—e.g., "This concludes this lesson." Look for this as you evaluate instruction to see if it makes sense. Include this kind of message if you are designing your own CBI.

Evaluating a CBI Lesson

This example is an evaluation example. It refers to the content of the lesson and contains notes requiring follow-up with the CBI course author/designer.

Title of the Lesson: Initial Firing

1. **Title Page** Boiler Startup: Initial Firing — ok as is	2. **Objectives** — seem too ambitious — more time is probably needed to manage all variables on line
3. **Directions/Instructions** — student performs a simulated initial firing—regulates valves, operates pumps and fans, fires burners — very clear instructions	4. **Relevant Prior Knowledge** — good use of "Information Blocks" to model pump, burner, and tank configurations of common company equipment
5. **New Content** — experiment with various percentages of output — choice between automatic and manual control — standards of oxygen content	6. **Guiding the Trainee** — good idea to build in a branch tutorial on valves for those who need it
7. **Practice** — pump and burner exercises are good — need more on valve regulation standards and cause and effect	8. **Test and Answer** — answers are too easily accessible—some should be harder to get in order to encourage more experimentation

Example 2: Designing a Lesson

Enlarging each "element box" allows you to use this worksheet as a design guide. "Element box" #6 is a design example.

> 6. **Guiding the Trainee**
>
> suggested valve branch tutorial:
>
> *Include these valves:*
> - vent valves
> - blowdown valves
> - waterflow valves
> - block valves
> - bypass valves
>
> *Create a table to include:*
> - valve labels and acronyms
> - valve functions
> - settings; what they mean
> - common errors; their effects
>
> *Create optional exercises using the table*

WORKSHEET 11–6

ELEMENTS OF A CBI LESSON

Title of the Lesson: _____

1. Title Page	2. Objectives
3. Directions/Instructions	4. Relevant Prior Knowledge
5. New Content	6. Guiding the Trainee
7. Practice	8. Test and Answer

CHECKLIST FOR EVALUATING CBI TESTS

Tests on line, like written tests or oral tests, are directly related to objectives for learning. When either evaluating tests embedded in CBI or creating your own computer-based tests, be sure that every test item, question, or exercise helps the student to accomplish a specific stated objective of the CBI course. Be careful that what's required of the student is not just a demonstration of the computer's speed or the software's cleverness.

It's a good idea to evaluate all the test questions at one session so that you see the overall structure of testing in this course. (This session might last several days, depending on the number of test items and length of the course.) Do this with the list of learner objectives for the course in front of you. Step through the course to find the test questions and apply this checklist to the course as a whole, lesson by lesson. A checklist for each lesson is a good idea.

Example

Title of lesson: Merging data, text, and lines in creating tables.
Objective 1: To create a 3 x 3 table with a box around it.

Good test item:

Are you ready to begin the test on section 6B of this course?

Choose (Y) Yes or (N) No after the ? prompt.

If you choose (N), page back to repeat any exercise you require more practice with. Answers to exercises are found by entering the command RETRIEVE*ANSWERS.

?

Test item 1:

Using the appropriate drawing commands found in lesson 6 (Tables), section B (Lines), create a 3 x 3 table including horizontal and vertical lines and a box around the entire table. Choose data from either the staffing handout or the marketing handout.

If you prefer to work entirely on line, you may access this staffing and marketing data by entering RETRIEVE*STAFFING or RETRIEVE*MARKETING. Follow exit procedures within these files to return to the test.

You have 30 minutes for this test item. You may print your table by entering the command PRINT*TABLE6B. This is optional.

(space to create table 6B)

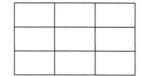

Troubleshooting message:

"To trainee Kristen:
Table 6B requires 3 spaces around the entire perimeter before drawing the box. Your response provides only 1 space. Not bad, but not correct. Please try again."

Trainee response tally:

"Your correct response was achieved in 23 minutes. This increases your total score by 7 points. You are in the category of advanced intermediate student. Congratulations on your progress!"

Bad test item:

Test item 1:

As the list of Create-a-Table commands flashes on the screen, choose all the commands you need to create a 3 x 3 table.

Enter the names of the commands in a series after the ? prompt.

You may vary the speed of flashing by entering the command MODIFY∗FLASH.SXX, where XX equals the number of seconds by which you wish to modify the flash, and S equals the sign plus (+) or minus (−) associated with the number of seconds.

Major problems with test item 1:

- Directions are not clear.
- System didn't provide a prompt or instructions on how to enter a "series."
- Instructional intent is not clear.
- No practice time is provided.
- Test item doesn't test the objective.
- It seems to be a test of the computer's flashing capability, not of the trainee's ability to create a 3 x 3 table with a box around it.
- This test item is so poor that most trainees will not even attempt it.

WORKSHEET 11–7

CHECKLIST FOR EVALUATING CBI TESTS

Title of Lesson: _____

When evaluating tests in CBI, look for these characteristics:

- _____ Clear directions
- _____ Clearly stated purpose
- _____ Mastery standards and scoring methods specified
- _____ Opportunity to practice before being tested
- _____ Feedback on the practice
- _____ Only one test question on a screen
- _____ Consistent test format
- _____ Easy access to all test questions
- _____ Capacity to change responses
- _____ On-line identification of troublesome items
- _____ Capability to return to troublesome items later
- _____ Lapse time indication, if time is important in testing
- _____ Detailed feedback on answers to all questions, especially incorrect answers
- _____ Optional hard copy test results
- _____ Capability for trainee to comment on line to the test administrator
- _____ Storage and score access guarantees
- _____ Student decision regarding when to begin testing.

Notes regarding revisions to the tests in this lesson:

STORYBOARD: WHAT IT IS AND HOW TO USE IT

A storyboard is the visual presentation that the trainee will later view on his or her computer screen.

Creating Storyboards

The storyboard is a paper representation of the screen. It is generally limited in size to 40 characters wide and 24 characters long for most CBI screens. Storyboarding is an exercise much like writing lines of software code with a pencil on a pad of coding sheets.

Using Storyboards to Check CBI Quality

When all storyboards are completed, check the scope and sequence of the course by viewing all the storyboards together. A good way to do this is to tape them to a wall or lay them out on a large conference table, in order. Be sure each storyboard is numbered and contains other identification in case they get shuffled or out of order.

Put yourself in the role of trainee and "take" the storyboarded course. Rearrange storyboards that are out of order and correct any errors. Use the corrected storyboards to input the course by using the authoring system.

Reviewing a course at the storyboard level is the best quality check for computer-based instruction before the course is actually produced. Include on a storyboard everything that a trainee could possibly see. This includes:

- Content, all options
- Questions
- Cues
- Feedback messages
- Tests and exercises
- Remedial problems and exercises
- Enhancements or advanced supplemental exercises
- Directions/instructions

Example

A sample storyboard, in reduced size, is reproduced below.

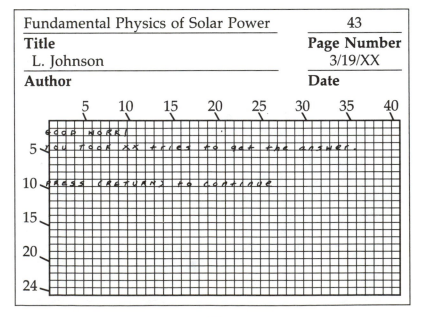

How To Use a Review Team to Evaluate a Storyboard

A good way to review a storyboarded CBI course is to use a review team. Follow these steps:

1. Post the storyboards on walls.
2. Give each review team member a clipboard and Storyboard Quality Review Form.
3. Stagger the start time of each review team member.
4. Instruct the team members to review each storyboard by walking around the room, noting any problems on the review form.
5. At an appointed time, convene the review team, course author, programmer, and instructional technologist for discussion based on the responses recorded on the review form.

WORKSHEET 11–8

STORYBOARD TEMPLATE

Title _____   Page Number _____

Author _____   Date _____

STORYBOARD QUALITY REVIEW

Worksheet 11–9 is a summary sheet for a review of all the storyboards in a course. This review aims to specify correctible problems in order to save time and money during revision of the storyboards. An individual reviewer uses this sheet as he or she evaluates the storyboards prior to purchasing or programming the course.

The storyboard quality review focuses on four key areas of CBI instructional design: instructions, new topics, tests/exercises, and displays. Several typical problem areas are noted, and a space is provided to add other problem areas as required. Being specific at review time—without creating mounds of paper notes—greatly facilitates the revision process.

Example

<table>
<tr><td colspan="3" align="center">**STORYBOARD QUALITY REVIEW**</td></tr>
<tr><td colspan="3">Aircraft Operation 304: Landing on Foam</td></tr>
<tr><td colspan="3">**Course Title**</td></tr>
<tr><td colspan="2">Carl Robertson</td><td>4/23/XX</td></tr>
<tr><td colspan="2">**Reviewer's Name**</td><td>**Date**</td></tr>
<tr><td colspan="3">Instructions: As you review the storyboarded course, place the number of any problem storyboard next to the applicable quality problem.</td></tr>
<tr><td colspan="2" align="center">**Focus Your Quality Review on These Areas:**</td><td align="center">**Numbers of Problem Storyboards**</td></tr>
<tr><td rowspan="4">**Instructions**</td><td>— Missing</td><td>38, 40, 41, 44</td></tr>
<tr><td>— Incomplete</td><td>67</td></tr>
<tr><td>— Unavailable when needed</td><td></td></tr>
<tr><td></td><td></td></tr>
<tr><td rowspan="4">**New Topics**</td><td>— Incomplete description/definition</td><td>5, 6</td></tr>
<tr><td>— Lack of explanation</td><td>6, 7</td></tr>
<tr><td>— Weak transitions</td><td>8, 9, 10</td></tr>
<tr><td></td><td></td></tr>
<tr><td rowspan="4">**Tests/Exercises**</td><td>— Not enough cues</td><td>40, 41</td></tr>
<tr><td>— Lack of trainee's ability to review prior to or during testing</td><td></td></tr>
<tr><td>— Trivial exercises</td><td></td></tr>
<tr><td>— Too difficult</td><td>40, 41</td></tr>
<tr><td rowspan="5">**Displays**</td><td>— Spacing problems</td><td>3, 14, 15, 72, 76</td></tr>
<tr><td>— Seldom or never used display</td><td>30, 32, 33</td></tr>
<tr><td>— Insignificant display (too much form; too little substance)</td><td>11, 12</td></tr>
<tr><td>— Redundant display</td><td>35, 36</td></tr>
<tr><td></td><td></td></tr>
</table>

Total problem storyboards   24

Total number of storyboards   88

WORKSHEET 11–9

STORYBOARD QUALITY REVIEW FORM

STORYBOARD QUALITY REVIEW

Course Title

_____

Reviewer's Name   **Date**

<u>Instructions</u>: As you review the storyboarded course, place the number of any problem storyboard next to the applicable quality problem.

	Focus Your Quality Review on These Areas:	**Numbers of Problem Storyboards**
Instructions	— Missing	
	— Incomplete	
	— Unavailable when needed	
New Topics	— Incomplete description/definition	
	— Lack of explanation	
	— Weak transitions	
Tests/Exercises	— Not enough cues	
	— Lack of trainee's ability to review prior to or during testing	
	— Trivial exercises	
Displays	— Spacing problems	
	— Seldom or never used display	
	— Insignificant display (too much form; too little sub-stance)	
	— Redundant display	

Total problem storyboards   _____

Total number of storyboards   _____

HOW TO USE A CBI GRAPHICS CHECKLIST IN CBI COURSE EVALUATION

A final phase of evaluation of your CBI course is one last look at the layout of the screens. This review is independent of content or instructional design reviews. It is best done by a graphic artist.

During this review, Worksheet 11–10 can provide a documentation guide. The experienced graphics eye can detect design flaws even if the artist does not have any experience with the subject matter of the course. The following design examples illustrate what to look for.

The Standards	*Bad Example*	*Good Example*

Information Flow

Does information flow left to right, top to bottom?

White Space

Is there adequate white space around chunks of information?

User Friendly

Are user interfaces located for convenience, clarity, attractiveness, and usefulness?

Graphics

Are graphs, charts, and diagrams legible and placed next to appropriate text?

Rule of 7

Are there no more than 7 separate pieces of information per screen?

236

WORKSHEET 11–10

CBI GRAPHICS CHECKLIST

Information Flow

_____ Does information flow left to right, top to bottom?

Comment: _____

_____

White Space

_____ Is there adequate white space around chunks of information?

Comment: _____

_____

User Friendly

_____ Are user interfaces located for convenience, clarity, attractiveness, and usefulness?

Comment: _____

_____

Graphics

_____ Are graphs, charts, and diagrams legible and placed next to appropriate text?

Comment: _____

_____

Rule of 7

_____ Are there no more than 7 separate pieces of information per screen?

Comment: _____

_____

CHAPTER 12

HOW TO SET UP WORKSHOPS AND CONFERENCES

Workshops and conferences are group-based alternatives to classroom training. Like classroom training, workshops and conferences are planned by starting with learning objectives for those in attendance. From these objectives, a workshop/conference theme or title is derived.

Remember that time away from the job costs the company money. Be sure that time has a payoff for the company in new knowledge, skills, or attitudes learned.

PROCESS VERSUS TASK: TWO CRITICAL FACTORS IN SUCCESSFUL GROUP TRAINING

Any meeting involving two or more people focused on accomplishing an objective has two essential characteristics, process and task. Successful group training requires designers to pay attention to both the processes of interaction among participants and the tasks that participants are expected to perform. This means that conference planners have to pay attention to not only the subject of speeches and small group sessions but also to the way in which individuals choose or are assigned to meetings, how they are seated during meals, and the skill of group session leaders, facilitators, and welcomers.

It's usually easy to get together to focus on a task—handing in a report, contributing ideas, making a decision, choosing the best option, solving a problem, collating materials, collecting money, or signing a get well card. In *task* focus, the emphasis is on the result or outcome—on the thing that is being done. It's easy to define and describe a task.

Process is a different matter. *Process* is harder to identify and describe. Process does not focus on an object or outcome. Process focuses on the way in which things happen. It is simply the interactions among participants. Process is how that report was derived, how ideas were sought and generated, and how the contributions of each participant were put forth and received.

239

Workshops and conferences depend heavily on the benefits of group dynamics to enable participants to accomplish the tasks of the workshop/conference. Workshops and conferences are not "information dumps." Design that carefully blends process techniques and opportunities for accomplishing tasks provides a variety of group-based activities and skillful leaders and facilitators. Workshops and conferences are ideal tools for learning through group interaction.

WORKSHOP VERSUS CONFERENCE: KEY DIFFERENCES

How Workshops Address Training Problems

A workshop is a structured group meeting of persons with a common job problem or need to know. These persons come together to solve a complex problem or to improve their proficiency on the job.

Examples of workshops show how several typical training problems can be addressed.

1. The Statistical Reliability Department is holding a workshop to learn the newest statistical procedure developed by mathematicians at Technical University.

2. Forty middle managers across three levels of management and a facilitator from QT Products are going away to a hotel for two days to come to consensus about restructuring middle management at QT to eliminate one of the levels.

3. Twenty-five account representatives from this county are holding a half-day workshop to learn techniques for and to practice demonstrating the new Total Body Conditioner home exercise machine.

At a workshop, practical skills are emphasized, although theory is sometimes considered in the context of practical application. Workshop leaders are facilitators and resource people. Learning is highly dependent upon contributions of each group member and mutual support of workshop participants for each other.

How Conferences Address Training Problems

A conference is a structured group meeting of persons with a common interest, generally from different companies/organizations representing different points of view.

Examples of conferences show how several typical training problems can be addressed.

1. Foreign competition challenges our support systems for manufacturing. We put together a conference for 200 supervisors in our southwest factories to get some new ideas about inventory control, trucking and transport, and automated warehouse management.

2. Three new product lines and peripheral devices in desktop publishing are ready for introduction. We have invited account reps and technical managers from eight states in the region to inspect and try out the new products. Approximately 300 products will be featured.

3. Miniature Gardens, an international association of suppliers of decorative designs and hardy plants for rock gardens, alpine gardens, Japanese gardens, English gardens, and urban pocket gardens, has scheduled a three-day conference at Fernwood Farm. They will exchange ideas about soil conditioning, organic pest control, effects of ozone layer depletion, results of new gene splicing experiments, constructing boulder beds, log step design, and ponds and fountains. Presentations from members are encouraged to complement the keynote speeches each day.

The major purposes of a conference are to exchange information, to improve communication, and to foster cooperation. Problems are often identified and solutions to them proposed at a conference.

OTHER TYPES OF STRUCTURED GROUP MEETINGS

Although workshops and conferences are the most common group-based alternatives to classroom training, other types of structured group meetings are also used in training. Worksheets in this chapter are useful for all types of group-based meetings. Unlike classroom training, the group-based alternative presents a major coordination task because of larger audiences, many topics, many logistical and people-moving problems, hospitality needs, and diversity of presentation media. Worksheets in this chapter will give you some help with these coordination and planning tasks.

In addition to workshops and conferences, the following kinds of structured group meetings are often sponsored by training organizations.

- *Convention*: A convention is a large group of representatives, usually from different companies, with similar interests. A convention relies on a combination of smaller group activities to accomplish its objectives. Speeches, panels, forums, workshops, and committee meetings often characterize a convention. It generally involves more than 100 people.

- *Forum*: A forum is a meeting structured to allow audience participation. This is usually done through questions written on cards and handed to a moderator who relays the concerns of the audience to a lecturer or panel. The success of a forum depends on the ability of the moderator to encourage audience participation and keep the responses to their concerns on target.

- *Institute*: An institute is organized around a specific body of knowledge and is often presented over time as a series of meetings. Expert or authoritative information is emphasized. It generally involves more than 50 people.

- *Panel*: A panel is a small group (no more than six persons) of people who discuss an assigned topic in front of an audience. The panel is usually seated at a table, with a moderator to start, facilitate, and conclude discussion.

- *Seminar*: A seminar is a meeting structured around current research on a topic, led by an expert in that subject. A seminar is characterized by exploration of a topic and examination of questions and problems in that topic.

- *Symposium*: A symposium is a set of short (about 30 minutes each) speeches made by experts to an audience. Symposium presenters generally do not confer with each other before the symposium; they are assigned related topics by the symposium chairperson. Symposium presentations are often run in parallel, allowing the audience to split into smaller groups according to their choice of presentation.

For ease of reading, forms and checklists on the following pages use the term *conference* as a generic label for any group-based structured meeting.

HOW TO USE THE WORKSHEETS IN THIS CHAPTER

The worksheets in this chapter are designed to facilitate the planning and evaluation of a workshop or conference.

Worksheet 12–1: Conference Chairperson's Responsibility Plan

Use this planning sheet to establish responsibilities for key areas of management, program, and facilities/food.

Worksheet 12–2: Conference Countdown Timeline

Use this six-month timeline as a planning guideline. Adapt it to the special tasks of your own conference.

Worksheet 12–3: Master Planning Checklist for Conferences and Workshops

This checklist poses important questions regarding the particularly complex planning tasks associated with publicity, audio/visual media, food, facilities, and speakers. Use it as a checklist at various points during planning.

Worksheet 12–4: Small Group Meeting Evaluation Form

Distribute this evaluation form to small group session presenters or facilitators right before the conference begins. They are generally responsible for handing them out to attendees at the small group session to complete at the conclusion of the small group meeting. Be sure your evaluation coordinator collects these completed small group session evaluations.

Worksheet 12–5: Conference Evaluation Form

Distribute this form to each conference participant, to be completed at the conclusion of the conference and returned to the conference chairperson (or to his or her designee). Print this form "back to back," so that only one sheet of paper is used.

Worksheet 12–6: After the Conference: a Follow-up Checklist

Use this checklist to remind yourself to attend to the details of clean-up after the conference. Try to get all follow-up work done within one month after the conference.

CONFERENCE CHAIRPERSON'S RESPONSIBILITY PLAN

Worksheet 12–1 is the chairperson's (often the training manager's) basic tool for overall conference planning. It is used at the very beginning of planning, and it becomes a quick-reference document throughout the planning.

Planning a structured group meeting involves three essential elements: management, program, and facilities/food.

Within each of these three major planning categories are other important elements of planning. These are:

Management	*Program*	*Facilities/Food*
budget, finances	schedule	meeting rooms
registration	content/topics	meals, coffee breaks
evaluation	speakers	accommodations
public relations	audio/visual media	parking
message center	exhibits	reception/hospitality
mementos	handouts	transportation

TRAINING TIP: Conference planning is a complex job. It works best if there is one overall manager of planning (conference chairperson) who is responsible for all of the management planning tasks.

In addition, one assistant manager is in charge of program planning tasks, and one assistant manager is in charge of facilities/food planning tasks. Tasks within each planning category are delegated as needed, and delegation is the key to success. Secretaries, training specialists, and managers and staff from related departments often work together planning and implementing conferences.

Worksheet 12–1 is the major "assignment" sheet, prepared by the conference chairperson. It is filled out as soon as the subject of the conference, its date, and location are confirmed.

Use this worksheet the first time you convene a conference committee meeting. Do these steps in order:

1. Fill in the title, date, and location of the conference.
2. State conference objectives. (This sometimes takes a little discussion!)
3. Define the conference audience.
4. Identify persons in charge of management, program, and facilities/food.
5. Delegate the job of assignment of responsibility within the three areas.
6. Establish start and end dates of all tasks. (Group consensus is good here.)
7. Assign persons to specific responsibilities, if the three managers can't do this themselves (step 5).
8. Notify each person of his or her responsibility, and start and end dates.

WORKSHEET 12–1

CONFERENCE CHAIRPERSON'S RESPONSIBILITY PLAN

Title: _____

Objective(s): _____

_____

Audience: _____

_____

Date: _____

Location: _____

Planning Element	Person Responsible	Start Date	End Date	Comment
Management:				
Budget, Finances				
Registration				
Evaluation				
Public Relations				
Message Center				
Mementos				
Program:				
Schedule				
Content/Topics				
Speakers				
Audio/Visual Media				
Exhibits				
Handouts				
Facilities/Food:				
Meeting Rooms				
Meals, Coffee Breaks				
Accommodations				
Parking				
Reception, Hospitality				
Transportation				

STARTING OFF ON THE RIGHT FOOT

These obvious planning items can stand additional emphasis—the wise conference chairperson will be sure to make the time for them in order to start off conference planning on the right foot.

1. *Title.* Get broad consensus on the title of the conference. Don't just pick a title yourself. Touch base with many different key people to be sure the title says what you want it to say in order to have the greatest appeal to the target audience. Do this formally through memos or questionnaires, or informally by a brief visit to a colleague's office, a cafeteria chat, or a phone call.

2. *Objectives.* Be sure each key member of your conference committee provides input to your statement of conference objectives and that, in fact, your entire committee understands and is satisfied with the conference objectives. It's much easier for people to charge ahead with planning if they can always bounce off a hard decision against a clear set of objectives.

   For example, good objectives help conference planners decide not to include a certain exhibitor, to try extra hard to get a certain speaker, to allow a certain presentor to use more time, to trip an audio/visual budget in a certain area, or to be sure certain newspapers or trade journals get early word about the conference.

   Good objectives save the conference chairperson a lot of headaches as planning accelerates and others need to make day-to-day decisions.

3. *Mailing list.* Assign your best secretary to the mailing list. Be absolutely sure names and titles are correct, and that there are no duplications. Make the recipient of a conference invitation feel "hand picked."

4. *Hot line.* Assign an unflappable, cheerful, knowledgeable person to receive inquiries about the conference. Involve this person in key planning meetings, provide this person with complete information about conference details, and rehearse this person in answering phone calls from inquirers well before the calls start coming in.

CONFERENCE CHAIRPERSON'S RESPONSIBILITY PLAN

Title: "EXPORT EXPERTISE"

Objectives(s): To exchange information and establish contacts re: export legislation, port administration policies and practices, international marketing, export accounting, software and data services, transport issues

Audience: 200 individuals/corporations from four coastal states who are just getting started in exporting

Date: October 10, 11, 19XX

Location: Seven Seas Conference Center

Planning Element	Person Responsible	Start Date	End Date	Comment
Management: (L. Walters)				
Budget, Finances	CN	4/10	11/30	(allow 30 days after the conf.)
Registration	KD	7/10	10/30	
Evaluation	DR	10/1	10/30	(work with KD)
Public Relations	DL	6/10	10/1	
Message Center	EN	10/1	10/10	
Mementos	JM	7/10	10/10	
Program: (P. Ricardo)				
Schedule	JD	6/10	10/10	
Content/Topics	MY	5/10	10/1	
Speakers	CD	5/10	10/10	
Audio/Visual Media	DJ	8/10	10/10	
Exhibits	JL	6/30	10/10	
Handouts	DS	7/1	10/20	(mail extras)
Facilities/Food: (J. Lucinda)				
Meeting Rooms	MD	4/10	10/10	
Meals, Coffee Breaks	PG	9/10	10/10	
Accommodations	JC	4/10	10/10	
Parking	JH	9/10	10/10	
Reception, Hospitality	LJ	10/1	10/10	(work with PG)
Transportation	NW	10/1	10/10	

TIMELINE FOR CONFERENCE PLANNING

Worksheet 12–2 highlights major planning activities in the month during which they should be done. Conventions or meetings of more than 100 persons may require more than six months' planning time.

As you plan a conference, be sensitive to the deadlines of the various service providers you will interface with during the planning and implementation of the conference. Some service providers include:

- Hotel accommodations managers
- Hotel food managers
- Speakers who might need to prepare papers, talks, and so on
- Airlines, travel agents
- Television and radio stations
- Newspapers, journals
- Printers
- Exhibitors
- Graphics and audio/visual specialists
- Your own staff who might be planning out-of-town engagements.

This timeline was used to develop the sample Responsibility Plan on the previous page for the conference titled "Export Expertise." Note that the conference scheduled for 10/10 required planning to begin during the fourth month, or six months in advance.

WORKSHEET 12–2

COUNTDOWN TIMELINE

Planning Activity	Month 6	Month 5	Month 4	Month 3	Month 2	Month 1	
1. Choose topic and dates	X						H
2. Identify audience	X						O
3. Specify needs of audience	X						L
4. Choose facilities	X						D
5. Set budget	X						
6. List items of content		X					C
7. Contact principal speakers		X					O
8. Get mailing list		X					N
9. Organize content into group sessions		X					F
10. Prepare preliminary agenda		X					E
11. Contact group leaders and facilitators			X				R
12. Send conference publicity and call-for-papers notice to potential audience			X				E N C E
13. Receive and review papers; notify chosen presenters				X			
14. Choose and notify exhibitors				X			
15. Prepare conference handouts—proceedings, program manual				X			
16. Order mementos				X			
17. Mail registration forms				X			
18. Inspect facilities					X		
19. Receive registrations; acknowledge them by mail					X		
20. Order all food and drinks					X		
21. Determine all room set-ups					X		
22. Send final agenda to speakers						X	
23. Make room and transportation arrangements for principal speakers and guests						X	
24. Review speakers' visuals and audio-visual equipment						X	
25. Establish sign-in procedures						X	
26. Prepare final program schedule						X	
27. Release media announcements						X	
28. Be sure facilitators and clerical staff know their jobs						X	
29. Be sure parking signs are visible (check bushes and trees)						X	
30. Assign someone to introduce each major speaker						X	
31. Design and print evaluation forms						X	
32. Assign someone to distribute and collect evaluation forms						X	

MASTER PLANNING CHECKLIST FOR CONFERENCES AND WORKSHOPS

Worksheet 12–3 is a five-part checklist of details that sometimes can "slip through the cracks" during planning.

This worksheet is organized into the major responsibility areas of publicity, audio-visual media, food, facilities, and speakers. Persons with planning and implementation responsibilities in these areas will find this checklist helpful. The conference chairperson distributes the appropriate page of the worksheet to the individual responsible for that area as soon as the individual is named to that responsibility.

WORKSHEET 12–3

MASTER PLANNING CHECKLIST FOR CONFERENCES AND WORKSHOPS

Checklist for Publicity Planning

Use this checklist to coordinate details of publicity planning for the conference, to uncover problems early in the planning cycle, and to find solutions.

		Notes
☐	1. Mailing list up to date?	
☐	2. Registration coordinated with publicity?	
☐	3. Exhibiting vendors on mailing list?	
☐	4. All name spelling and titles verified?	
☐	5. Photos and biographies of key speakers available?	
☐	6. Advance copies of key speeches available?	
☐	7. Press conference required?	
☐	8. Radio coverage desired?	
☐	9. TV coverage desired?	
☐	10. Follow-up news release required?	
☐	11. Exhibiting vendors encouraged to promote conference?	
☐	12. Photographer needed at conference?	
☐	13. Delivery of proofsheet arranged?	
☐	14. Budget available for reprints of conference photos?	
☐	15. Copies of key speeches for registration table?	
☐	16. Exhibiting vendor list available?	
☐	17. Any parts of conference open to the public?	
☐	18. Videotaping desired?	
☐	19. Budget available for copies of videotapes?	

WORKSHEET 12–3 (continued)

MASTER PLANNING CHECKLIST FOR CONFERENCES AND WORKSHOPS

Checklist for Equipment and Audio-Visual Media Planning

Use this checklist to plan for the many details of support for A/V services. This checklist is helpful in planning and during the conference itself. Remember, in A/V planning, seeing is believing. Be sure each small room and auditorium has the specific pieces of equipment, supplies, and services it requires for the presentation that will occur in that room.

		Notes
☐	1. All equipment plugged in and tested?	
☐	2. Flipcharts and markers plentiful?	
☐	3. Blackboard, markerboard have chalk, markers, erasers?	
☐	4. Backup equipment, spare lamps, fuses, cables accessible?	
☐	5. Lenses clean?	
☐	6. Transparencies, slides, films, videotapes legible when projected?	
☐	7. Test visual in focus, no glare?	
☐	8. Pointer available?	
☐	9. Adequate power and cables for computer hookup?	
☐	10. Microphones/speakers tested?	
☐	11. Exhibit area safe, wires taped down?	
☐	12. Dates/times for exhibit setup and takedown?	
☐	13. Display cloths, backdrops available?	
☐	14. Extra insurance needed?	
☐	15. Push pins, masking tape, stapler available?	
☐	16. Knife, scissors, 3-hole punch available?	
☐	17. Typewriter available?	
☐	18. Copy machine available?	
☐	19. Tape recorder, blank tapes available?	
☐	20. Tables available to hold visuals, extra slide trays?	
☐	21. Product samples, kits available?	

MASTER PLANNING CHECKLIST FOR CONFERENCES AND WORKSHOPS

Checklist for Food Planning

Use this checklist to coordinate food and beverage details before and during the conference. These are the details that help the conference run smoothly, and are sometimes not specified by hotel personnel. These details require early coordination and cooperation between your training staff and the hotel staff.

	Notes
☐ 1. Menu choices confirmed?	
☐ 2. Head table defined?	
☐ 3. Place cards needed?	
☐ 4. Liquor policy?	
☐ 5. Coffee/juice breaks established?	
☐ 6. Food variety at coffee/juice breaks?	
☐ 7. Minimum guarantee required?	
☐ 8. Cocktail hour?	
☐ 9. Bar, bartenders required?	
☐ 10. Cancellation policy?	
☐ 11. Reservations include all meals?	
☐ 12. Coffee, tea, soft drinks needed in small-group meeting rooms?	
☐ 13. Water and glasses in all meeting rooms?	
☐ 14. System for seating?	
☐ 15. Meal choice tickets?	
☐ 16. Food in hospitality room?	
☐ 17. Guard service/escort to parking lot required after dinner?	

MASTER PLANNING CHECKLIST FOR CONFERENCES AND WORKSHOPS

Checklist for Facilities Planning

Use this checklist to verify that the facilities will, in fact, facilitate the movement of people and support the learning that you expect to occur at this conference. These are details which are sometimes overlooked at the earliest stages of choosing a facility. They become more important after the registrations have been received and you know how many people will be coming.

		Notes
☐	1. Heat, light, air conditioning working?	
☐	2. Meeting rooms well marked?	
☐	3. Know how to darken the rooms?	
☐	4. Seating plans/room set-ups firm?	
☐	5. Seating plans arranged for learning?	
☐	6. Actual registration match room sizes?	
☐	7. Water pitchers and glasses available?	
☐	8. Smoking area available?	
☐	9. Wastebaskets well placed?	
☐	10. Coat check room available?	
☐	11. Restrooms nearby?	
☐	12. Message center have enough phones?	
☐	13. Exhibit area have adequate power and lighting?	
☐	14. Restrooms, snacks convenient to exhibit area?	
☐	15. Lectern and handouts table provided?	
☐	16. Sleeping accommodations confirmed?	
☐	17. Hospitality rooms needed?	
☐	18. Parking adequate?	
☐	19. Recreation areas, events available?	
☐	20. Flowers, plants needed?	
☐	21. Interior traffic and movement patterns convenient?	
☐	22. All rooms safe, fire exits well marked and convenient?	
☐	23. Insurance adequate?	
☐	24. Registration tables efficiently set up?	

WORKSHEET 12–3 (continued)

MASTER PLANNING CHECKLIST FOR CONFERENCES AND WORKSHOPS

Checklist for Speakers Planning

Use this checklist to guide your interactions with your chosen speakers. This checklist is useful after the speakers have agreed to participate in your conference. Paying attention to these details will help your speakers be prepared, and will help your staff attend to the support that your speakers might need to make their stay more comfortable and their message well-received.

		Notes
☐	1. Invitations sent?	
☐	2. Confirmations received?	
☐	3. Conference registration made?	
☐	4. Overnight accommodations made?	
☐	5. Meal reservations made?	
☐	6. Travel/transportation provided?	
☐	7. Someone to greet speakers, guests upon arrival?	
☐	8. Limo service required?	
☐	9. Preliminary agenda sent to speakers?	
☐	10. Speakers notified of exact presentation time?	
☐	11. Photos and biographies available?	
☐	12. Press conference or advance publicity convenient for speakers?	
☐	13. Someone to introduce speakers?	
☐	14. Speakers need special equipment?	
☐	15. Visuals of good quality?	
☐	16. Speakers trained to use equipment?	
☐	17. Speakers briefed on audience characteristics?	
☐	18. Final conference agenda sent to speakers?	
☐	19. Conference memento given to speakers?	
☐	20. Conference feedback provided to speakers?	
☐	21. Honorarium/fee paid?	

SMALL GROUP MEETING EVALUATION

Worksheet 12–4 is appropriate for attendee evaluation of a paper presentation, panel discussion before a small group, or other speaker-led presentations to small groups within a larger conference.

It is the responsibility of the person in charge of evaluation for your conference to prepare, distribute, and collect completed evaluation forms. This means that this person will have to get from room to room quickly at the beginning of each speaker's session in order to give a pile of forms to that speaker. It is often a good idea to delegate this distribution of evaluation forms to the person from your own training staff who will be introducing the speaker for that session. It is generally not a good idea to make the guest presenter responsible for the forms—they have enough to do to remember to bring with them their handouts, visuals, and copies of their papers. It's your responsibility to get good evaluations of the small group sessions.

The form is a two-sided form, asking the audience to rate the three major areas, speaker(s), content, and facilities, on a scale of 1 to 4. In addition, space is provided for narrative comments on the value of the small group session.

WORKSHEET 12–4

SMALL GROUP MEETING EVALUATION FORM

Instructions: In order to help plan future small group sessions, please respond to the items below according to the four-point scale. One is low; four is high. Place an X on the scale line, indicating your evaluation of items 1 through 11. Respond to items 12–16 in narrative form.

	Unsatisfactory 1	Poor 2	Good 3	Excellent 4

How do you rate these elements of this small group session?

Speaker(s)

1. Knowledge of subject
2. Organization of presenta-tion
3. Enthusiasm
4. Use of media
5. Rapport with attendees

Content

6. Quality of content
7. Value to my job
8. Appropriateness to this con-ference
9. Handouts

Facilities

10. Meeting room
11. Audio-visual system

Please elaborate on any item above. _____

_____

_____

_____

_____

Worksheet 12–4 has been adapted from the NSPI Conference Session Evaluation form. It is reprinted here with permission from the National Society for Performance and Instruction.

SMALL GROUP MEETING EVALUATION FORM

12.   How do you expect to use what you learned in this session in your job?

_____

_____

_____

_____

13.   What was of most value to you in this session?

_____

_____

_____

_____

14.   What was of least value to you in this session?

_____

_____

_____

_____

15.   Suggestions for improving this session:

_____

_____

_____

_____

16.   Additional comments:

_____

_____

_____

_____

> *TRAINING TIP*: Always prepare about 20 percent more evaluation forms per small group session than you have registrants. This is to accommodate strays and folks who've changed their minds once they arrived at the conference. Some small group session presenters have reputations which precede them, accounting for changes in the number of attendees at a particular session. Use registration lists only as a general guideline, and prepare for the reality of attendance by "overplanning" by about 20 percent.

CONFERENCE EVALUATION

It is important, while planning and implementing a conference, to remember that a conference is one way to learn—it is a very good alternative to classroom instruction. If the training department is to be true to the principles of instructional systems design (see Chapter 6), evaluation must be a vital part of the "system" that is the conference.

Evaluation forms are prepared well in advance of the conference. Be sure to check the wording on the forms to be sure it is appropriate to this particular conference, and make any necessary changes. (Generic evaluation forms are sometimes copied without this "relevance" check.)

As part of your planning, assign two people to distribute and collect evaluation forms. Position these people at a visible spot and introduce them during a session when all conference attendees are assembled in one place. Give a serious introduction to the evaluation forms, and allow ample time for your staff to distribute and collect them.

Worksheet 12–5 is a two-sided form, providing space for the attendees to rate 15 elements of the conference on a scale of 1 to 4. There is also opportunity for the attendees to elaborate on the value of the conference as a whole.

WORKSHEET 12–5

CONFERENCE EVALUATION FORM

Conference Title: _____

Conference Date(s): _____

Name (optional): _____

Address (optional): _____

Instructions: In order to help plan future conferences, please respond to the questions below according to the four-point scale. One is low; four is high. Respond to items 16–20 in narrative form.

How Do You Rate These Elements of the Conference?	Unsatisfactory 1	Poor 2	Good 3	Excellent 4
1. Overall quality				
2. Registration				
3. Conference publicity				
4. Schedule/agenda				
5. Content, topics				
6. Principal speakers				
7. Small group presenters				
8. Small group facilitators				
9. Audio-visual media				
10. Exhibits				
11. Handouts				
12. Meeting rooms				
13. Food				
14. Accommodations				
15. Other _____				

Please elaborate on any item above. _____

_____

_____

_____

_____

_____

Worksheet 12–5 has been adapted from the NSPI Conference Session Evaluation form. Reprinted with permission.

CONFERENCE EVALUATION FORM

16. How do you expect to use what you learned at this conference in your job?

_____

_____

_____

_____

17. What was of most value to you in this conference and why?

_____

_____

_____

_____

18. What was of least value to you in this conference and why?

_____

_____

_____

_____

19. Suggestions for improving this conference:

_____

_____

_____

_____

20. Additional comments:

_____

_____

_____

_____

WORKSHEET 12–6

AFTER THE CONFERENCE: A FOLLOW-UP CHECKLIST

Within one month after the conference, all follow-up should be completed. These tasks complete the management job of running a successful conference:

☐ Prepare and send list of attendees to all attendees.

☐ Thank speakers and other key participants (leaders, facilitators, moderators, chairpersons, registrars, facility manager, and so on).

☐ Pay final bills.

☐ Synthesize evaluation comments and other feedback.

☐ Meet with key conference planners to go over evaluation and feedback.

☐ Prepare brief narrative report for file to accompany evaluation forms, conference press releases, manuals and handouts, attendance list, and final agenda/schedule.

TRAINING TIP: Immediately after a conference, the conference manager can be overwhelmed with "people problems"—misplaced briefcases, equipment needing to be shipped, attendees requesting follow-up information, requests for lunch dates, extra handouts left behind in departure haste, and so on. It's a good idea, therefore, for the conference manager to delegate post-conference details to someone from the training organization who will do all the planned follow-up, leaving the conference manager free to troubleshoot the inevitable people problems that arise.

CHAPTER 13

GUIDELINES FOR PURCHASING AND MAINTAINING TRAINING EQUIPMENT AND FACILITIES

Purchase, maintenance, and repair of equipment are major costs of operating a training function. When too much or the wrong kind of equipment is purchased, costs soar—storage or display space is wasted, users become frustrated, and profits can be lost by "throwing good money after bad." When too little equipment is purchased, time is wasted and productivity is slowed while employees continue to have to do their jobs the same old way.

TRAIN FOR PRODUCTIVITY: MAKE IT "PAY"

The equipment required for training ranges from simple calculators and terminals to advanced simulators of complex chemical, medical, mechanical and other processes. Training equipment has to be related to equipment used in the rest of the corporation, and often the equipment used for training is equipment that will eventually be used in production operations.

Whenever possible, keep training equipment and operations equipment in separate budgets. Dedicate or earmark enough equipment so that you can effectively train the workforce. Be astute in your planning and scheduling of use of equipment in training—coordinate training with the operations managers who will benefit from well-trained employees. Using equipment advantageously can reap big rewards in productivity.

RULE OF THUMB FOR PURCHASING EQUIPMENT

As in other training decisions, the decision to purchase new equipment or embark upon a training program that uses a lot of equipment has to be made on the basis of learner objectives for specific target groups. Don't be misled by salespersons pushing "bells and whistles" on products.

All the analysis, design, and evaluation techniques discussed previously in this book apply to decision-making regarding skills training using equipment. A good rule of thumb to follow is *Buy services first, not goods.* That is, when making decisions about equipment for training, look beyond the box, the widget, and the hardware to see if the primary purpose of the goods is to serve your specific needs.

Take Advantage of Opportunities to Purchase New Equipment

It's a good idea to keep a file folder on equipment you'd like to purchase, so that when money becomes available, you can act quickly. Often the purchase of new equipment is tied to unexpected increases in revenue rather than to a carefully planned budget. Be especially sensitive to the month after the close of a fiscal quarter—it's during this month that the accounting figures are compiled and available.

How to Protect All Parties Who Interface with Equipment

Equipment purchase or lease is a legal contractual agreement that has to be executed properly by a corporate attorney or contract specialist. Quality of manufacture and safety of operations are only two of many concerns of buyers and sellers of equipment.

These measures are among the most common:

- Be sure equipment for training is installed according to federal Occupational Safety and Health Administration (OSHA) standards.
- Be sure equipment for training is installed following state and local building codes (e.g., strength of floors, ceilings, adequacy of ventilation, power, and so on).
- Protect trainees with safety glasses, masks, smocks, lead aprons, rubber soled shoes, hard hats, gloves, or any other appropriate specialized apparel. Anticipate that trainees will make mistakes—be sure to order enough items for all trainees with plenty to spare.

Often the job of ordering specialized apparel and checking for safe training installations falls to the trainer. Don't let these safety considerations fall through the cracks. Trainers have the ultimate responsibility to plan for the possibility of error and to protect trainees from potentially harmful situations during training. Often only the trainer (not general management) understands how trainees can be expected to interact with equipment. The trainer is usually the best person to plan and implement the safety guarantees for training. Trainers understand how people make mistakes and learn from them.

HOW TO SET UP FACILITIES TO MAXIMIZE OBJECTIVES

Replicate or simulate the operational environment of the job as much as possible, but allow space to create a teaching and learning environment too. At training sites:

- Have adequate table space for spreading out manuals and training aids,
- Arrange comfortable seating to minimize stress, and
- Provide carrels or lab areas for individual practice or tutoring.

Recognize that many people are intimidated by complex equipment and are afraid to use it. Many people lack confidence when it comes to trying a new piece of equipment, especially when it means having to do their jobs in a new way. Most of us have been schooled in learning by "turning the phrase," not by "turning the wheel." Our cognitive skills are often more finely tuned than our motor skills. Trainers need to be sure that a thorough analysis of trainees' skill levels has been done, and that training equipment and facilities are set up to enable trainers to deliver training to fill in the gaps where trainees are deficient. First and foremost, training facilities have to be designed for learning—not for use as employee lounges, sales offices, board rooms, or storage rooms.

HOW TO USE THE WORKSHEETS IN THIS CHAPTER

The following forms and guidelines are included to help you keep track of equipment needs and use within your training facilities, and to help you provide for adequate training facilities.

Worksheet 13–1: Training Equipment Needs Analysis

This form is designed to help you "cover all the bases" regarding the equipment needs of your various training constituencies. It is especially useful at annual planning and budgeting times. Be sure to check all these sources, and others unique to your business, before generating your training equipment order.

Worksheet 13–2: Equipment Inventory Form

This form is designed to record your training equipment inventory. It can be used as a paper form or can be entered into your computerized system for inventory control. It is important to maintain such a list, not only for your convenience, but also for your accountant, since federal tax laws regarding depreciation, capital expansion, and tax credits change every few years.

Worksheet 13–3: Computer Equipment Inventory Form

This form is included because many training centers have extensive computer equipment. Much of this equipment is under warranty, service contract, or is leased. Often many different manufacturers/vendors are represented. It is important to know where each manufacturer's/vendor's equipment is located so you can expedite service and maintenance.

Worksheet 13–4: Equipment Agreements/Contracts

This form is especially useful at the beginning of the lifespan of a piece of training equipment. Remember that you are responsible for using this new tool to boost your company's productivity and profit. You have a challenge to get the most possible use from this piece of gear. Plan for all contingencies at the time you acquire it.

Worksheet 13–5: Equipment Deployment Form

This form is useful in large training operations as you plan the equipment needs of specific courses for an extended period of time, for example, a semester or a year. Use a separate form for each course.

Worksheet 13–6: New Equipment Training Schedule Projection

This form is useful in planning the working life of a new piece of training equipment. It is particularly useful when you are faced with a single piece of expensive equipment (e.g., flight simulator, computer, CAD terminal, lathe, camera, and so on) that must be used by many trainees. Specifying a schedule of this type is necessary to get the most use out of equipment. It is invaluable when training sessions are split between lecture time and lab time on the equipment.

Worksheet 13–7: Training Facility Floor Plan

Two generic facility floor plans are suggested in this chapter because training effectiveness often depends upon the trainee's total level of comfort in a learning situation. No matter how big or how small your training operation is, three essentials must be provided: classroom, lounge, and staff office.

Worksheet 13–8: Facility Expansion Guidelines

Guidelines for expansion of the training operation conclude this chapter. The focus of this expansion is equipment and facilities that are desirable as a training operation grows. These guidelines can apply to small, mid-size, and large training operations, and to situations of growth in numbers of courses, numbers of trainees, or "lateral" expansion into other training services such as running conferences, developing a library, or providing a consulting service.

TRAINING EQUIPMENT NEEDS ANALYSIS

Use this form to focus on your company's training needs as they relate to equipment. Following this form can lead you to specific sources of training problems as you and your fellow workers look at equipment with which they interact as they do their jobs.

When you identify a piece of equipment for which there is a training need, list it on the form. Use this completed form to plan your training program. Purchase identified equipment for your training center if that seems appropriate and the budget will allow it.

Example

	Item	Contact Person	Date Interviewed
Maintenance Department	Pager	W. Sheppley	5/1/XX
Purchasing Department	—	—	—
Finance Department	Checkwriter # 5458	N. O'Neill	5/15/XX
Personnel Department	Personal History Input form	S. Costenza	5/6/XX
Operations			

Sample Training Follow-up

- three-hour workshop on *Pager Use—All the Bells and Whistles*
- two weeks of on-the-job training on checkwriter # 5458 using a supervised buddy system
- weekly one-hour seminar for the next month on using the Personal History Input form plus new 24" x 36" wall chart job aid posted throughout the personnel department.

Purchase a checkwriter #5458 to be placed in the training center for use as a lab machine. Develop a training program to begin second quarter next year.

WORKSHEET 13–1

TRAINING EQUIPMENT NEEDS ANALYSIS

	Item	Contact Person	Date Interviewed
Maintenance Department			
Purchasing Department			
Finance Department			
Personnel Department			
Operations			
Engineering Department			
Research and Development			
Sales Department			
Training Plans			
Training Reports (job studies, safety reports, career path profiles)			
Union Contracts			
Corporate Business Plan			
Competitors' Positioning			

EQUIPMENT INVENTORY FORM

Use this form to record your training equipment inventory, keeping in mind that some of your inventory will be in storage and some will be in classrooms or labs in current use. If equipment is used for both training and operations, be sure it is inventoried properly for tax purposes.

In any size training operation, it is a good idea to review inventory at least twice per year to be sure everything is still available, not obsolete, and in good working order for instruction and trainee use.

This paper form can be easily entered into your computer system.

Example

Quantity	Description	Year	Size	Features	Storage Location	Notes
6	M3 overhead projectors	1989	Standard	folding arm	room C bin 2	this kind best for travel
3	DAK slide projector	1980	100-slide tray	slide-tape capacity	room C shelf 14	old model
20	PSC tape recorder	1990	mini	remote micro-phone	room C shelf 7	used to be 30 at last inventory (?)
10	desktop computers	1988	1 meg	hard disk	in use in classrooms P, Q, S, T, U	classroom Q has a wiring problem

WORKSHEET 13–2

EQUIPMENT INVENTORY FORM

Quantity	Description	Year	Size	Features	Storage Location	Notes

COMPUTER EQUIPMENT INVENTORY FORM

This is a special use form to keep track of computer equipment in your training center. This form is laid out to facilitate locating computer equipment in an office environment or a training center where different types of equipment from different vendors are used side by side (terminals, modems, personal computers, printers, and so on).

Save yourself a lot of troubleshooting time by listing items according to the floor plan of your office/training center—that is, room by room instead of alphabetically by vendor or hardware type.

Use Worksheet 3–3 in conjunction with your floor plan. Clip the two sheets (worksheet and floor plan) side by side to a large clipboard, and fill out the form while you walk around your facility. This will save you time in planning, and the documentation on the form will facilitate maintenance, repair, and replacement of equipment later.

Large Clipboard

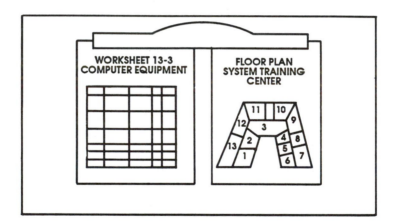

Example

Location/ Room Number	Person Responsible	Equipment Identification	Port	Notes
3	D. Wang	JCN9000 terminal	26	2 of these in room 3
4	M.J. Chew	TTA8510 PC	3	—
5	S. Lee	SummitXZ29 desktop publisher	1	used only here by her
6	M.J.Chew	TTA8512 PC +	4	—

WORKSHEET 13–3

COMPUTER EQUIPMENT INVENTORY FORM

Location/ Room Number	Person Responsible	Equipment Identification	Port	Notes

EQUIPMENT AGREEMENTS/CONTRACTS

Use this worksheet at the beginning of the training lifespan of a new piece of equipment. This completed form will help you keep track of vendors who are responsible for assuring that a piece of equipment works. Training can be hard on equipment—it is critical that you know who can help keep that equipment in good working order.

Example

	Manufacture	Delivery	Installation	Maintenance	Repair	
Item of Equipment: Enlarger						
Date of Purchase: 2/1/XX						
Training Purpose: technician training in developing lab						
Start date of contract	—	2/1XX	2/5XX	8/1/XX	2/1/XX	
In-house contact who executed the contract	—	ACJ	PVS	PVS	PVS	
Vendor	Vision	o-Nite	Vision	Vision	Vision	
Vendor contact person	K. Hanna	G. Andrews	S. Lawrence	S. Lawrence	S. Lawrence	
Insurance carrier	Best	Best	Best	Best	Best	
Will seller provide training on this phase?	yes	—	yes	no	no	

WORKSHEET 13–4

EQUIPMENT AGREEMENTS/CONTRACTS

Item of Equipment: _____

Date of Purchase: _____

Training Purpose: _____

	Manufacture	Delivery	Installation	Maintenance	Repair	
Start date of contract						
In-house contact who executed the contract						
Vendor						
Vendor contact person						
Insurance carrier						
Will seller provide training on this phase?						

EQUIPMENT DEPLOYMENT FORM

Use one form for each course at equipment planning time. You'll need a form for each course to be offered. It's a good idea to have your master schedule of courses on hand as you focus on items of equipment and where you'll need them.

Use Worksheet 13–5 for annual or quarterly planning. By coordinating the item of equipment with the other variables on the form—number of trainees, classroom location where the item is needed, and time of the training—you will be able to see quickly what your equipment deployment requirements are for the coming planning period.

At the end of planning, you'll know exactly which and how many pieces of equipment you'll need for training, and if there is any scheduling conflict for major items. This kind of equipment planning is essential in technology-based operations.

Example

Closing the Sale (S101)

Title of Course

August and September 19XX (10 sessions, one day each)

Expected Time Frame for Delivery of Course

Item	Number of Trainees Per Session	Classroom Location	Time of Training Session	Total Needed of This Item
VCR	16	C 10 and breakout rms J,K,L	9–5	4 (1 per rm)
Video Camera	16	C 10 and breakout rms J,K,L	9–5	4 (1 per rm)
Video tapes	16	C 10	9–5	12
TV monitor	16	C 10 and breakout rms J,K,L	9–5	4 (1 per rm)
Sound-slide projector	16	C 10	morning only	1

Example

Inventory Management Using Your Personal Computer

Title of Course

Every Friday morning August through June

Expected Time Frame for Delivery of Course

Item	Number of Trainees Per Session	Classroom Location	Time of Training Session	Total Needed of this Item
PC2001	Self-paced, individualized 2–4 at a time	training lab D	8–12 A.M.	minimum 2

WORKSHEET 13–5

EQUIPMENT DEPLOYMENT FORM

Title of Course

Expected Time Frame for Delivery of Course

Item	Number of Trainees Per Session	Classroom Location	Time of Training Session	Total Needed of This Item

NEW EQUIPMENT TRAINING SCHEDULE PROJECTION

Use this worksheet to plan the working time of a new piece of training equipment. This is a useful document to project when service or replacement might be required because of training wear and tear over time. Projecting the scheduling for trainees per item of equipment is especially useful at start-up time for a particular piece of equipment.

Example

Fork Lift
_____

Item of Equipment

October
_____

Time Period of Use for Training

How many hours per day can this item be used? _3_____

Number of persons to be trained on this item
within the specified time period   _____40 (in pairs, 20 days)_____

Percentage of equipment actually installed and ready
for operating at start of training (minimum 40%)   _100%_____

Target date for all equipment to be operational   _one only, September 15___

Target date for all training to be completed _October 28_____

Instructions: Divide the number of persons to be trained into operational groupings each week of the month (e.g., persons from the same work group, persons expected to work on the same production job, and so on). Enter your projected number of trainees in either morning or afternoon time slots. Fill out a monthly schedule for each month you expect to offer training.

		Week 1	Week 2	Week 3	Week 4	Week 5
Mon.	A.M.			2	4	2
	P.M.					
Tues.	A.M.					
	P.M.	2	2	2	2	
Wed.	A.M.	2		2	4	
	P.M.					
Thurs.	A.M.					
	P.M.	2	2	2	2	
Fri.	A.M.	2	2	2	2	
	P.M.					

WORKSHEET 13–6

NEW EQUIPMENT TRAINING SCHEDULE PROJECTION

Item of Equipment

Time Period of Use for Training

How many hours per day can this item be used? _____

Number of persons to be trained on this item _____
within the specified time period

Percentage of equipment actually installed and ready _____
for operation at start of training (minimum 40%)

Target date for all equipment to be operational _____

Target date for all training to be completed _____

Instructions: Divide the number of persons to be trained into operational groupings each week of the month (e.g., persons from the same work group, persons expected to work on the same production job, and so on). Enter your projected number of trainees in either morning or afternoon time slots. Fill out a monthly schedule for each month you expect to offer training.

		Week 1	Week 2	Week 3	Week 4	Week 5
Mon.	A.M.					
	P.M.					
Tues.	A.M.					
	P.M.					
Wed.	A.M.					
	P.M.					
Thurs.	A.M.					
	P.M.					
Fri.	A.M.					
	P.M.					

TRAINING FACILITY FLOOR PLAN

A successful training operation advances the company's position in many ways. The training facilities are part public relations and part environment for learning. Considerable care should be taken in the layout and decor of all training spaces, keeping in mind this dual purpose of the facilities. Training can be like "motherhood" and "apple pie"—learning is a valued part of American culture. The image that training facilities project can be an excellent reinforcer of corporate values for those engaging in learning.

When designing a training facility, think of yourself as a student. What do you need in order to learn efficiently and effectively? Persons who come into your training facility will form an impression about your company when they react to the feeling of comfort or discomfort they get when they arrive.

The Essentials

The essentials of a training center are:

- A classroom,
- A lounge, and a
- Staff office.

Two generic training facility floor plans are shown on the following page. The first plan is for a mid-size company or training operation running only one or two courses simultaneously. Larger training operations will simply expand this plan, adding more of each type of space.

Small training operations have to compress the spaces, but must include the three essentials—classroom, lounge, and staff office. In operations pressed for space or in small operations, it is especially important to consider the emotional needs—the comfort level—of the student learner. Training, in a sense, takes away something from many learners—it "levels" trainees in relationship to their peers. The adult learner needs a place to relax, to attend to his or her own business during breaks or lunch hour, and to meet privately with a classmate or the instructor for extra help, counseling, or sometimes confidence-building.

Even in a small training operation, these spaces must be provided. If you can't provide a class copy machine, telephones, or separate lavatories and lounge, make arrangements for your trainees to share this equipment and these facilities with your regular employees. Often, a quiet space in the staff office will accommodate the trainee's needs for reflective or private time.

In a small training operation, often you need to compromise regarding classroom space too. The most flexible arrangement if you have only one room in which to deliver all kinds of training (lecture, lab, small groups, demonstrations) is to set up the room with easily movable rectangular tables and sturdy stackable straight back chairs. Chairs can be rearranged in many ways: side by side in rows theatre style, in a circle for large group discussion, around individual tables, and so on. Groups of four or five chairs can be moved to corners of the room for "breakout" or problem solving tasks during class. Tables can be pushed together to form a square, angled to form a "V," or pushed against the wall to allow space in the center of the room for physical movement or demonstrations.

WORKSHEET 13–7

TRAINING FACILITY FLOOR PLAN

Mid-Size Training Operation

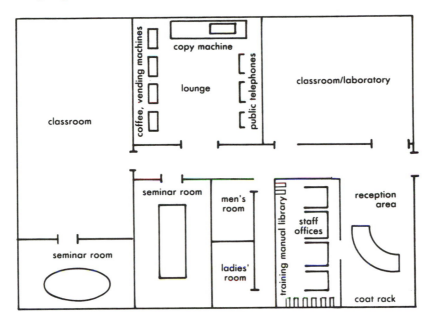

Small Training Operation

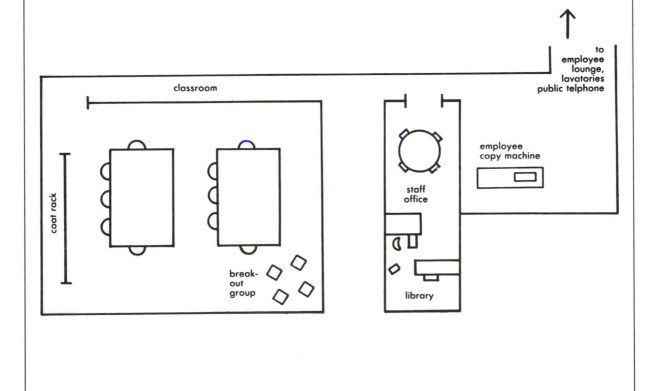

FACILITY EXPANSION GUIDELINES

Use these guidelines to plan for expansion of training facilities as your need arises, and as company profits allow. The guidelines encourage you to tie expansion to a training plan, not just to a temporary increase in business. They suggest specific ways in which you can provide support to your staff, your curriculum, your instructional systems, your trainees, and your company's finances.

Read these guidelines from time to time to remind yourself that training is a viable and visible business operation whose development and growth contribute to and should benefit from corporate profits.

WORKSHEET 13–8

FACILITY EXPANSION GUIDELINES

1. Relate facility expansion plans to a training plan.

2. Create spaces that can be flexible during periods of change, either growing or downsizing.

3. As the client base for training and the training staff expand, be sure you have adequate office and conference rooms.

4. Create spaces for individual study, e.g., carrels, alcoves.

5. House these items together in a room with a lock: personal computer, a supply of paper, a supply of acetates, transparency maker, simple graphics software for personal computer, printer/plotter, audio tape supply and recorder, videotape supply, recorder, and camera, monitor or TV set, and 35 mm camera and film.

6. A separate training library room containing all course materials, periodicals, books, software, and purchased videotapes should be created.

7. An auditorium with movable seats to accommodate workshops and conferences is a good addition to a training facility when course revenue is high enough to support its construction.

8. Add a terminal room or PC network for 8–20 trainee positions. Allow plenty of space for the instructor to walk around the room and between trainees. Be sure visibility from each trainee chair is good. (Terminals often obstruct lines of vision to the front of a terminal classroom.)

9. Add a demonstration room to help market your company's products. An adjunct to training is presentations. Work with sales staff to promote your company's products and services in such a way that potential customers will want to learn how to use them.

CHAPTER 14

HOW TO ATTRACT EMPLOYEES TO YOUR TRAINING PROGRAMS

Training is seldom considered a primary business operation, as are sales, manufacturing, and accounting. In fact, training costs are often computed in terms of hours away from an employee's "real" job.

However, training is central to effective business operation. It is provided to employees to serve a variety of purposes. It must be carefully promoted in relation to a specific business goal.

HOW TO GENERATE A FAVORABLE RESPONSE TO YOUR TRAINING PROGRAM

Training is often motivated by a new technology, a major competitor, or a need for retraining during a time of rapid organizational change (growing or downsizing). The presentation of training opportunities to employees has to address the correct reason in order for employees to respond positively.

Informational materials about training have to answer the question, "Why are we offering you this training?" It is not enough to simply describe the training. Training always has to be justified on the basis of the corporate bottom line: It will cause us to do something better and therefore enable us to stay in business longer.

Employees will respond more favorably to training opportunities if you spell out the justification in your promotional literature. Your justification might include:

- To learn about a new technology
- To learn about a new policy, operation, or business direction
- To learn how to perform a new skill
- To learn how to accomplish a new procedure
- To do a current task in a different way
- To learn about a new product
- To explore a new career opportunity.

WAYS TO SPREAD THE WORD

This chapter provides guidelines and formats for various print and nonprint communications to tell employees about training. These include:

Policy Statements

A policy statement helps promote training because it focuses on the fundamental image the organization wants to portray. Training program publicity that "piggy backs" a policy statement can engender a favorable response because the training program seems to be designed to help further the company image. Employees generally like the opportunity to be team players.

Brochures

A brochure is used to promote a training program when a complete description is required. Brochures are typically used when a new course has just been developed (especially around a new product or a new technology), when you are trying to beat out a competitor with a similar course, or when you are reviving an old course. A brochure gives you a chance to be salesy, and can be expected to generate phone calls of inquiry or registration.

Catalogs

A catalog is a reference document, meant to be kept by an employee and used for browsing. It contains general information about all training courses and services and how to enroll in them. The catalog entry for your specific course follows a prescribed format like all other entries in the catalog. The catalog promotes your course because employees can see your course in relation to all the other courses and services training has to offer. Employees often respond to a catalog when they need to fill a gap in their expertise.

Bulletins/Announcements

Bulletins and announcements promote training when you are in a hurry or when timing is critical. They immediately follow a major change or unexpected event. Bulletins and announcements are designed so that employees can respond to them immediately. They contain only essential facts, presented succinctly. Bulletins and announcements focus on the event that triggered the communication, and make it clear that you want the employee's response right away.

Newsletters

A newsletter helps advertise training before it occurs or publicize it after it has occurred. Newsletter articles generally feature a special person, group, or event in training, and are meant to spark the reader's interest. Employees respond to newsletters by voicing an opinion about the subject of the article, by discussing the article with colleagues, and often by being persuaded that training is something they'd like to participate in.

Electronic Mail and Electronic Bulletin Boards

Although print is the preferred and most common way to promote training, other media may be used. These media are usually electronic; most often, these are electronic mail and electronic bulletin boards. Electronic media can be used effectively to promote training only if all employees are networked together electronically. When this is the case, training bulletins and announcements can be transmitted quickly and efficiently. If employees are in the habit of reading their electronic mail and responding to it, electronic media can be very useful in notifying employees of last-minute course cancellations, over-enrollments, or changes in course location or instructor. If electronic communication is used, it's a good idea for the sender to require an electronic response indicating that the message was received. Electronic media are generally used to notify rather than to promote.

Audio-Visual Media

Training can also be promoted through custom-made videotapes, films, slides, and radio and television programs. Casting and scripting for these highly specialized promotions are generally contracted out to professional studios. While design of such items is beyond the scope of this book, some general guidelines for their use are included in Chapter 7.

YOUR SUCCESSFUL PROMOTIONAL EFFORT

A well-planned, systematic promotional effort will result in well-informed and challenged employees. It's a good idea to build the employee's expectations about training by, for example, always using brochures to introduce new product training, by issuing new catalogs at the same time every year, and by publishing a training newsletter at the same time each quarter. Always look for opportunities to publicize enhancements of existing courses, to reach potential trainees at locations you hadn't thought of before, and to describe training in fresh and lively terms. Choose promotional media carefully so that the distribution channels are efficient and effective, and so that you get a timely employee response to your message.

HOW TO USE THE WORKSHEETS IN THIS CHAPTER

The worksheets in this chapter will help you spread the word about your training program and the courses you offer. These worksheets can be used independently of one another.

Worksheet 14–1: Training Policy Statement

Use this worksheet to write a policy statement that conveys your company's commitment and explains how training supports it. Show that training is proactive by your development of a policy for training that governs your training actions.

Worksheet 14–2: Brochure Copy

Use this worksheet to prepare a brochure promoting a course, special training conference, or new training service such as internal consulting, video self-study, or on-the-job training program.

Worksheet 14–3: Format: Catalog Entry

Use this worksheet to write a description of a course for your course catalog. Catalogs are often overlooked opportunities to promote training.

Worksheet 14–4: Catalog Entry

Use this worksheet to layout the essential elements of your catalog entry. Clarity and consistency are foremost concerns. It is difficult to synthesize and separate information about a course using a highly structured format. This worksheet will help.

Worksheet 14–5: Bulletin/Announcement

Use this worksheet to issue bulletins and announcements about upcoming courses. Save this for last minute courses and programs or for training activities that require an immediate response.

Worksheet 14–6: Newsletter Article

Use this worksheet to write an article or press release about your company's training program. Use the newsletter to announce or promote an upcoming event or course and to report on training activities that have occurred.

Worksheet 14–7: Using Electronic Mail and Electronic Bulletin Boards

Follow these guidelines to send electronic messages about training to employees' computer screens. Be careful to tailor your message to the electronic medium. Use this worksheet as a guide to content and format.

Worksheet 14–8: Using Audio-Visual Media

Consult these guidelines to promote training via video, slides, teleconferencing and other audio visual media. Don't overlook the possibilities for promoting training through various corporate media that typically reach wide audiences. Find promotional opportunities in many places throughout your company. These media guidelines will help.

TRAINING TIP: Write down in "5W" outline form the key points that you want to promote before you telephone a newspaper reporter, editor, photographer, advertising manager, or company public relations staff member.

Talk enthusiastically from your outline and don't ramble. Remember that these people are interested in news—interest the person on the other end of the conversation by telling him or her *why* your training is newsworthy. Then go on to the other "Ws"—*who, what, when, and where.*

HOW TO WRITE A TRAINING POLICY STATEMENT

1. Statement of Commitment

In this section, state:

- an action that will result in attaining some common good
- a pledge of corporate support for a specific value.

Example: Starbright Cleaning Corporation is committed to retraining each employee every other month in using new ecologically safe products. We share the corporate commitment to providing customers with proven alternatives to unsafe chemicals in our environment.

2. Statement of Belief

In this section, state:

- what you believe will result from good training
- your perception of the effects of facts and feelings about training.

Example: Jones Ltd. believes that each employee has a right to be informed about every new product approved for sale. We believe that employees "in the know" are employees "on the go," and that better communication results in better implementation.

3. Succinct Policy Statement

In this section, synthesize your statement of commitment and statement of belief and tell what the training organization intends to do in response to these statements.

Example: It is, therefore, the policy of Corporate Training to provide all managers and assistant managers with four courses in quality processes and productivity improvement during the next calendar year in order to maintain our competitive edge in an increasingly shrinking market.

WORKSHEET 14–1

TRAINING POLICY STATEMENT

1. **Statement of Commitment**

   This organization is committed to _____

   _____

   _____

   _____

   _____

2. **Statement of Belief**

   We believe that _____

   _____

   _____

   _____

3. **Succinct Policy Statement**

   It is, therefore, the policy of this organization to _____

   _____

   _____

   _____

   _____

HOW TO WRITE A TRAINING POLICY STATEMENT (continued)

4. Challenge to Employees

In this section, list actions you want employees to take in order to implement the policy.

Example: In order to implement Excel Software's policy of "walking in your moccasins," we challenge each employee to take the following steps during the next six months:

- Identify a colleague whose work is similar to yours
- Identify a colleague whose work is very different from yours
- Arrange a "shadowing experience" to last two days with each of the above colleagues
- Enroll in and take two of the following three courses: Software Evaluation, Building R&D Teams, Software Quality Improvement.

5. Organizational Responsibilities

In this section, list the responsibilities of the training organization or company to the employee in order for the policy to be accomplished.

Example: In order to carry out Ace Manufacturing's policy of simplifying the paperwork associated with performance reviews, the training organization will:

- Provide each employee with a "Performance Review Standards" card to be inserted in the front pocket of your current employee information binder
- Schedule a one-to-one information session with you to show employees how to fill out the new form and to show them which forms to take out of their current binder
- Provide your work group with a 15-minute presentation on the new corporate concept of workflow and give them the opportunity to ask questions about the new process.

Note:

Every company has its own "buzz words." When you sit down to write a policy statement, write in the "buzz words" of your particular company culture. Some examples are: quality management, quality measurement, customer satisfaction, technology transfer, peer support, facilitation, human resources, quality of worklife, excellence.

TRAINING POLICY STATEMENT

4. Challenge to Employees

In order to implement this policy, we challenge our employees to:

- _____
- _____
- _____
- _____
- _____

5. Organizational Responsibilities

The responsibilities of the organization/company in carrying out this policy are:

- _____
- _____
- _____
- _____
- _____

POLICY STATEMENTS CAN BE USEFUL IN MANY AREAS
OF TRAINING

Look in many areas of training practice for opportunities to develop policy statements.

Here are some examples:

- training to ensure employee safety
- training to increase literacy among target groups
- training to guarantee affirmative action
- training to improve quality
- training to foster teamwork
- training to increase productivity
- training to serve customers better
- training to cut down on overruns
- training to streamline procedures
- training to improve communications

TRAINING POLICY STATEMENT
Loan Officer Development Training Policy

Statement of Commitment

The Loan Officer Development Training Program is committed to providing each trainee with an individualized competency-based training experience. This new training program parallels the new corporate focus on "Strategic Concern for Customer Uniqueness."

Statement of Belief

We believe that each Development Officer in the Loans Division can contribute to the bank's profit more quickly by working to achieve specified performance levels succinctly spelled out for his or her assigned function. Because our functional assignments are determined by customer category, we believe that the focus on individualized competencies will result in more highly satisfied customers and more successful customer contacts.

Succinct Policy Statement

It is, therefore, the policy of the Loan Officer Development Training Program to customize the training offered to each person in the program in order to serve our customers better.

Challenge to Employees

In order to facilitate the success of this policy, we challenge each participant in the training program to:

- Prepare a list of desirable behaviors for his or her function
- Become familiar with the desirable behaviors of at least two other functions
- Prepare a description of his or her typical customers, identifying their needs and wants.

Organizational Responsibilities

The responsibilities of the Loan Officer Development Training Program in implementing this policy are to:

- Incorporate input from all manager-mentors regarding competent Loan Officer behaviors
- Seek trainee input through a questionnaire one month prior to start of training
- Provide trainees with a copy of the current "performance qualities" checksheet
- Devise an individualized training schedule to coincide with each trainee's "customer milestones" plan.

WHAT TO INCLUDE IN A BROCHURE

1. Purpose

On the cover page or in the first words on the second page of a brochure, state a single, clear purpose.

Example: To be an effective supervisor of technicians, you need updated problem-solving skills. This two-day course presents the latest skill-building techniques in a hands-on workshop format.

2. Promotional Title

A brochure's title can be catchy, and should incorporate in it the course's name or key words in the course's name. Spell out the title in large letters accompanied by eye-catching graphics.

Example: "PITCHING FAST FOODS TO THE SENIOR MARKET"

3. Main Points

Use text sparingly and make it motivational. List the course's main topics or main points you expect the training to address. Tell three to five things the trainee will be able to do as a result of buying this course. Identify each point with a large dot, bullet, small square, star, arrow, or some other graphic symbol. Your goal is to hit the reader hard with only the main content thrust.

Example: You'll graduate from the Camera 1 Advanced Short Course with these finely tuned skills:

- Knowing when to zoom and pan
- Compensating for natural back-lighting
- Balancing color intensity and hue
- Steady shooting of moving targets
- Judging drains on the battery pack.

WORKSHEET 14–2

BROCHURE COPY

1. **Purpose**

2. **Promotional Title**

3. **Main Points**

   -
   -
   -
   -

WHAT TO INCLUDE IN A BROCHURE (continued)

4. Company Name and Logo

Put the full company name and logo on the front and back of the brochure.

Example: Pyramid Projects, Inc.

5. Name and Number of the Course

Be sure to identify the course completely. Include the exact name as it appears in the catalog and on the training schedule. Include the course number, if the course is numbered as part of its identification. This simplifies inquiry response, cross reference, and registration.

Example: Better Business Writing (TC 32)

6. Contact Person's Name, Address, and Phone Number

Include a knowledgeable customer service-type person as a contact. Responding to brochure inquiries is best done by someone in the registrar's office, so that simple inquiries can be efficiently turned into registered trainees.

Example: For more information on "Pampering Your Pet through Perfect Grooming" contact:

> Carla Katz, Information Officer
> School for Obedience and Grooming
> 56 Campus Parkway
> Hometown, Wisconsin 00020
> (715) 222-9988

7. Time and Place the Course Will Be Offered, and Cost

Put the time and place details somewhere near the name of the contact person, either directly before it or after it. These are the essentials that turn interest into dollars.

Example: "Negotiating Strategies for Salespeople" will be offered on three Wednesdays from 2:30–4:30 P.M. in Training Room B, West Campus. February 2, 9, and 16 or April 11, 18, and 25.

BROCHURE COPY

4. **Company Name and Logo**

   Suggested front placement: Suggested back placement:

5. **Name and Number of the Course**

6. **Contact Person's Name, Address, and Phone Number**

7. **Time and Place the Course Will Be Offered, and Cost**

TRAINING TRIP: Save money when printing your brochure by choosing paper, ink, and type styles ahead of your brochure design efforts. There are generally many design approaches that can convey your message, so know your budget and the printing possibilities before you do the brochure design.

Sit down with your printer first, so that you can give your designer the working parameters of the brochure before design work begins. You'll save time and money in the long run!

BROCHURE COPY
Machine Operators' Course

Purpose

This course in shop practice and machine setup is offered through the government-funded Job Training Consortium to entry-level aircraft machinists residing within a 50-mile radius of the Power Crafter's plant. Come grow with us!

Promotional Title

SHOP PRIDE, PRACTICES, AND MACHINE SETUP

Main Points

This is the chance you've been waiting for. Contribute to area redevelopment through pride in shop work. You can get in on the ground floor of this major employment opportunity by signing up for training to develop your skills in:

- Shop safety and courtesy
- Monitoring production and quality control
- Handling cutting tools
- Achieving quality in surface finishing
- Setting up lathes, drills, and milling machines.

Company Name and Logo

Offered by

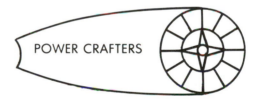

POWER CRAFTERS

Name and Number of the Course

This course, Shop Practices and Machine Setup (EL 2), is the second in a series of four courses offered under the Job Training Consortium's local incentives program.

Contact Person's Name, Address, and Phone Number

For more information, contact:

> Michael Duke, Employment Development Manager
> Power Crafters
> 100 Corporate Park West
> Plainville, Oregon 00030
> (503) 987-6543

Time and Place the Course Will Be Offered, and Cost

The six-hour course is offered every Saturday from 9:00 A.M. to 4:00 P.M. during September and October at Power Crafters, Building 3. Cost: FREE.

HOW TO WRITE A CATALOG ENTRY

Approximately two-thirds of the way through designing a course, the course author is given a format for the catalog description of the course. The training manager's responsibility is to provide the format; the course author's responsibility is to provide the information in an acceptable form.

The standard training catalog is a compendium of all courses given by a training organization and a set of general instructions for registering for a course. Course descriptions form the bulk of material in the catalog. All these course descriptions are written in the same style and format. The catalog's primary characteristics are clarity and efficiency.

Catalog Structure

- Date of catalog and catalog title
- Table of contents, generally listing courses by curriculum group
- Brief narrative overview of training services
- Steps to follow to register for a course
- Individual entry for each course, presented as a group in the order in which they are listed in the table of contents. Group listings are often preceded by a curriculum chart.

It helps to see your specific catalog entry within the larger framework of the catalog.

TRAINING TIP: Print the catalog using a light screen over or boxes around the sections Course Description, Objectives for the Trainee, and Major Topics, in order to break up the monotony of page after page of text. Use this printing technique to attract your readers to those highlighted sections.

WORKSHEET 14–3

FORMAT: CATALOG ENTRY

_____ _____

Course Number   Course Title

_____

Name of Curriculum in which this Course Is Found

Course Description:

Objectives for the Trainee:	*Major Topics:*
.	.
.	.
.	.
.	.
.	.
.	.

Target Audience: _____

_____

Prerequisites (knowledge, skills, experience, courses): _____

_____

_____

Instructional Delivery Mode (self-paced, computer-based, lecture, and so on): _____

_____

_____

Course Length: _____

HOW TO WRITE A CATALOG ENTRY (continued)

Catalog Entry

Follow these steps when you write a catalog entry:

1. Course Identification

In this section of the catalog entry, identify the course by:

- number
- title
- name of curriculum in which this course is found.

Example:

AWP 3 Creating Tables and Charts
Advanced Word Processing Curriculum

2. Course Description

In this section of the catalog entry, describe the course purpose and special features. Use sentences. Use present tense.

> *Example*: This hands-on course presents step-by-step maintenance techniques for "summerizing" your Snow Panther snowmobile. The course emphasizes the learning team, and is structured around pairs of mechanics working together.

3. Objectives for the Trainee (Learner Objectives)

In this section, list about five major objectives that the trainee will be able to accomplish as a result of having taken this course.

> *Example*: This course enables the trainee to:
> · Use an overhead projector
> · Produce two-color transparencies
> · Use two flip charts during the same lesson
> · Facilitate two small work groups meeting simultaneously
> · Choose and use appropriate handouts.

WORKSHEET 14—4

CATALOG ENTRY

1. Course Identification

_____ _____

Course Number   Course Title

_____

Name of Curriculum in which this Course Is Found

2. Course Description:

3. Objectives for the Trainee:

-
-
-
-
-

HOW TO WRITE A CATALOG ENTRY (continued)

4. Major Topics

In this section, list the major topics of the course. List no more than ten topics.

Example:

> - Intro to process operations
> - Reading engineering drawings
> - Safety fundamentals
> - Basic instrumentation
> - Startup and shutdown
> - Troubleshooting
> - Heaters
> - Compressors
> - Boilers

5. Target Audience

In this section of the catalog entry, specify the intended target audience for this course.

Example: Women who have been out of the workforce for five to ten years and women who are changing careers after ten years in the same career.

6. Prerequisites (knowledge, skills, experience, courses)

In this section, specify any prerequisites you expect trainees to have met before registering for this course.

Example: Trainees are required to have an MBA degree or have attained the position of director before registering for this course.

7. Instructional Delivery Mode (self-paced, computer-based, lecture, and so on)

In this section, simply state the way in which instruction will be delivered.

Example: Lecture accompanied by videotaped examples.

8. Course Length

In this section, state the course length.

Example: Five days, including two evenings.

CATALOG ENTRY

4. Major Topics
-
-
-
-
-
-
-
-

5. Target Audience:

6. Prerequisites:

7. Instructional Delivery Mode:

8. Course Length:

TRAINING TIP: If you need to rely on a variety of instructors to write catalog entries for you, give them a lot of help before they sit down to write their copy. Each instructor will be tempted to include too much information, might get objectives and topics mixed up, and might have trouble being consistent in written expression.

The wise training manager will make a project of the catalog entries and assign a training staff member who is a good (that is, clear and succinct) writer to the task of managing the project. The wise training manager will also allow enough time for individual conferences between the catalog entry project manager and instructors, for writing, and for editing.

Clarity and consistency are the focus of the catalog entry. Someone needs to be in charge to see that this focus happens.

CATALOG ENTRY

CP 300 FORTRAN PROGRAMMING

This is one of five programming courses in the Computer Programming curriculum.

Course Description: This course presents the fundamentals of computer programming using the FORTRAN language. The course covers concepts of writing programs using a high-level language as well as techniques of programming in FORTRAN. Desired outcome of the course is a working program involving at least three mathematical operations.

Objectives for the Trainee:
- Assemble and input data
- Perform math operations
- Perform data manipulation
- Store data
- Retrieve data

Major Topics:
- Organizing data
- Algorithms
- Mathematical logic
- Input/output techniques
- Memory structure
- Storage and recall
- Programming economies
- Programming style

Target Audience: Programmers with at least six months of programming experience.

Prerequisites: Trainees are required to know one programming language other than FORTRAN and have demonstrated on-the-job competency in programming. This course is for programmers. (Persons with no knowledge of or experience in programming are referred to course CC 1, Essentials of Computer Programming.)

Instructional Delivery Mode: Lecture, small group work, labs. Two hours per day in the classroom; three hours per day in lab.

Course Length: Four days.

HOW TO WRITE A BULLETIN/ANNOUNCEMENT

When to Issue Bulletins/Announcements

Bulletins and announcements are the preferred choice for communication with employees under the following conditions:

- A "big name" instructor is available
- A new group of employees needs to be trained quickly
- A course specifically addresses a technology breakthrough
- A course specifically addresses unexpected competition
- A new course didn't make the printing deadline to be included in the catalog
- A course is underenrolled or overenrolled according to preliminary enrollment information
- A specific course could use more visibility in general
- Production and distribution of the bulletin/announcement can be accomplished quickly and inexpensively.

What to Include in a Bulletin/Announcement

1. Headline and Reason for Bulletin/Announcement

Write a clear, factual, and eye-catching headline followed by an explanation.

Example: DUNCAN SCOTT IS COMING TO TEACH BAGPIPES!

Dr. Duncan Scott, world-renowned bagpipe performer and teacher, has an open afternoon in his itinerary and has agreed to conduct a master class at the conservatory.

2. Course Identification and Content Brief

Identify the course in the same way as you would list it in a catalog. Briefly tell what is included in the course.

Example: Q 704 Process Quality Planning. This seminar presents the new technique for process quality assurance known as "Process Mapping." Attendees will have the opportunity to work with the new technique under guidance of the creators of Process Mapping.

3. Location, Date, Duration, Fee

List these important details.

Example: St. Louis, Linwood Hotel, March 9, 19XX, 9:00 A.M.–5:00 A.M. Fee $100.

4. Contact Person

State the contact person's name and phone number.

Example: Contact Cathy Douglas, Holiday Hotel, (312) 876-5000.

WORKSHEET 14–5

BULLETIN/ANNOUNCEMENT

1. Headline

   Reason for Bulletin/Announcement

2. Course Identification

   Content Brief

3. Location, Date, Duration, Fee

4. Contact Person

SAMPLE

BULLETIN/ANNOUNCEMENT

Registration Reopened!

Registration for "Keep the IRS Happy—Use the Short Form" is reopened because we were oversubscribed the first time. We have been able to secure an additional instructor, and can therefore offer this additional course before the IRS deadline for filing.

"Keep the IRS Happy—Use the Short Form" is a two-hour workshop course that steps you through the Short Form. The goal of the workshop is to enable you to correctly fill out this simplified form with only the necessary and sufficient data.

The course will be offered at the Newtown Public Library on March 30, April 3, and April 7, 19XX from 7:00–9:00 P.M. Fee $20.00.

For more information, contact:

> Liz Claret
> AccountServe
> (201) 777-8000

HOW TO WRITE A NEWSLETTER ARTICLE

Format

A newsletter is written in the style of an article. It is, actually, a collection of articles written in journalistic style. The typical newsletter is printed on a single sheet of paper, 11" x 17", folded once to make four 8½" x 11" pages.

Newsletters that are published frequently generally have a recognizable "look" in terms of graphics and placement of articles. The look often includes standard special features such as a calendar of events, a quotable quotes column, a helpful hints section, a glossary, a directory of names, a featured employee, and so on.

Other common elements of newsletter format are:

- three or more type styles to emphasize various kinds of text
- two colors of ink
- photographs and graphics
- address section as part of page four
- set up in two or three columns.

Example:

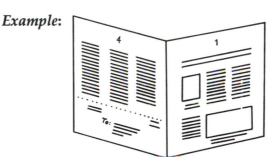

How to Write a Newsletter Article

Newsletter articles follow journalistic writing style. They are meant to be read quickly: The most important information is near the beginning of each article.

The following graphic illustrates the concept of journalistic writing:

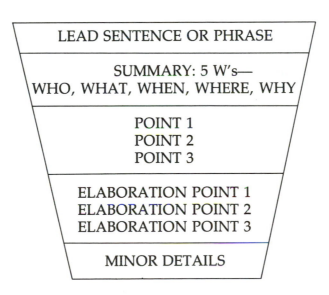

LEAD SENTENCE OR PHRASE

SUMMARY: 5 W's—
WHO, WHAT, WHEN, WHERE, WHY

POINT 1
POINT 2
POINT 3

ELABORATION POINT 1
ELABORATION POINT 2
ELABORATION POINT 3

MINOR DETAILS

1. Lead Sentence or Phrase

Begin each article with an informative lead sentence or phrase. Use a person's name or the name of an organization that will be familiar to the readers.

Example: Mark Smith Gets Flight Instructor License

2. Summary: 5 W's—Who, What, When, Where, Why

Start the descriptive part of the article with a summary of what happened. Readers will often read only the first paragraph of a newsletter article, so be sure you get the whole message across now.

Example: At the quarterly meeting in Denver last week, the Board of Directors voted to build a Software Development and Training Center to meet the competition of Software Designs, Inc. head-on in their own territory.

3. Main Points

Next, briefly describe several main points of the message.

Example:

Point 1: The decision to turn the training operation into a cost center was prompted by the acquisition of the corporation by Prime Movers. Training at Prime has traditionally been a cost center, and the intent of the corporation is to fold our operation into theirs.

Point 2: For years Prime Movers has implemented an internal pay-back accounting system in which costs are distributed among divisions according to a use and benefit formula.

Point 3: Before the change occurs, Prime has authorized us to distribute the current year's training center profits to our own employees under our profit-sharing plan.

WORKSHEET 14—6

NEWSLETTER ARTICLE

1. **Lead Sentence or Phrase**

2. **Summary: 5 W's—Who, What, When, Where, Why**

3. **Main Points**

   <u>Point 1:</u>

   <u>Point 2:</u>

   <u>Point 3:</u>

HOW TO WRITE A NEWSLETTER ARTICLE (continued)

4. Elaboration

If you have room, this is the place to add details. Do this additional writing in the same order in which you listed and described the main points. This elaboration section includes a greater level of detail that only the truly interested and persistent reader will read.

Example:

Elaboration Point 1: Barbara Jones, Acquisitions Manager at Prime Movers, is planning to meet with our corporate Vice President for Human Resources August 10 to begin putting together a transition planning team.

Elaboration Point 2: Prime's accounting system and use/benefit formula have been credited by many observers as the reason for Prime's outstanding track record of success as a take-over company. Most folks believe that Prime Movers is the most target-sensitive corporation of its type. Prime received the annual citation of excellence from *Business Today* magazine earlier this year.

Elaboration Point 3: Controllers from both corporations will draft the plan for distribution of this year's profits about mid-way during fourth quarter. Preliminary estimates indicate that approximately $784,000 will be available for distribution among our 3,250 employees.

5. Minor Details

End the article with any minor details that can be used to close the article.

Example: Results of the employee poll taken last quarter seem to support the current action. Feedback and discussion sessions will probably be held in approximately five weeks. Supervisors will notify each work group.

NEWSLETTER ARTICLE

4. **Elaboration**

Elaboration Point 1:

Elaboration Point 2:

Elaboration Point 3:

5. **Minor Details**

SAMPLE

NEWSLETTER ARTICLE

BISCUIT DIVISION RUNS WILDLY SUCCESSFUL CONFERENCE!

National Treat's Biscuit Division held a New Product Conference January 5–8, 19XX in Orlando. Stars of the show were the new chocolate striped "ZOOPERS" cookies and the reformulated "PARTY PERFECTION" marbleized crackers of pumpernickel and rye.

As usual, conference attendees were satiated with a tummy full of treats of all sorts, both sweet and salty. ZOOPERS seemed to appeal to every type of conference-goer, and easily won the prize for best new product.

Our old stand-by, PARTY PERFECTION, was given a new recipe, a new shape, and new packaging, and reintroduced to a targeted Yuppie crowd.

Prior to setting up the conference, the ZOOPERS product introduction team attended four weekly training sessions here in Pittsburgh. These sessions focused on how to accurately assess the buying motivation of diverse customer types, and on how to use teamwork to promote a product.

Before the PARTY PERFECTION product was prototyped, that product introduction team met here in the training center to brainstorm with our chemists on the subject of the decreased salt content in the formula.

Kids seem to love the chocolate stripes on ZOOPERS' zebras, tigers, and tropical fish. Parents seem to appreciate the fact of low sugar content. Grandparents get a kick out of the antics of the kids as they mimic the cookies. And folks of all sorts just seem to go for the taste.

The training center takes pride in the success of the conference because we were here to help, and we did!

WORKSHEET 14–7

USING ELECTRONIC MAIL AND ELECTRONIC BULLETIN BOARDS

1. <u>Choose to inform, but be aware of complications.</u>

   Employees in networked workplaces can benefit from information transmitted electronically. Information transmitted should be spare, because it very often shares the computer's memory with critical business data. Avoid trivial or lengthy messages.

   Messages sent via electronic mail or bulletin boards to each computer screen have the potential to reach employees quickly and inexpensively, but are limited by the habits and abilities of employees regarding receiving electronic messages.

   As in all communication, the receiver of the message must view the medium of transmitting the message as an appropriate instrument for communication. If this does not happen, the medium itself becomes the focus of contact and the message is garbled by the attention to the instrument.

   Electronic media are particularly subject to this communication conflict. Messages that inform, rather than promote or persuade, are appropriate for electronic transmission.

   Example:

   To all members of Department 123:
   Please be advised that the CPR course given by the Red Cross has been postponed until next Tuesday at 11:30 A.M. It will meet in Lionel Auditorium, as usual.

2. <u>Follow the instructions in your computer user's manual.</u>

   When you input an electronic message, be sure you use the system to its fullest capacity. Program the system to feed back to you an electronic "return receipt" so that you know who has read the message. Know your way around your manual. An electronic mail instruction might look something like this:

   Example:

   mail
   sender cdn
   mesg -frwd nwn ejn sjm knd rcd lnd jck gib
   rr < cdn

   A note of caution concerning electronic media: Training is often considered to be an opportunity of employment. Using electronic media carries with it more than the usual risk of not reaching all persons equally. Tracking electronic messages is trickier than tracking print messages. Don't use an electronic medium for its "Wow Factor" just because it's there. Be sensitive to issues regarding equal employment (training) opportunity.

WORKSHEET 14—8

USING AUDIO-VISUAL MEDIA

1. <u>Use audio-visual media to persuade or to inform.</u>

    A multi-sensory approach to communication can quickly engage the viewer/listener and motivate that employee to act. Multi-sensory involvement with your message is likely to produce a stronger and more immediate employee response to the message. Audio-visual media are often used together with print media (for example, a videotape and a questionnaire) for maximum motivational purposes.

    Example: These are some standard audio-visual media used to promote training:

    - In-house closed-circuit television
    - Commerical TV or cable TV
    - Videotape, played through a VCR
    - Film
    - Slides and transparencies
    - Audio tape
    - Radio
    - Telephone conferencing.

2. <u>Verify the ability of your target audience to receive your message.</u>

    Before you embark on an audio-visual communication project, be sure that your target audience will still be there at the receiving end of the message when the project is finished.

    Example: These kinds of things can happen to negate the effect of your message:

    - Organizations and people move, but the closed-circuit television remains with the old building
    - VCRs are not available or are the wrong size
    - Television sets/monitors are not conveniently placed
    - Viewing and listening spaces are poorly designed
    - It took too long—the concept (e.g., excellence) you're promoting was hot last year but not this year
    - Your schedule slipped and the actor's contract expired.

    A note of caution concerning audio-visual media: Only choose commercially prepared custom videos, tapes, films, or slides if you have six to twelve months lead time before you need to use them. It takes time to work with agents, graphic artists, and actors.

CHAPTER 15

HOW TO WRITE A BUSINESS PLAN

TWO KEY MANAGEMENT GUIDELINES FOR TRAINING MANAGERS

In addition to all the normal management problems associated with running a business operation that is heavy in client interface, the training manager faces several special challenges.

These major challenges specific to training are:

- *Choosing whether to be a cost center or a profit center.*

  Longevity in a corporation generally depends on your department's ability to make a profit, but training frequently is positioned within the corporate structure to be a cost. It's easier to be a cost center, but corporate mentality usually says that the real business is done in a profit center. Training managers can influence the decision to be a cost center or a profit center. This decision will determine the way you manage the training operation.

- *Targeting the right audience for training services.*

  Trainers face a common problem of delivering a course to the wrong audience. This is because people come to training for a variety of reasons: It's company policy, they want to get out of the office for a few days, they are curious but don't know anything about the topic, somebody said the instructor was great, it's a slow time for production and they have the time now, or they need to learn a new skill.

  Training designers and people who write courses must have a specific audience identified in order to efficiently develop an effective course. Training delivered to the wrong audience is doomed to fail. It's a major challenge to the training manager to assure that training serves the client.

CULTIVATING A GOOD REPUTATION FOR YOUR TRAINING DEPARTMENT

Training suffers from having both a good and a bad reputation—bad because courses are often badly designed and badly delivered, and good because training is generally seen as an opportunity for growth and as something that is "good for you."

The best technique for straddling the middle ground suggested by the above comment is to behave like a business. Have a business plan; use project management tools; deploy resources wisely; build quality into courses, programs, and development processes; and keep complete records.

The business of training should be run with the rigor of a production operation, the accountability of a payroll department, and the enthusiasm of a sales force.

The Training Business Plan

The Training Business Plan is a planning document tied to the training market and to marketing considerations regarding cost and pricing. It specifies products and services within a profit context. It generally tries to convince its readers that additional money is needed for training or that money should be spent in a certain targeted way.

It is a persuasive document loaded with figures, facts, and control points. Three major elements it contains are:

- An innovative training product or service that addresses real need or opportunity,
- A proven record for good management, and
- Potential for profit.

When to Write a Training Business Plan

A Training Business Plan should be written annually, even in a small training organization, because training is so heavily client centered and has continuous potential for growth as the people in an organization change and grow.

Training markets are very "fluid," reflecting changes in corporate attitudes, personnel, economic realities, new systems, and needs for new skills and information.

Because the Training Business Plan is market driven, it can be appropriate to write one at any time when the training market is favorable to a change in training products or services. Often a Training Business Plan is the major document launching an entrepreneurial training effort within an existing training operation or as a new business venture.

It is a document of hope, backed up by solid data from a source who knows training's potential, operational constraints and capabilities, and financial requirements.

Who Should Write a Training Business Plan

The training manager generally writes a Training Business Plan because it is the manager who understands how the training operation—whether cost center or profit center—can contribute to corporate operations.

Advantages of Writing a Training Business Plan

These are the major advantages of writing a Training Business Plan:

- Clients have been studied—actual client needs and wants have been analyzed. A better understanding of the client(s) never hurt any organization!
- The market has been analyzed—success factors and pitfalls have been identified and recent trends have been defined.
- Competitors outside the company have been studied.
- Competing organizational demands within the company have been analyzed.
- Development plans for training have been specified to take advantage of client studies, market studies, and organizational studies.
- Lines of responsibility, timelines, and controls have been specified to guide developmental efforts.
- Changes in the training operation are cast within the "bottom-line" concerns of the company.
- Through the Training Business Plan, training takes its place as an initiating, contributing corporate citizen.

HOW TO USE THE WORKSHEETS IN THIS CHAPTER

The worksheets in this chapter are designed to be used sequentially, in step-by-step fashion, to write a complete Training Business Plan.

Worksheet 15–1: Executive Summary Worksheet

Identify your readers and prepare an executive summary for them. Begin by knowing exactly who will read your business plan and anticipate the kinds of decisions they will make regarding your requests. Write the plan for a specific audience, often no more than three or four people.

As you create parts of the document, abstract out of each part an essential idea or several key sentences to put into an executive summary for this target readership. Complete the executive summary as you complete the total Training Business Plan.

Worksheet 15–2: Introduction and Reasons

Succinctly state your reasons for this Training Business Plan. Define precisely what you are trying to persuade the readers to do. Limit your reasons to about three major ideas. These can be expressed as goals backed up by brief but well-supported rationale statements.

Worksheet 15–3: Operational Plan

Specify an operational plan. Take a page or two to construct a chart or timeline establishing a date by which each major decision has to be made in order to make the plan operational and thereby accomplish the stated goals. Coordinate each decision date with a decision issue.

Worksheet 15–4: Business Analysis Worksheet

Present back-up information (business analysis). Use this section of the Training Business Plan to present an evaluative analysis of factors driving you to write this plan. Support the reasons for the plan (Worksheet 15–2) with narrative about your market for training, competitors outside the company, internal organizations competing for the same dollars, your capacity for service, your ability to contribute to the bottom line, evidence of your reputation for excellence, specific client needs, stages of growth as you see them, and so on.

Organize these pages carefully, clearly, and logically, building your case for funding or organizational support by making your reasons self-evident through this powerful business analysis. Use consistent, structured writing and avoid wordiness in this section.

Worksheet 15–5: Controls

Design the controls. Specify measures, points of measurements, and person responsible for monitoring the implementation of your business plan. Write these into the plan in chart form.

Worksheet 15–6: Resources Required

Identify resources needed. Specify people, materials, and dollars required to accomplish your plan.

Following the layout of the Training Business Plan, instructions, examples, and worksheets for constructing a Training Business Plan are presented for further illustration.

FORMAT FOR A 20-PAGE BUSINESS PLAN

Executive Summary	1–2 pages
Reasons for the Plan	2–4 pages
Operational Plan (Issues and Decision Dates)	1–2 pages
Business Analysis (Support Text)	4–6 pages
Controls (Measures, Person Responsible)	2–3 pages
Resource Requirements	2–3 pages

LAYOUT OF A TRAINING BUSINESS PLAN

1

Cover

2

Table of Contents

3

Executive Summary

1.

2.

3.

4.
-
-
-

5.

6.

4

Introduction:

Reasons for this plan:

1.

2.

3.

These goals are possible because:

1.

2.

3.

LAYOUT OF A TRAINING BUSINESS PLAN (continued)

5

Operational Plan

	15	30	15	30	15	30	15	30
Decision 1...								
Decision 2...								
Decision 3...								
Decision 4...								
Decision 5...								

6

Business Analysis

-
-
-
-
-
-

7

Controls

Event	Date	Person Responsible

8

Resources Required

-
-
-
-
-

Example

TRAINING BUSINESS PLAN:
EMPIRE CONSULTING SERVICES
December 19, 19XX

Distribution:

R.C. Dorfman, VP Human Relations
L.N. Joyce, Director of Training Operations
P.D. Bettcher, Director of Project Planning
V.J. Johnson, Controller

Cover

Example

TRAINING BUSINESS PLAN
Table of Contents

Table of Contents

IDENTIFY YOUR READERS AND PREPARE AN EXECUTIVE SUMMARY FOR THEM

Begin by addressing your Business Plan to a very specific audience—generally these are the people with financial decision-making responsibilities. List their names and titles on the cover of your plan.

Then, as you complete the various sections of the Business Plan, on a separate piece of paper, construct an Executive Summary of the entire plan for this readership. The Executive Summary highlights the important elements of the plan these readers need to be informed about in order to decide whether or not to support you in your analyses and requests. Keep it simple; no more than two pages.

Example

The example on the following pages contains elements of a Business Plan to initiate a consulting services division within the overall training department which, to date, has received revenues only from teaching courses. The proposed name of the new consulting division is Empire Consulting Services.

Executive Summary

New Training Service: This Business Plan presents opportunities for corporate growth through the start up of a consulting services division to be called Empire Consulting Services. Empire will operate out of the vacated Language Lab and will be administered by our existing Training Department. Minor refurbishing of the Language Lab is required.

Operational Plan: We can begin client services within 30 days of facility renovation, redecorating, and moving the consultant staff into their new offices.

Business Analysis: We believe the time is right for this venture because

- 20 percent of our trainees over the first three months requested "consulting services" on their end of course evaluation forms.

- We currently have 28 percent of market share with our seminars and courses. Empire could be one way to increase our market share.

- Last year's corporate profits were up, possibly freeing up some internal venture capital. Training operations contributed an unusually large share to profits because of our very popular Process Quality Workshop.

Controls and Staffing: We currently have an exceptionally talented staff that works well together. They will respond favorably to this kind of challenge and added responsibility.

Resources Required: Start-up costs (for nine months) are estimated at $54,000, including refurbishing and moving consultant staff. The first full year of operation is projected to yield 15 percent profit.

TRAINING TIP: Reproduce a copy of the single page Executive Summary Worksheet on a piece of colored paper so it stands out among your other draft pages as you work. Discipline yourself to stay within the confines of this single sheet of paper so that you keep the Executive Summary spare and readable.

WORKSHEET 15–1

EXECUTIVE SUMMARY WORKSHEET

Who will read this Training Business Plan?

Name	Position
_____	_____
_____	_____
_____	_____
_____	_____

Introduction:

Reasons:

Operational Plan:

Business Analysis:

Controls:

Resources Required:

SUCCINCTLY STATE YOUR REASONS FOR THIS TRAINING BUSINESS PLAN

Introduction

Begin this section of the Training Business Plan with a statement of the plan's subject. This is done in two or three short, clear sentences. Be careful to write in a simple style. Don't be tempted to try to sound lofty in this introductory section. Remember that this is a business venture, not the Bill of Rights. Leave no room for interpretation in the structure of your language.

Example

This document is a Business Plan for Empire Consulting Services. These services will be tailored to specific clients and will include training design, test development and administration, and delivery of instructional services at client sites. Empire Consulting Services will be administered by our existing Training Department.

Reasons

Follow up this introduction with a description of the reasons why you are seeking support. Make sure that these reasons are business reasons, not statements of esoteric principles of general goodness. Support these reasons with additional rationale statements if you need to elaborate.

Example

1. The start up of Empire Consulting Services within the Training Department is an opportunity for corporate growth because our training client base is strong and our potential for profit is increasing due to higher gross margins in consulting services.

2. An outstanding facility, the Language Lab, is available to us and can be refurbished at minimal expense. By acting now, we can take advantage of substantial savings in the costs of facilities.

3. On our end-of-course evaluation forms, clients have consistently requested that we develop training consulting services. This is a vote of confidence in our current talented professional and support staffs.

WORKSHEET 15–2

WORKSHEET FOR INTRODUCTION AND REASONS

Introduction:

Reasons:

1.

2.

3.

Additional Rationale Statements:

SPECIFY AN OPERATIONAL PLAN

Construct an operational plan in chart form. Coordinate major decisions with dates. A typical date breakdown is the 15th and 30th of each month. The purpose of this plan is to give the plan's readers a quick, clear idea of how long it will take for this Business Plan to pay off for the business.

Example

Operational Decisions	March 15	March 30	April 15	April 30	May 15	May 30
1. Define organization structure, position descriptions, compensation	x					
2. Renovate facilities		x				
3. Move			x			
4. Begin client services				x		
5. Send out first billing					x	
6. Receive first revenue						x

WORKSHEET 15–3

OPERATIONAL PLAN

OPERATIONAL DECISIONS

Months

	15	30	15	30	15	30	15	30	15	30
1.										
2.										
3.										
4.										
5.										
6.										
7.										
8.										
9.										
10.										
11.										
12.										
13.										
14.										
15.										

ANALYZE BUSINESS FACTORS AND PRESENT BACKUP INFORMATION

Business Analysis

Present an evaluative analysis of all business factors that are driving you to write this Training Business Plan. Consider any of the following:

- Market segmentation
- Availability of market channels
- Stated needs of targeted clients
- Probable volume of sales
- Probable gross margin
- Competitors' current activity
- Internal organizations competing for corporate resources
- Corporate profits
- Strength of the training organization
- Projected stages of growth for the new venture.

Use Worksheet 15–4 to list the major sections of your business analysis and write brief notes to yourself. Use the completed worksheet as a guide when you write the Business Analysis section of the plan. Try to complete the full analysis in 4–6 pages.

Example (*Notes on Worksheet 15–4*)

Market segmentation:

- 90 percent of current clients got quality courses for managers—need still exists for engineers and technical professionals.
- we have concentrated only on delivery—to stay ahead of competition, we should revise many of our courses and get into customized services.

Example (*Full analysis based on these notes*)

Market segmentation: During the past three years, we have seen a clear segmentation of the training market in our area of corporate expertise. Our focus has been delivery of courses in quality methodology, including process quality and product (statistical) quality. Ninety percent of our clients wanted and received courses in quality for management employees.

We now see a need for updating those courses and for providing customized consulting services for these clients and others like them. We see the market segments as:

- course delivery (process and product courses),
- course design/development (process and product courses), and
- customized consulting services in quality and productivity design.

Information Sources

Use this section of Worksheet 15–4 to list your allies who can provide you with good supporting information. Consider who has the facts and success stories that you can use to build your case.

338

WORKSHEET 15—4

BUSINESS ANALYSIS WORKSHEET

List of Business Factors and Notes:

1.

2.

3.

4.

5.

6.

Information Sources:

Name	Phone Number	Type of Information

DESIGN THE CONTROLS

Specify control events and measurements, the date of implementation, and the person responsible. Write these into the plan in chart form.

Example

Event/Measurement	Date	Person Responsible
Get HRD okay on organization chart and compensation plan	2/1	Manny
Get Facilities Management engineer to okay computer installation	2/27	Carla
Get general contractor to okay renovation prior to city building inspection	5/1	Zack
Complete training all word processing operators at the new facility	9/17	Jeanne

WORKSHEET 15–5

CONTROLS

Event/Measurement	Date	Person Responsible

Identify Resources Needed

Specify people, materials, and dollars required to accomplish your plan.

Example

Personnel (in addition to current staff):

2 part-time clerks to work 5–9 P.M. @ $7,500 . . . . $15,000

Materials:
- 6 additional personal computers @ $5,000 30,000
- 6 copies Project Management software (floppy disks) @ $300 1,800
- 6 pocket dictating machines @ $200 1,200

Facility Renovation:
- Construction 3,000
- Decorating 1,000
- Moving 2,000

TOTAL $54,000

WORKSHEET 15–6

RESOURCES REQUIRED

- <u>Personnel:</u> $

- <u>Materials:</u> $

- <u>Facilities:</u> $

- <u>Services:</u> $

-

-

TOTAL $

The Business Case

The Business Case is a smaller, specialized version of the Business Plan. It contains the same elements as the Business Plan, but because it is smaller in size, the Business Case generally concludes with an Action Plan which is similar to the Operational Plan in the Business Plan. Pared down in scope, a Business Case focuses on one product or service. Like the broader Business Plan, its goal is to persuade management or funding sources to finance a business venture. It is structured around analysis of competition. The suggested length for a Business Case is three pages.

A Business Case generally can become operational within a short time frame, as contrasted with the typical yearly cycle of Business Plans. A Business Case is usually about a project that can be handled by current staff within current facilities. The major expense of personnel and facilities is frequently missing from the Business Case in training.

Some likely topics for a Business Case in training are:

- A new piece of equipment
- A new piece of software
- Videotaped courses from vendors
- Reference books
- Instructor manuals
- Films
- Development of a new course
- A conference
- A seminar series.

Contrasts Between the Business Case and the Business Plan

Business Case	*Business Plan*
six videotapes on customer service techniques, from CCC Sales Trainers Inc. (Cost $4,000)	transfer of the customer service training function from the Sales and Marketing VP area to the Personnel VP area (cost $650,000)
twenty Spanish-English dictionaries and audio tape pronunciation lessons (cost $600)	new program of reading, writing, and conversational English for persons of Hispanic background for whom English is a second language (cost $250,000)
two-day conference on fabrics and fashions for fall (cost $3,500)	construction of a new Fashion Technologies Wing onto the textile development laboratory (cost $3 million)

CHAPTER 16 _____

PROJECT MANAGEMENT: _____
HOW TO KEEP _____
CONTENT, COST, AND _____
SCHEDULING UNDER _____
CONTROL _____

This chapter is especially useful for training organizations that function like a consulting group—that is, a business enterprise that organizes its business activities around specific products and services for specific clients.

This kind of organization makes a profit on specific projects and works against an anticipated revenue figure for each specific, well-defined product or service. This kind of organization's "business health" is measured by the accumulated profits from all of its various projects.

PROJECT MANAGEMENT AS CHANGE AGENT: MOVING TRAINING FROM A COST TO A PROFIT CENTER

Any training operation can be run this way, although bureaucratic organizations and cost centers generally are not as entrepreneurial as a project orientation suggests. On the other hand, a project management focus can be used to move a training operating from a cost center to a profit center within a larger corporate environment. In large companies, the principles of project management are sometimes expanded so that the concept of a "project" becomes the concept of a "line of business" or a "business unit," competing against each other as projects tend to do.

Project management techniques are the accepted management methodology for training consulting practices. Training operations that want to function like a consulting company can adopt project management with good results.

PITFALLS OF PROJECT MANAGEMENT

The danger to effective management inherent in project management is that projects invariably are compared with one another. A project manager whose project provides only four percent profit will not be valued as much as a project manager whose project brings in 40 percent profit. Project managers must have action orientation, profit motivation, and a strong, independent sense of self worth. Organizations that operate as a collection of projects are seldom collegial organizations. Loyalty is first demonstrated to the project, and second to the company as a whole. Openness, sharing, and creation of corporate image have to be systematically worked on if these characteristics are important to the business, because these do not naturally occur in an organization that operates as a group of projects.

EXAMPLES OF TRAINING PROJECTS

A training product or service can be considered a project; that is, a complex "deliverable" whose development has a beginning and an end. Some examples of training projects are:

- designing a new course
- revising an old course
- teaching a week of classes
- running a conference
- writing a user guide
- creating a job aid
- producing a videodisc
- developing a curriculum.

THE FOUR ELEMENTS OF PROJECT MANAGEMENT

Four basic elements of project management are:

- Content
- Cost
- Schedule
- Control.

Each training project—whether for an internal client such as a neighboring department or for an external client such as a major corporation that wants to buy a seminar series from you—is defined around these four basic elements.

The essential motivation for project managers is to make a good profit by providing clients with high quality products and services, prepared efficiently and within a reasonable time frame. The more defined, more finely-tuned each of the four elements is, the better the project as a whole will be—and the greater its chance of greater profit will be.

The following chart lists the standard components of each of these four elements.

CONTENT	Objectives Scope Staff Tasks List of products/services

COST	Salary, expressed as person-days Materials Computer time Purchased services (accounting, legal, photography, art) Overhead

SCHEDULE	Milestones Person-days to complete each task, and total person-days Lapse-time to complete each task, and total lapse-time

CONTROL	Roles and responsibilities Relationships among project staff, tasks, and time Communications, correspondence, status reports to clients In-process reviews End-of-project evaluation

CREATING A PROJECT JOURNAL TO HELP YOU ORGANIZE INFORMATION

An essential project management tool is the project journal or notebook. This journal is kept in a standard 3-ring binder, and is comprised of daily documentation about the project. Information in the project journal is organized behind the four tabs, Content, Cost, Schedule, and Control, which provide space to document and study the four basic elements of the project.

The chart above contains a list of components that should be kept in the project journal. Other project-specific items may be added as appropriate, and appendices may be included to contain memos or reports that do not fit into any particular category but are relevant to the project.

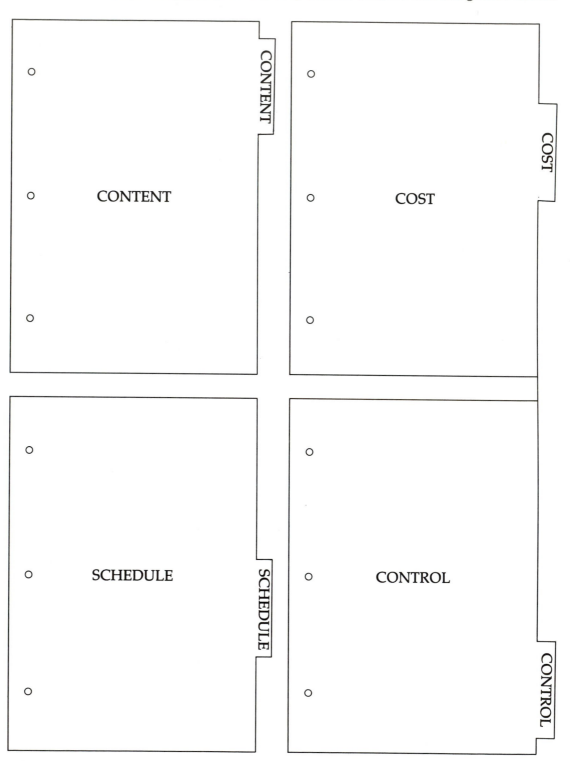

HOW TO USE THE WORKSHEETS IN THIS CHAPTER

The Project Journal, described on the previous page, provides documentation of the project details as the project is being implemented. In addition to this, there are several kinds of planning and monitoring tools which the training manager or manager of all projects can use. Four tools are described and illustrated on the following pages. These are:

Worksheet 16–1: Project Planning Summary Sheet

This is a summary of the project at its initial implementation stage. It is a planning document to be used as a reference as the project takes its place with other projects in your company.

Worksheet 16–2: Project Flowchart

A project flowchart is suggested as a planning guide and guide to implementation for staff. By seeing a graphic representation of the project as a whole, those involved in making it work can often relate better to other members of the project team. The importance of meeting deadlines is often dramatically apparent when the project is represented as a flowchart of interrelated parts.

Worksheet 16–3: Project Regular, Periodic Report (Status Report)

The status report is a project monitoring tool as well as a communication to the client who is paying to have this project done.

Worksheet 16–4: Project Monitoring Form

This form is useful to the training manager or company executive whose task it is to certify that a project is or has been successful. It is useful as a monitoring tool at a project's halfway point or as an evaluation tool at a project's conclusion. It could be a piece of documentation in the project manager's personnel folder, to indicate strengths and weaknesses of the project manager.

HOW TO CREATE A PROJECT PLANNING SUMMARY SHEET

Often it is useful to have a single-sheet summary of a project. This is frequently requested by your management, by client management, by your company's salespeople and account representatives, and by the project team members. It can be helpful to office administrators who schedule project staff and who assign project managers.

This summary sheet is best prepared by the project manager, who can realistically estimate critical variables such as end date, cost summary, and person-days required. It should not be prepared by the sales staff, who tend to estimate these variables too low.

The Project Planning Summary Sheet is a concise single sheet of information that can be used for meeting handouts, overhead presentations, or discussion guides with management or project staff. A project is a complex effort; summarizing it at the planning stage can help you inform key people about the project without overwhelming them with all the operational details.

The Project Planning Summary Sheet is placed at the beginning of the Project Journal. Information in the Project Journal can be helpful to the project manager as he or she prepares the summary sheet.

Example

A sample Project Planning Summary Sheet is on page 353. Worksheet 16–1 has several key areas requiring careful attention. These are:

Objectives and Scope: Be sure to define the scope of the project, stating the *client's* major objective or goal.

Cost Summary: This section summarizes *your* costs. When you estimate person-days, you can generally assume that more than one member of your staff will be working on the project at the same time. In the sample, for example, 200 person-days are required to complete the project in approximately 4½ months. These 200 person-days cost your project an average of $200 per day—against the rate you are charging BSL of $540 per day. Likewise, the cost and price figures are given for production work ("Other Costs"), and your cost is totalled at $40,000.

Revenue Projection: This is the amount of money you expect to be paid during the life of this project. In the sample, it is calculated by multiplying the 200 person-days by the per diem rate of $540, to equal $108,000 plus $750 for production.

Since this is a planning summary, profit is not calculated at this point. These dollar figures are used primarily for planning, not for preparing a corporate balance sheet.

Milestones: It is important to identify the major activities of the project in a systematic way, in order to schedule personnel and production resource use.

The sample indicates one way to do this; the two examples which follow are additional ways. The first lists project milestones for developing a new course:

January	April	July	October
1.0 VERIFY NEED	3.0 DEFINE LEARNING TASKS	6.0 WRITE LESSONS	7.0 PRODUCE
1.1 Collect data	4.0 WRITE COURSE OBJECTIVES	6.1 Design aids	COURSE
1.2 Analyze data	5.0 WRITE COURSE OUTLINE	7.0 CONDUCT DESIGN	
2.0 IDENTIFY AUDIENCE	5.1 Organize into units	REVIEWS OF UNITS	
2.1 Conduct job study	6.0 CONDUCT DESIGN REVIEW		

The second represents project milestones by using a Gantt chart:

	January	April	July	October
1. Verify need	-----------			
2. Collect data	------			
3. Analyze data	-----------			
4. Identify audience	---			
5. Conduct job study	-------------			
6. Define learning tasks	-----------------			
7. Write course objectives	-------------------			
8. Write course outline	-------------------			
9. Organize into units	-----------------------			
10. Conduct design review	----------------------			
11. Write lessons	---------------------------------			
12. Design aids	----------------------------------			
13. Conduct design reviews	--			
14. Produce course	--			

WORKSHEET 16–1

PROJECT PLANNING SUMMARY SHEET

Project Name _____

Objectives and Scope: _____

_____

_____

_____

_____

_____

Start Date–End Date　　　　**Project Manager**　　　　**Telephone**

Milestones:

•	•	•	•
•	•	•	•
•	•	•	•
•	•	•	•
•		•	

Cost Summary:

_____　　　$_____

Person-days Required　　　　　　　　　　**Revenue Projection**

　　　　　　　　$_____

Per-diem Rate

　　　　　　　　$_____

Other Costs

_____

_____

_____

TOTAL COST　$_____　　　　　　**Approval to Begin Project**

　　　　　　　　　　　　　　　　　　　　_____

　　　　　　　　　　　　　　　　　　　　Date

PROJECT PLANNING SUMMARY SHEET
"The New Nutrition"

Project Name

Objectives and Scope: This is a two-day seminar for Business Services Ltd. (BSL). We are creating the seminar for BSL and training their instructors to deliver it for 20 groups of employees at the rate of two or three groups per week over a two-month period. Goal is for employees to choose more nutritious food, ultimately increasing their energy levels off and on the job.

9/2/XX–1/17/XX	R. D. Pearl	539-9600
Start Date–End Date	**Project Manager**	**Telephone**

Milestones:

Sept.	Oct.	Nov.	Dec.	Jan.
• verify client groups	• draft the seminar	• identify BSL instructors	• assist with the first two seminars at BSL	• compile results of all evaluations
• study absentee & medical data	• pilot test seminar at BSL	• train BSL trainers in their facility		• conduct feedback session with all BSL instructors
• study productivity charts for last 18 mos.	• use feedback to revise			
	• product seminar materials			

Cost Summary:

200

Person-days Required

average $200 (BSL pays $540)

Per-diem Rate

production $400 (BSL pays $750)

Other Costs

TOTAL COST $40,400

$108,750
Revenue Projection

H. R. Wilson
Approval to Begin Project
8/10/XX
Date

WORKSHEET 16–2

PROJECT FLOWCHART

There are several simple conventions to follow when constructing a flowchart to represent a training project. These are:

- Use a box to represent an activity.
- Use a diamond to represent a decision point.
- Use a circle to represent tangible output (e.g., draft documents, reports, manuals, charts, graphic output).
- Connect all parts of the flowchart, paying special attention to what happens at a decision point.
- Arrange boxes, diamonds, and circles in the order in which things are expected to happen in a project, from top to bottom on the page.

Using a Flowchart to See "The Big Picture"

Persons responsible for implementing a project often see only a part of the project. Work generally progresses more smoothly if those involved in a project understand the big picture of the work effort. A flowchart of the project as a whole is helpful.

Be sure such a flowchart is given to each person working on the project. Posting it in 24″ x 36″ size where all can see it, or entering it on the computer system for easy "call up" are also ways to disseminate the information.

Using a Flowchart for Project Control

By adding time constraints and person responsible to a flowchart, the project manager can create an effective and efficient tool for project control. Good management of small, discrete parts of a project generally has good payoff in terms of time and dollars saved.

Example

The project illustrated on the next page is a production project for a new course manual. This flowchart could also be used to represent writing a user guide or book.

PROJECT CONTROL USING A FLOWCHART

Project Title: Managing Employee Performance Course

	Time Constraint	**Person Responsible**
Create directory and file structure for the course	10/1	Kristin
Use format standards	10/1	Katy
Call up the tracking system	10/1	Mitch
Generate text	10/1–10/20	Jamie Mary Kristin
Output to author and editor	10/20	Jamie
Edit	10/20–10/25	Nancy
Revise — Yes / No	10/25–10/30	Dick Annie
Save and store master file and directory	10/30	Kristin
Print course hardcopy	10/30	Kristin

HOW TO WRITE A PROJECT STATUS REPORT

This report has a dual purpose: (1) to communicate to the client how the project is progressing, and (2) to enable the project manager to monitor current progress against all previous progress. Copies of status reports are placed in the Project Journal as they are sent to the client. (Control section). Send out status reports at regular intervals (e.g., every 2 weeks).

Be brief when writing a status report. Be factual and non-evaluative in your listing of "Accomplished" and "To Be Accomplished." Express constraints and concerns clearly, indicating your reponsibility as well as the client's responsibility to work on any problems you foresee.

Example

Accomplished:

- Estimated length of each section of the User Guide to System 36.
- Drafted System Overview (to be used in presentation to management).
- Got approval from CDN on format.

To Be Accomplished:

- Take over supervision of word processing group.
- Complete the section on System Maintenance.
- Complete the section on Change Management.

Constraints and Concerns:

- Due date seems unreasonable due to client supervisor's illness. Can we renegotiate this or replace her within two weeks?
- Our move to new facilities will not impact delivery of the draft to you.

TRAINING TIP: The period for the periodic status report varies according to the duration of the project. Issue a status report at the end of each week for projects of six weeks or less; issue a status report at the end of two weeks for projects longer than six weeks. Status reports are often timed to reach a client at the same time your bill for services reaches him or her. Be sensitive to this, and time your reporting to your best advantage, but always report in the same interval.

WORKSHEET 16–3

PROJECT REGULAR, PERIODIC REPORT (STATUS REPORT)

_____   _____

Project Name   **Date of Report**

_____

Time Period Covered by this Report

Accomplished:

-

-

-

-

To Be Accomplished:

-

-

-

Constraints and Concerns:

-

-

-

_____

Project Manager Signature

TRAINING TIP: Before you send the status report to a client, double check the language of each section.

The *Accomplished* section should be written in past tense verbs.

The *To Be Accomplished* section should be written in present tense verbs, with the assumption that these actions will be accomplished within the period between the date of this status report and the date of the next status report.

The *Constraints and Concerns* section should reflect both the client's position and your position.

STATUS REPORT

Tuning Manual for Apprentice Organ Builders   August 10, 19XX
Project Name   **Date of Report**

July 27–August 9, 19XX
Time Period Covered by this Report

Accomplished:
- Observed small-scale metal pipecrafters in the shop

- Received samples of sleeve-tuned pipes

- Drafted the two units on stopped and capped pipes

- Ordered four books on reed and string tuning

To Be Accomplished:
- Need decision about whether or not to include units/appendix on French and Spanish reed pipe tuning

- Draft the unit(s) on reed pipe tuning

- Draft the units on string pipe tuning

- Circulate capped pipe unit to three apprentices for review

Constraints and Concerns:
- Additional money might be required for heavy-duty binding. We assume conventional binding in our estimate. We need to meet within 10 days to decide this issue.

N. N. Wood
Project Manager Signature

USING THE PROJECT MONITORING FORM

The training manager or company executive to whom project managers report will find Worksheet 16–4 useful. It is a brief documentation tool, covering three major areas of a project manager's responsibility: management, finances and record-keeping, and performance.

This form can be used as an interim documentation and monitoring tool before the project is completed, or as an end-of-project evaluation tool. It can be effectively used during personnel discussions regarding performance standards and expectations for project staff, and as one kind of evaluation base for analysis of corporate support that might be required for successful project implementation across the company.

Keep in mind that this is a very brief documentation; complete records and backup information should be available in other project file cabinets or in the Project Journal.

Example

Commendations and Concerns		Not at All	Some-what	To a Large Extent
	MANAGEMENT			
–P.M. could be less wordy	1. Planned tasks have been completed on schedule.	☐	☐	■
–our instructor was terrific— rave reviews	2. Changes are consistent with original project objectives.	☐	☐	■
	3. Reports are succinct and nontrivial.	☐	■	☐
	4. Staffing has been effective.	☐	☐	■
	FINANCES AND RECORD-KEEPING			
–financial stuff is clearly *not* his strength	1. Expenditure records are current.	■	☐	☐
	2. Revenue records are current.	☐	☐	■
	3. Records indicate that resources have been allocated in support of deliverable products/services.	■	☐	☐
	4. Costs have been justified.	☐	■	☐
	PERFORMANCE			
	1. Required information has been assembled.	☐	■	☐
	2. Data is accessible and easy to use.	☐	■	☐
	3. Deliverables have been produced according to design.	☐	☐	■
	4. Deliverables are available for review.	☐	☐	■
	5. There is evidence that the target audience accepts the project as complete.	☐	☐	■

WORKSHEET 16–4

PROJECT MONITORING FORM

Date: _____

Project Name: _____

Project Manager: _____

Commendations and Concerns		Not at All	Some-what	To a Large Extent
	MANAGEMENT			
	1. Planned tasks have been completed on schedule.	☐	☐	☐
	2. Changes are consistent with original project objectives.	☐	☐	☐
	3. Reports are succinct and non-trivial.	☐	☐	☐
	4. Staffing has been effective.	☐	☐	☐
	FINANCES AND RECORD-KEEPING			
	1. Expenditure records are current.	☐	☐	☐
	2. Revenue records are current.	☐	☐	☐
	3. Records indicate that resources have been allocated in support of deliverable products/services.	☐	☐	☐
	4. Costs have been justified.	☐	☐	☐
	PERFORMANCE			
	1. Required information has been assembled.	☐	☐	☐
	2. Data is accesible and easy to use.	☐	☐	☐
	3. Deliverables have been produced according to design.	☐	☐	☐
	4. Deliverables are available for review.	☐	☐	☐
	5. There is evidence that the target audience accepts the project as complete.	☐	☐	☐

CHAPTER 17 _____

PLANNING _____
THE TRAINING BUDGET _____

Different companies use different budgeting systems. The training operation, of course, has to fit within the accepted budgeting and accounting framework of the company as a whole.

This chapter provides some basics regarding the training budget and suggests ways to plan how much training will cost. Worksheets in this chapter can provide useful budget planning information, not only to the training department, but also to the accounting and personnel departments. Planning the training budget requires close working relationships with these other departments in your company.

HOW TO USE THE WORKSHEETS IN THIS CHAPTER

Forms and guidelines in this chapter include the following:

Worksheet 17–1: Guidelines for Estimating the Cost of Development Time and Delivery Time

This worksheet suggests a formula for estimating the amount of days that have to be budgeted for developing your own course and for delivering a course. To figure out the cost, multiply the days by the person's salary plus benefits (often called the person's "loaded rate").

Worksheet 17–2: Training Department Annual Budget Planner

This worksheet breaks down costs of training into three columns: development, implementation, and maintenance. It is helpful to project the costs of the various parts of training operations (administration, instruction, equipment, marketing, and so on) in terms of costs in each of these phases: development, implementation, and maintenance. It often helps for corporate accountants and human resources administrators to see the sometimes hidden costs of training projected at annual budget planning time, so they allow enough money in the budget to cover these costs. This kind of planning is also particularly useful to training managers who set prices that trainees will pay for courses.

Worksheet 17–3: How to Use Account Numbering for Budget Planning

This worksheet suggests a three-digit account numbering system. This worksheet will be especially useful in a large corporate training operation, in which "line item" accounting and budgeting are required by corporate financial planners. Small training operations can easily adapt this accounting system by eliminating line items that are beyond their scope. Training managers are encouraged to check with accountants regarding the latest tax laws concerning allowable business expenses and depreciation deductions. Training account numbers might change as tax laws change.

Worksheet 17–4: Task-By-Objective Budget Worksheet

This worksheet is meant to be used as a monitoring tool which documents expenditures by training account number. These costs are objective-specific, providing a check for the training manager to see how much it is costing to accomplish a particular objective.

Strategies for Saving Money in Training Design and Delivery

Before sitting down to prepare an annual training budget, the wise training manager will consider alternative methods for designing, delivering, scheduling, and supporting courses. The following are some strategies to keep the costs down:

- Shorten the length of a course, that is, tighten the course design.
- Adopt a standard format for visuals using only three point sizes. Design visuals using inexpensive graphics software rather than custom graphics houses.
- "Suitcase" a course whenever possible, that is, send an instructor (with the course materials in a "suitcase") to a trainee site, instead of bringing all the trainees to the instructor. Travel time and expenses are much less for only one person.
- Set up computer practice time after hours, when more students can have access to the system and processing time is less expensive.
- Use job aids instead of manuals.
- Use a lending library of course manuals, together with a folder of handouts. Trainees keep only the folder of handouts, and return the manuals to the library.
- Conduct design reviews at several points early in the development process. Keep a list of items that need to be changed. Errors cost more, the longer they go uncorrected.
- Provide support to the instructor during his or her preparation for teaching (e.g., word processing support, printing and binding support, briefings about the target audience, level of prerequisite knowledge/skills expected in the target audience, classroom setup assistance). Save instructor time for teaching.

WORKSHEET 17–1

GUIDELINES FOR ESTIMATING THE COST OF DEVELOPMENT TIME AND DELIVERY TIME

Putting time estimates in print is risky business. The following guidelines are included here as a suggested starting point; they are conservative figures. An inexperienced course developer, instructor, or manager will cause the figures to rise. These estimates are based on years of experience with hundreds of course developers and instructors. They are meant to guide the training manager in preparing the workload and the staffing of a training operation.

These guidelines are for professional staff only, and don't include secretarial, clerical, graphics, or production time. They are based on a single individual. If a course developer is paired with an instructional technologist, or if multiple authors are developing a course together, the time will increase by 25–50 percent. If quality control is built in, an additional 10–15 percent should be added for periodic design reviews, run-throughs, pilot tests, and use of feedback.

Course Development Time

single author	40 person-days	for	1 day of class
paired	60 person-days	for	1 day of class
quality	70 person-days	for	1 day of class

As a training manager, do not underestimate the time it takes for good analysis, good design, good writing, good communication during development, and good quality control of the process.

Course Delivery Time

Per instructor, new course: 3 person-days preparation for 1 day of class (this can include a course pilot, evaluation, and feedback session).
Per instructor, existing course: 1 person-day preparation for 1 day of class.

TRAINING DEPARTMENT ANNUAL BUDGET PLANNER

Managers sometimes get in trouble because they neglect maintenance costs or implementation costs of the various elements of running a training department. People naturally pay attention to the earliest or first stages of a process or operation. It's hard for most folks to plan accurately for phases of operation beyond development—most people have energy for the initial stages of activity, but that energy often dissipates as an activity progresses.

It takes time and money to "keep things going." The Budget Planner chart on the following page can help you to separate the elements of costs in order to plan a realistic budget that won't surprise you with hidden costs as the year progresses. Estimate each item as an annual cost.

Example

	Development Cost	Implementation Cost	Maintenance Cost
Software	$100,000	$ 3,000	$20,000[1]
Hardware	$ zero	$10,000[2]	$ 4,500
Marketing	$ 20,000[3]	$ 6,000[4]	$ 4,000[5]
Secretarial Support	$ 6,000	$ 2,000	$ 7,000

Notes:
  (1) one person, one-fourth of her responsibility
  (2) includes dedicated telephone (data) lines during classes
  (3) consultant fee
  (4) printing and mailing costs
  (5) direct mail listing maintenance contract

WORKSHEET 17–2

TRAINING DEPARTMENT ANNUAL BUDGET PLANNER

	Development Cost	Implementation Cost	Maintenance Cost
Course Administration			
Course Instruction			
Course Design			
Software			
Hardware			
Graphics			
Instructional Materials			
Equipment			
Facilities			
Marketing			
Secretarial Support			

Notes:

Worksheet 17.3 is both an example of the accounts in a typical training operation and a worksheet to guide you in organizing your accounts in a similar way.

Pay special attention to the 100s, 200s, 300s, and so on—the major areas of cost. Note the number breakdown within each major area. As you construct your own account numbering system, be sure to allow enough digits between items.

Use this kind of record keeping by accounts to keep track of the costs associated with each part of your training program. It's an invaluable aid at budget planning time because it allows you to be accountable all during the year in a very specific way. Your boss and your corporate accountants will thank you for your thoroughness and accuracy.

WORKSHEET 17–3

HOW TO USE ACCOUNT NUMBERING FOR BUDGET PLANNING

Use a three-digit account number for each cost item. Assign major items an account number with a zero for the right digit (or a five or a zero in larger organizations). A sample account numbering system for training is shown below.

100s   Generic Programs/Courses

110	Company Orientation	133	Quality Control
120	Train the Trainer	140	Management Training
130	Quality Training	150	Sales Training
131	Quality Principles	160	Better Writing
132	Quality Measures and Tests		

200s   Custom Programs/Courses

210	Personnel System Conversion Procedures	220	How to Design Job Aids for the ABC Project
211	Data Entry Skills and Methods	230	Optimization Techniques at the KQZ Processing Plant

300s   Instructional Materials

310	Classroom Supplies	332	Packaged Videos
320	Visuals	340	Textbooks
321	Overhead Transparencies	350	Trainee Manuals
322	Slides	360	Instructor Manuals
323	Film	370	Handouts
324	Wall Charts, Job Aids	380	Other Consumable Student Aids
330	Videotapes	390	Evaluation Forms
331	Blank Tapes		

400s   Staff Salaries and Fringe Benefits

410	Training Director	450	Training Specialist(s)
420	Training Manager(s)	460	Graphic Artist(s)
430	Instructor(s)	470	Editor(s)
440	Instructional Technologist	480	Secretarial and Clerical Support

500s   Purchased Services

510	Professional Memberships	544	Meals
520	Subscriptions and Books	545	Entertainment
530	Professional Development Courses	550	Outside Consultants
540	Travel and Entertainment	560	Honorariums
541	Auto	570	Legal
542	Air	580	Accounting
543	Lodging	590	Printing and Binding

600s   Equipment

610	Audio/Visual Rental	622	Word Processing
611	Camcorder	630	Classroom Equipment
612	VCRs	631	Rear Projection System
613	Monitors	632	Fixed Mount Cameras
620	Office Equipment Rental	633	Terminals
621	Copy Machines		

700s   Facilities

710	Space Rental	723	Heat
720	Utilities	724	Telephone
721	Power	730	Postage
722	Water	740	Insurance

800s   Capital Outlay

810	Audio/Visual Equipment Purchase	830	Classroom Equipment Purchase
820	Office Equipment Purchase		

TASK-BY-OBJECTIVE BUDGET WORKSHEET

Training program audits will evaluate expenditures against program objectives. In training design, this usually means an objective for learning, rather than an objective for administration.

The following form can help you document how much it costs to help trainees learn new skills which will contribute to corporate profits. This kind of planning by learning objective provides the training department and corporate human resources planners with information about the costs of a trained workforce.

This kind of information is often helpful to personnel administrators who write "Help Wanted" advertisements and contract with "Head Hunters" and placement agencies. If projected costs seem too high, it might be worth hiring persons who already have the skills in question, rather than incurring the costs of training.

Note that this accounting is based on a specific objective, and may contain many different training line item numbers.

Training budget administration is an on-going activity that documents how money is being spent. The most informative way to collect budget information is to collect it in relationship to an objective for the learner. Collect data periodically, for example, quarterly (March, June, September, December) or semi-annually at the midpoint and end of your fiscal year.

A completed sample worksheet follows the blank form. It follows the account numbering system suggested on Worksheet 17–3.

WORKSHEET 17–4

TASK-BY-OBJECTIVE BUDGET WORKSHEET

Date: _____

Objective: _____

Task (Cost Item)	Account Number	Expenditure/ Encumbrance		Account Balance
		Date	Amount	
1.				
2.				
3.				
4.				
5.				
6.				
7.				
8.				
9.				

SAMPLE

TASK-BY-OBJECTIVE WORKSHEET

Date: June 30, 19XX

Objective: To install the spa in a laboratory setting with 100 percent accuracy.

Task (Cost Item)	Account Number	Expenditure/ Encumbrance		Account Balance
		Date	Amount	
1. Purchase spa for lab demonstrations	630	4/3	$2,000	$ 8,000
2. Purchase two power panels for trainee practice	630	4/10	$ 500	$ 7,500
3. Create wall chart of the electrical system	324	5/1	$ 250	$ 250
4. Hire evaluation consultant to provide one-to-one testing at the end of lab sessions, beginning 6/1	550	5/15	$6,000	$24,000
5. Hire video contractor to tape each individual trainee during final practice exercise	550	5/15	$2,500	$21,500
6. Purchase blank notebooks for each trainee to use as a lab record	380	5/15	$ 100	$ 400
7. Prepare evaluation forms (with consultant input)	390	5/15	$ 250	$ zero

CHAPTER 18 _____

HOW TO SURVIVE AN _____ OPERATIONAL AUDIT _____

At some point in the life of a training operation, someone external to training will make a judgment about how well you've done. When this judgment is formalized, documented, and used for planning or budgeting decisions, it is an operational audit.

BE AWARE OF SAGES AND STAKEHOLDERS

One of the difficulties in training is that most people believe they know a lot about training. Everyone has learned, has applied that learning, and has many instructional role models.

Most people, however, do not know how training design and development processes can be systematized, or how the products of these processes can be evaluated against standards. Most people do not think of training as project management. Most people think of training delivery as "platform skills" instead of the ability to facilitate transfer of learned skills to the job situation. Many people do not understand that training support systems—registration, scheduling, production—often operate under severe time constraints and need to be staffed with performance-driven and flexible professionals.

Operational audits are generally done by people who care about training and who have a stake in the outcome of the audit. There seldom is an impartial operational audit of training. Operational audits are conducted by a variety of people. In a small training operation, the results of training and the processes of training operations are generally audited by a company vice-president or president. In a large training operation with several levels of training managers, training specialists, and instructional designers, an operational audit of parts of the training operation is often done by a specialized training manager, such as the manager of management training, the manager of sales training, or the manager of data processing training projects.

A rule of thumb is that if the highest responsible person for training operations is called "manager," then an internal operational audit is done by someone called "director."

An external operational audit could be done by a client manager or director, or by an outside consultant hired specifically for the auditing task.

When Does an Operational Audit Occur?

There is no particular time for an operational audit. Some common events that trigger an operational audit are a change in training management, a change in top management, completion of a major client service or project, reduction in force, merger, IRS audit, major change in federal tax law, decline in business, upsurge in business, venture into a new technology base, major change in employee base, or new client base. Whenever it happens, training management has to be prepared.

BUILD IN A BIAS FOR ACTION

The training manager, therefore, has a responsibility to provide those making judgments about training (auditors) with information that presents the training operation as objectively as possible. All persons concerned with the results of an audit should be able to come away from it with a list of action items for making improvements.

The following pages present forms, guidelines, and checklists to help you collect and document information that will keep you afloat operationally, and assist you in helping those "significant others" to understand what it takes to make training work.

ETHICAL CONDUCT DURING AUDIT

The following guidelines can be useful as you interact with your auditor at audit time. Share the two-part Code of Ethics with your auditor ahead of time to ensure a smooth-running look at your training operations.

Trainer's Code of Ethics

- I have led the training department in self-evaluations during the year.
- I have considered feedback from employees and clients in a timely and responsible way when it was provided to me.
- I have been accountable in areas of money, time, personnel, and program.
- I have represented training operations accurately and fairly.
- I have made an honest attempt to define my problems and to devise solutions to them.
- I will listen carefully in order to answer the audit questions appropriately, realizing that providing too much information is as poor a response as providing too little information.

- I will devise corrective actions that address specific audit points and that are achievable within my planning and budget framework.
- I welcome the opportunity for improvement that is inherent in an operational audit.

Auditor's Code of Ethics

- I have done my homework before the operational audit begins—reviewed relevant documents to get the big picture, and drafted a set of questions in order to provide a fair framework for investigation.
- I have an open mind to sources of information, written and oral, that I might have overlooked.
- I respect the confidentiality of sources.
- I appreciate the efforts of training employees to do a good job.
- I seek to clarify, facilitate, and improve.
- I will ask questions that can be answered and that point to realistic and do-able corrective actions.
- I will provide timely, focused, and comprehensive feedback to those who participated in the audit.

HOW TO USE THE WORKSHEETS IN THIS CHAPTER

Worksheets in this chapter help you provide information that is useful during an operational audit. Some of these forms help you gather the right kind of information; some help you identify and describe results of training operations; some provide you with feedback from others who are interested in helping you improve the way you do things.

A good operational audit begins with introspection—a hard look by the training department itself into its own operations. This inward self-evaluation is done several weeks before the formal audit.

Worksheets 18–1 through 18–4 can be helpful tools during this self-evaluation. All members of the training department participate in the self-study, and all are expected to contribute to operational improvements. These worksheets can then provide excellent documentation for use during the formal operational audit.

Worksheet 18–5 can be used effectively during a departmental self-study or during a formal audit. It is an efficient way to focus on improvement.

Worksheets 18–6 and 18–7 are standard forms that should reside in training files. Course evaluations from the trainees and instructors provide a baseline of information about course design and delivery, generally the primary operational processes of training. It is important to keep these files current, because the accumulated data on these forms represents an ever-changing operational baseline. These files are useful during self-study as well as during a formal operational audit.

Worksheet 18–8 is one way of presenting the formal auditor's summary of findings.

The Secrets of Survival

You will survive an operational audit if you demonstrate that you do these things:

1. Take the initiative to look at your operations objectively.
2. Seek and use feedback from employees and from those you serve.
3. Clarify, specify, and document problems to be solved.

The following worksheets are examples of "survival gear."

Worksheet 18–1: Planning Worksheet for Results-Oriented Training

Use this planning worksheet to focus on the results you expect to achieve. Auditors will look for evidence that training made a difference. Course designers or training managers are responsible for completing this planning document when a new course is about to begin.

Worksheet 18–2: Value Calculation Worksheet

Use this worksheet to put a price tag on the benefits of training operations. Seek out data to translate training problems, training solutions, and training results into dollars. Training managers generally do this job, although an interested training specialist could do it instead.

Worksheet 18–3: Discussion Notes

Use this worksheet during a small group meeting to take notes in a structured fashion. This saves time and focuses the energy of the group on actions for improvement. Each person in the group uses a worksheet for personal note-taking.

Worksheet 18–4: Discussion Tally Sheet

Use this worksheet when small groups meet simultaneously and report back to each other as a large group. This form focuses on the four parts of the "training system"—analyze, design/develop, implement, and evaluate. Training operations are grouped within each of these four parts to assure discussion of a systems nature. This form is completed during a group discussion by an appointed recorder. This form is best used during a self-evaluation by a training department.

Worksheet 18–5: Auditor's Open Items

Use this worksheet to summarize the "to do" list that results from either a departmental self-study or an actual formal audit. It can be filled out by anyone who has participated in the evaluation of operations. The open items listed on this form should represent a consensus of all evaluation discussions and findings.

Worksheet 18–6: Trainee Course Evaluation Questionnaire

This is a standard form to be filled out by trainees at the conclusion of training. It can be used during a field test of a course or during a course "for paying customers." An on-going file of trainee course evaluations should be open for perusal by those engaged in self-evaluation or formal audit.

Worksheet 18–7: Instructor Evaluation of the Course

This is a standard form to be filled out by any instructor who teaches a course in your department. The form can be used during a field test of a course or during a course "for paying customers." An on-going file of instructor evaluations should be open for perusal by those engaged in self-evaluation or formal audit.

Worksheet 18–8: Summary Operational Audit Profile

This is the summary profile sheet to be filled out by the formal auditor. It is always backed up by specific documents or reports. A collection of these forms provides a simple and succinct record of audit activity.

PLANNING WORKSHEET FOR RESULTS-ORIENTED TRAINING

The following worksheet presents training from a before-and-after perspective. Use this worksheet to focus on results of training, noting the specific conditions both before and after training. It is a useful planning tool when initiating a new course, program, or strategy.

Information above the double line is required at the beginning of planning. Information below the double line is required at the end of training.

Example

Name of Proposed Course/Program/Strategy: WORKSHOP FOR NEW HOME HEALTH AIDES	
Objectives In a six-month period, 150 new home health aides will be prepared to provide home health care in five basic areas (food preparation and feeding, bathing and grooming, medications, conversation and cognitive skills, recreational and occupational therapy) and will be able to refer clients to appropriate resources within the new legislative framework.	
Specific Conditions Before Training	New state legislation has just been enacted to provide funding incentives to our agency and to persons desiring to become home health aides. No training has been provided to date.
Types of Records We Need to Maintain	• attendance of trainees • list of probable client placements for home health aides • legislative updates • criterion tests and individual test results
Specific Conditions After Training	• One hundred thirty-seven of the original group successfully completed training. • Add-on legislation provided more incentive funding. Two hundred new people have indicated an interest in our training program. • We need to hire and train four more instructors.
Results	With minor adjustments to our program in the cognitive skills area of training, we have a training program that meets the needs of our target audience. Replication is desirable and possible if we can find more instructors.

WORKSHEET 18–1

PLANNING WORKSHEET FOR RESULTS-ORIENTED TRAINING

Name of Proposed Course/Program/Strategy:

_____

Objectives

_____

Specific Conditions Before
Training

_____

Types of Records We Need to
Maintain

_____

Specific Conditions After
Training

_____

Results

GUIDELINES FOR ASSIGNING DOLLAR VALUES TO
TRAINING OPERATIONS

In preparing for an operational audit, a training manager or designee can provide a "financial benefits" picture of training operations for evaluators. Do this by placing a dollar value on the problem, the solution, and the result.

Examples

1. *Put a Price on the Problem*

   Define in dollars how much the problem costs the company.

   Example:

400 rejected widgets at our manufactured cost of $30 each	= $12,000
1200 hours of downtime on the training simulator at our cost of $5 per hour (downtime costs us; runtime does not for the first year)	= $ 6,000

2. *Put a Price on the Solution*

   Define in dollars how much the solution will save the company.

   Example:

   Course QU100, Quality Control Techniques, for 3 key line workers at our cost of $150 per course, plus their salaries during training ($80 × 3 = $240)
   $150 + $240 = $390 for a savings of 12,000 − 390   = $11,610
   Offer "Simulator Hands-on for Nontechnicians" during downtime at a tuition rate of $100 per course 1200/4 = 300
   × $100 = $30,000, less our cost to run the workshop ($4,000) = $26,000

3. *Put a Price on the Result*

   Define in dollars how much the company saved by implementing the solution.

   Example:

   From 400 to zero rejected widgets   savings = $11,610
   Plus, increase in perfect widget production of 120 over standard, at a profit of $40 per widget   = $ 4,800
   TOTAL SAVINGS $16,410

   "Simulator Hands-on Workshop" attracted only ⅔ of the target audience. Actual savings were $20,000 less $3,000
   TOTAL SAVINGS $17,000

WORKSHEET 18–2

VALUE CALCULATION WORKSHEET

The Problem:

$ _____

The Solution:

$ _____

The Result:

$ _____

DISCUSSION NOTES

Each person who participates in a discussion about operational issues/problems in training should have a "Discussion Notes" form in front of him or her as a personal record of discussion.

If your organization encourages group problem-solving, have a pad of these note forms available for each group member. A local printer can inexpensively make a 25–30 sheet pad of forms for you to use during group problem-solving activities.

This is a personal note-taking tool. Be sure to record the names of all participants in the group, so that you can contact them later when you begin to work on the action items. Problems get solved faster when solutions and action items are directly related to stated problems.[1]

Example

Issue/Problem	Solution	Action Items
1. Engineering Research Center laboratory tables are too narrow.	1. See if salesman can arrange a good deal on exchange and upgrade. 2. See if maintenance can build cantilevered table extensions.	1. Charlie will phone salesman and get price. 2. I will contact Barney and meet him in the lab and get his price.
2. Course 413 had to be cancelled because of underenrollment.	1. Promote it better. 2. Redesign the content (rearrange? update?). 3. Get a different instructor. 4. Check all evaluation forms to find the reasons for falling interest.	1. Ann will convene a task force to study evaluation forms and propose a solution. 2. This group agrees to meet again to act upon results of task force.

---

[1] For a lively, easy-to-read, and comprehensive discussion of problem solving, see Roger Kaufman's *Identifying and Solving Problems: A System Approach*. La Jolla, CA: University Associates, 1976.

WORKSHEET 18–3

DISCUSSION NOTES

Group Participants: _____   Date: _____

_____

_____

Issue/Problem	Solution	Action Items

DISCUSSION TALLY SHEET

This tally sheet is useful in situations where small discussion groups report back to a larger group, or task forces come back to a manager with their reports. In the case of small groups reporting to the larger group, the recorder for the large group checks which training functions are affected by each issue defined by the small groups. This tally sheet can be used by an audit committee or a self-study task force.

This tally sheet is best used during a self-evaluation by a training department, although it can also be used by an audit committee. In either case, it provides a quick analysis of the training operation from a "systems" perspective. Training operations are grouped under the system parts: analyze, design/develop, implement, and evaluate.

When the tally sheet is used as a tool in self-study, department members should be encouraged ahead of the meeting to write down several issues or problems that are especially troublesome.

Example

Issue/Problem	ANALYZE			DESIGN/DEVELOP					IMPLEMENT					EVALUATE			
	Market	Client Needs	Internal Organization	Subject Matter Experts	Instructional Technologists	Computer Support	Graphics	Editing	Instruction	Facilities	Catalog	Registration	Production	Meetings/Processes	Forms	Feedback	Maintenance
Need more copy machines for trainees		√	√	√		√			√		√				√		
Course 258 too long				√	√		√		√	√	√	√			√		
Need to raise rates	√	√	√						√	√	√						
Need another secretary			√							√		√		√			

WORKSHEET 18–4

DISCUSSION TALLY SHEET

Issue/Problem	ANALYZE			DESIGN/DEVELOP							IMPLEMENT						EVALUATE		
	Market	Client Needs	Internal Organization	Subject Matter Experts	Instructional Technologists	Computer Support	Graphics	Editing		Instruction	Facilities	Catalog	Registration	Production		Meetings/Processes	Forms	Feedback	Maintenance

AUDITOR'S OPEN ITEMS

This is a "to do" list, with identification of a person responsible for taking action on each specific item. This worksheet is used to distill a variety of comments made during operational audits or departmental self-studies. It is meant to be a summary list of open items that surfaced during operational evaluations. It can be filled out by anyone designated as a recorder, or by a training manager or auditor. Items listed should represent a consensus of open items discussed at group meetings or should represent the majority or significant operational issues defined on various recording forms such as the other worksheets in this chapter.

Example

Date of Audit: 8/15/XX

Auditor: B.H. Small

Name of Audited Project/Department: Pet Store Sales Training

Date of Next Audit or Follow-up Meeting: 9/15/XX

List of Open Items	Person Responsible for Corrective Action
1. Redesign magazine ad to focus on kids, ages 8–15.	Pinky
2. Develop two more suburban mall pet stores.	Susan
3. Purchase "Love a Goldfish" video for each store (20 copies).	Bert
4. Write handout for kids to accompany the video.	Lily
5. Design a one-day workshop for store managers around the theme of pet displays that attract kids (include training in how to get the most out of "Love a Goldfish").	Mark
6. Do a cost-benefit analysis of specialized market in Skinnerian boxes and behavioral training (rats, mice, birds, squirels, etc.).	Bert

WORKSHEET 18–5

AUDITOR'S OPEN ITEMS

Date of Audit: _____

Auditor: _____

Name of Audited Project/Department: _____

Date of Next Audit or Follow-up Meeting: _____

List of Open Items	Person Responsible for Corrective Action

TRAINEE COURSE EVALUATION QUESTIONNAIRE

This is an example of a simple course evaluation form for a trainee to complete at the end of a course. Remember to tell trainees at the start of class that they will be asked to fill out an evaluation questionnaire and that their comments will be appreciated. Keep a current file of all completed questionnaires to use during data collection at operational audit—and planning—times.

TRAINEE COURSE EVALUATION QUESTIONNAIRE

The information you supply will be used to improve the quality of instruction. An instructional technologist may want to contact you for clarification or elaboration of your comments. We appreciate your name and telephone number.

Course evaluation is done in the spirit of peer review. Thank you for your participation.

Name: Daniel Kirk   **Employee Number:** 2213

Department: Consumer Safety   **Telephone:** 3161

Course Number and Title: 369 Collision Testing

Date of Course Completion: 8/8/XX

Instructor: Manny Cristiani

Check the number in each answer box which most nearly reflects your opinion. Use the back of this form if you have additional comments.

1. Were the objectives of this course relevant to the knowledge/skill requirements of your job?

   | 1 | 2 | 3 ✓ | 4 |
   (not at all)   (very)

2. Were the course materials useful and of good quality?

   | 1 | 2 | 3 | 4 ✓ |
   (low)   (high)

3. How would you rate the delivery skills of the instructor?

   | 1 | 2 | 3 | 4 ✓ |
   (ineffective)   (outstanding)

4. Was the course content presented in a clear and understandable manner?

   | 1 | 2 | 3 ✓ | 4 |
   (obscure)   (very clear)

5. What is your confidence level to use what you learned in this course back on the job?

   | 1 | 2 | 3 | 4 ✓ |
   (low)   (high)

Additional Comments: _____

_____

Courtesy of Bell Communications Research. Reprinted with permission.

WORKSHEET 18–6

TRAINEE COURSE EVALUATION QUESTIONNAIRE

The information you supply will be used to improve the quality of instruction. An instructional technologist may want to contact you for clarification or elaboration of your comments. We appreciate your name and telephone number.

Course evaluation is done in the spirit of peer review. Thank you for your participation.

Name: _____   **Employee Number:** _____

Department: _____   **Telephone:** _____

Course Number and Title: _____

Date of Course Completion: _____

Instructor: _____

Check the number in each answer box which most nearly reflects your opinion. Use the back of this form if you have additional comments.

1. Were the objectives of this course relevant to the knowledge/skill requirements of your job?

1	2	3	4

   (not at all)   (very)

2. Were the course materials useful and of good quality?

1	2	3	4

   (low)   (high)

3. How would you rate the delivery skills of the instructor?

1	2	3	4

   (ineffective)   (outstanding)

4. Was the course content presented in a clear and understandable manner?

1	2	3	4

   (obscure)   (very clear)

5. What is your confidence level to use what you learned in this course back on the job?

1	2	3	4

   (low)   (high)

Additional Comments: _____

_____

_____

Adapted from Student Feedback Form, Bell Communications Research. Reprinted with permission.

INSTRUCTOR EVALUATION OF THE COURSE

This is an example of a simple course evaluation form to be filled out by the instructor at the end of the course. Training operations sometimes forget to include this type of evaluation. Good learning involves good teaching—don't ignore these interrelationships. The instructor will generally want to pack up and leave immediately after class—be sure that you, the training manager, stick around long enough to get this completed form from each instructor you employ. Keep all completed instructor evaluations of the course in a file for use during operational audit and planning activities.

INSTRUCTOR EVALUATION OF THE COURSE

Instructor: Joan Leslie   **Telephone:** 6–2700

Course Number and Title: R100 Fundamentals of Retailing

Course Date(s): 5/21/XX

Course Location: 5 Morris   **Class Size:** 50

1. Did all students have the specified prerequisite skill/knowledge? If no, what did they lack?   ___ yes   ✓ no

     13 lacked prerequisite Sales Accounting Seminar

2. Did students achieve the objectives for the course? If no, which ones were not achievable?   ___ yes   ✓ no

     about ⅔ of class had trouble with
     "Electronic Inventory Input"—perhaps
     this unit should be rewritten

3. Were there any instructional delivery problems? If yes, please explain.   ✓ yes   ___ no

     larger screen would have been nice—
     seems a bit small for this large room

4. Would you make any changes to the content or lesson structure of the course? If yes, please explain.   ✓ yes   ___ no

     yes—see #2

5. Were the course materials accurate, legible, useful, appropriate? If no, please describe the problems.   ✓ yes   ___ no

6. Were the facilities adequate? If no, please explain.   ___ yes   ✓ no

     too hot—fix air conditioning

WORKSHEET 18–7

INSTRUCTOR EVALUATION OF THE COURSE

Instructor: _____ Telephone: _____

Course Number and Title: _____

Course Date(s): _____

Course Location: _____ Class Size: _____

1. Did all students have the specified prerequisite skill/knowledge? If no, what did they lack?

    ____ ____
    yes   no

2. Did students achieve the objectives for the course? If no, which ones were not achievable?

    ____ ____
    yes   no

3. Were there any instructional delivery problems? If yes, please explain.

    ____ ____
    yes   no

4. Would you make any changes to the content or lesson structure of the course? If yes, please explain.

    ____ ____
    yes   no

5. Were the course materials accurate, legible, useful, appropriate? If no, please describe the problems.

    ____ ____
    yes   no

6. Were the facilities adequate? If no, please explain.

    ____ ____
    yes   no

SUMMARY OPERATIONAL AUDIT PROFILE

This is the summary profile sheet to be filled out by the formal auditor. It is a graphic representation of the auditor's findings. This profile can be used to summarize a project or a department. It must be backed up with specific data, reports, findings, and conclusions.

It can be a useful tool for a training manager to use with his or her staff to initiate improvement activities. It can easily be turned into a slide or overhead transparency for use in a meeting or as a discussion aid.

Space is left on the profile itself for the auditor to add specific areas of the training operation that deserve special attention.

Example

Project/Department Identification: Trade and Technical Services

Company Name: Regional Trade and Technical Schools, Inc.

Project/Department Manager: Ken Roberts

Auditor: Nils Kristensen   **Date:** 8/20/XX

Audit Profile

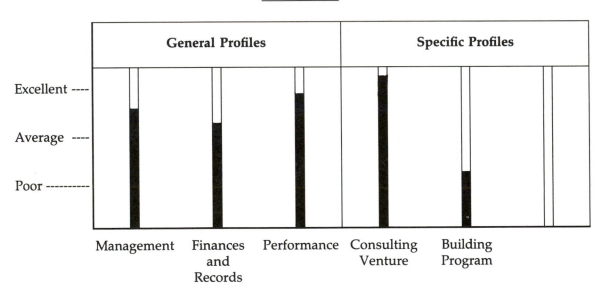

WORKSHEET 18–8

SUMMARY OPERATIONAL AUDIT PROFILE

Project/Department Identification: _____

Company Name: _____

Project/Department Manager: _____

Auditor: _____   **Date:** _____

Audit Profile

	General Profiles			Specific Profiles		
Excellent ----						
Average ----						
Poor ----------						

Management   Finances   Performance
                 and
                 Records

CHAPTER 19

WAYS TO STREAMLINE TRAINING ADMINISTRATION

Managing the training operation includes training administration. Major administrative tasks in training include:

- Staffing the organization
- Creating and managing the files
- Scheduling courses and services
- Registering students.

In a large training operation, a training administrator, staff specialist, and registrar are often hired to relieve the training manager of these administrative responsibilities. These persons generally report to the training manager, but often are not management employees.

In a small training operation, the training manager and a secretary often share these training administration responsibilities.

HOW TO USE THE WORKSHEETS IN THIS CHAPTER

Worksheets in this chapter help those with administrative responsibilities to attend to the many details of these important tasks. Each worksheet can be used independently of the others.

Worksheet 19–1: Training Organization Chart

This worksheet is included to provide a new training manager with some ideas for staffing. Levels of positions are suggested, and a variety of training specialties are presented. Use this worksheet to create an organization that is best for you.

Worksheet 19–2: Characteristics of Key Training Jobs

Use this worksheet to prepare a job description. Do this in coordination with your company's personnel organization. Worksheet 19–2 is included in this chapter to help you differentiate responsibilities of some key training jobs.

Worksheet 19–3: Checklist for Contract/Letter of Agreement with Outside Consultant

Use this worksheet as a guide for preparing a contract or letter of agreement with an outside consultant. Such a person typically works for you for a short period of time. A well-constructed, thorough, specific letter of agreement will help you maximize the benefits of using consultants as supplementary staff.

Worksheet 19–4: Training Time Sheet

Because training is an enterprise that includes development and implementation, staff support work, and work for clients, it is important that a careful record of expended time be kept. The best way to do this is weekly, on the individual employee's time sheet. Use this form to keep track of how your employees are spending their time. This is important documentation for client billing purposes and for calculating training's contributions to corporate profit. Each employee completes his or her own time sheet.

Worksheet 19–5: Training Files

Use this filing system to provide easy access to the many variables of the training operation. A secretary usually sets up the files.

Worksheet 19–6: Training Master Schedule

Use this format to schedule all your courses for a quarter, six-month period, or year. This is the large comprehensive schedule often found posted on the wall in the training manager's office or registration area of a training center.

Worksheet 19–7: Training Monthly Schedule

This schedule typically looks like a calendar, with days of the week across the top, and columns of boxes below to accommodate which courses are running on which days during that month.

Worksheet 19–8: Weekly Course Schedule

This kind of schedule is used on a course-by-course basis, to indicate the events of the course that are scheduled to happen on each day of the week. Each course being run in a training center has this kind of schedule. This schedule is generally given to students at the start of class.

Worksheet 19–9: Daily Course Agenda

This is a listing, by time, of the daily events of a course. Post this on the door of the classroom, turn it into a page of a flip chart, or write it on a chalkboard at the start of each day of class. Have a pile of daily agendas available for students at the start of each day.

Worksheet 19–10: Course Registrar's "To Do" List

Use this checklist to focus on the many details and critical timing of the registration process. The registrar's job is to get the students into the classroom—this involves initiating and processing all the necessary paperwork, supporting the instructor with materials, and attending to all follow-up paperwork and coordination activities on behalf of each student and instructor.

Worksheet 19–11: Course Attendance and Billing Record

This form is used to record course attendance information that is necessary for billing purposes. This kind of form is passed around at the beginning of class—generally right before the first break, to allow late comers to arrive. It is the instructor's responsibility to collect this information for the registrar and to pass it along to the registrar at the conclusion of the course. It is very important that all information is correct.

Worksheet 19–12: Course Enrollment Form

Use this form to send to a potential student after he or she inquires about the course, to include as a tear-off sheet in a brochure or catalog, or to have as a "pick-up piece" on a reception area coffee table. This is the form that an interested person fills out, gets a supervisor's signature for billing purposes, and sends in to a registrar. This form initiates a specific class of students.

Worksheet 19–13: Course Enrollment Confirmation

This form is sent by the registrar to the student confirming his or her place in an upcoming course.

TRAINING ORGANIZATION CHART

There are some major blocks in a training organization chart. Placement of these blocks within the organization varies because of differences in organizational cultures, mission of the business, and management practices.

The blocks below represent persons in the training organization chart. As you staff your organization, be sure the functions represented by these persons are included in your definition of responsibilities. The positions suggested here can be found in large training departments with many managers probably reporting to a director of training. Most organizations, however, are considerably smaller.

In small training organizations, the instructor often is the person who wrote the course, functioning as both the course developer and the instructional technologist. In small training organizations, the training secretary often functions as registrar, editor, graphic artist, and media specialist. In some small training operations, the training manager functions as an employer and coordinator of consultants who do all the development work and instructional delivery.

The training manager can adapt this organization chart to his or her particular training organization.

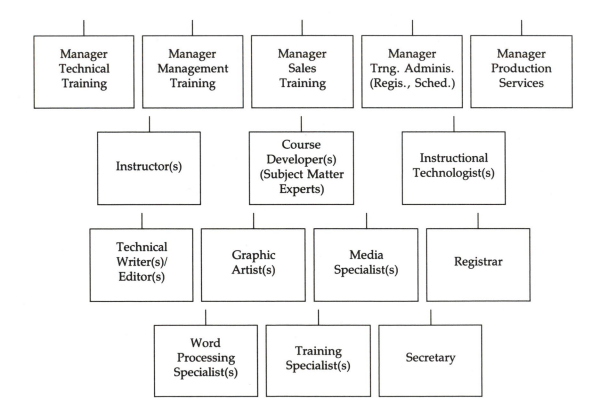

WORKSHEET 19–1

TRAINING ORGANIZATION CHART

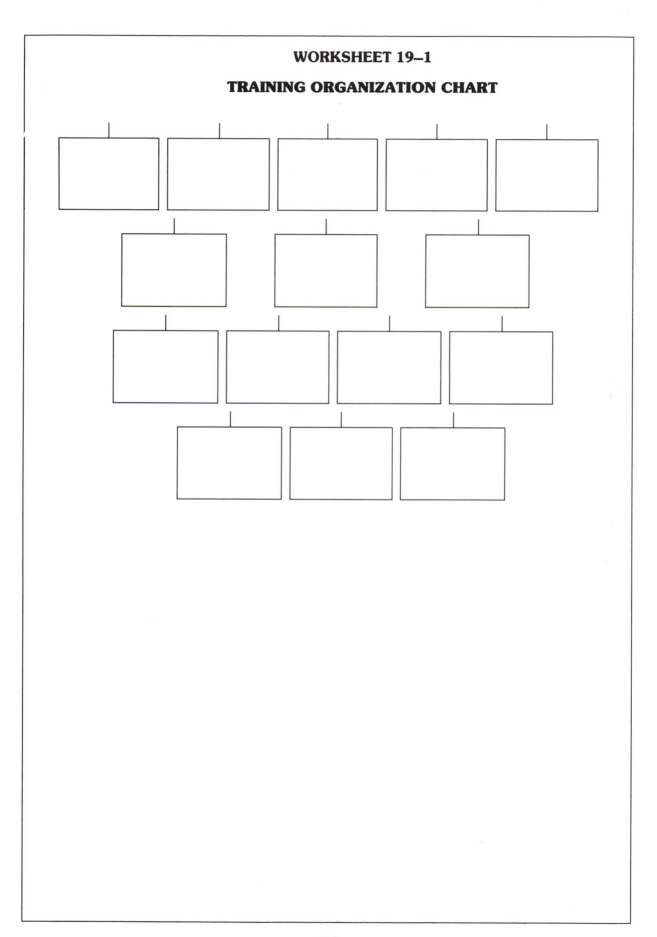

CHARACTERISTICS OF KEY TRAINING JOBS

Worksheet 19–2 is useful to the training manager who is hiring staff or who is changing the responsibilities of existing staff. This worksheet contains a listing of characteristics of four key training jobs. In consultation with your company's personnel department, write these characteristics into a job description. These characteristics can also be useful to those who write job advertisements for newspaper "Help Wanted" sections.

The following example is one way to use the characteristics in a job description.

Example: Course Developer

JOB DESCRIPTION

Job Title: Course Developer, "Chemistry of   **Level:**   3
            Fragrances"
Reports to: Curriculum Manager   **Salary Range:** $35,000–45,000

Major Responsibilities:
- Brings subject matter expertise to the task of writing a course.
- Works within a given format for designing a course, with guidance from an instructional technologist.
- Writes objectives, content outlines, lessons, visuals.
- Works with editing and production staff to produce course in a timely and accurate way.
- Seeks and uses feedback from peers and supervisors during the course development process.

Background Desired:
- M.S. or Ph.D. in chemistry
- 3–5 years laboratory experience in cosmetics industry
- Proven ability to work in a development team
- Knowledge of process quality methods and formative evaluation methods
- Strong interpersonal communication skills

WORKSHEET 19–2

CHARACTERISTICS OF KEY TRAINING JOBS

Training Manager:
- Manages all phases of instructional systems: analysis, design, development, delivery, evaluation.
- Manages all operations of training: registration, scheduling, production of materials, facility use.
- Controls the budget.
- Makes staffing decisions; hiring, terminating, reviewing performance.
- Represents training in other corporate contexts: sales, marketing, manufacturing, research and development, personnel.
- Promotes training services through internal and external communication channels.

Instructor:
- Is thoroughly familiar with course content.
- Prepares the classroom: seating, charts, job aids, trainee manuals, handouts.
- Checks equipment, lights, heating, air conditioning, facility layout.
- Delivers instruction.
- Takes attendance, distributes and collects evaluation forms and tests, forwards completed forms to instructional technologist or training manager.

Course Developer:
- Brings subject matter expertise to the task of writing a course.
- Works within a given format for designing a course, with guidance from an instructional technologist.
- Writes objectives, content outlines, lessons, visuals.
- Works with editing and production staff to produce course in a timely and accurate way.
- Seeks and uses feedback from peers and supervisors during the course development process.

Instructional Technologist:
- Supervises course developers in translating subject matter expertise into a structured course.
- Guarantees quality in design of instruction.
- Promotes principles and practices of a systematic design for instruction.
- Initiates and oversees course evaluations (in-process and end-of-course evaluations).
- Designs tests and proficiency exercises for trainees.
- Conducts dry runs and pilot testing of courses.
- Suggests options in design and delivery of courses.

CHECKLIST FOR CONTRACT/LETTER OF AGREEMENT
WITH OUTSIDE CONSULTANT

There are times when hiring an outside consultant is the best way to get a job done. Often, effective and efficient use of a consultant depends on the agreement with him or her at the time the consultant is engaged.

Training managers need to be aware that often a crisis precipitates the hiring of a consultant, and that the internal organization is often in trouble when the decision to hire a consultant is made. A good letter of agreement between you and the consultant can be helpful to everyone concerned with solving your particular problem.

Use this checklist as you draw up the letter of agreement for the selected consultant to sign. Do this well in advance of the time you expect services to begin, in order to give the consultant and your company's attorney or personnel officer a chance to review it.

An example of how to write these items into a letter of agreement follows. The point is to be specific, and to use the checklist as a guide.

(Date)

(Consultant name and address)

Dear Dr. LeClaire:

This letter authorizes the provision of consulting services by Diane W. LeClaire to CDN Training, Inc. These services are described below.

1. *Project Description*–Designing, writing, and delivering the course, "Tax Law Changes and Retirement Planning."

2. *Consultant's Role*–This assignment will require independent authoring work, weekly consultations with our staff course developers in the accounting curriculum, weekly reviews with our instructional technologist, and participation as requested in department task forces. The consultant is expected to deliver the first two sections of the completed course, after which course evaluations will be reviewed and continuation plans discussed.

3. *Duration of Engagement*–Work will commence on Monday, August 10, 19XX. The final draft of the course is due September 30, 19XX. Section one of the course is scheduled for October 20; section two is scheduled for October 30, 19XX. This engagement will be considered complete at the conclusion of the October 30th course.
   The consultant is expected to work on site at CDN Training, Inc. offices between 8:00 A.M. and 4:30 P.M. Half an hour lunch is suggested.

4. *Rates*–CDN Training, Inc. will pay Diane W. LeClaire $1,000 per diem for these services, on the basis of an eight–hour day.

5. *Overtime*–No overtime is authorized.

6. *Travel Expenses*–All travel expenses will be reimbursed upon submission of an authorized voucher. Your contact is N.W. Lasso.

WORKSHEET 19–3

CHECKLIST FOR CONTRACT/LETTER OF AGREEMENT
WITH OUTSIDE CONSULTANT

_____ 1. Brief (1–2 sentences) description of the project.

_____ 2. Description of the consultant's role (e.g., provide technical writing support to three course developers; test the system).

_____ 3. Specific time requirements that consultant is expected to work (e.g., part-time three mornings per week, 8 A.M. to noon, for six weeks).

_____ 4. Estimated rates per hour, per day, and total (e.g., at $50 per hour, $400 per day, or 40 days at $16,000 total).

_____ 5. Overtime restrictions and rates.

_____ 6. Travel expense agreement. Rates, contact person, conditions of travel.

_____ 7. Expectations regarding office space, and secretarial and word processing support.

_____ 8. A staff contact/internal project manager.

_____ 9. Project start date and end date.

_____ 10. Contract extension conditions.

_____ 11. Billing procedures and formats.

_____ 12. Protection of intellectual property, or nondisclosure statement (i.e., consultant guarantees he or she will not disclose any of your company's proprietary information to any other person or corporation).

_____ 13. Contract acceptance signatures and dates—yours and the consultant's.

TRAINING TIME SHEET

Each employee in the training department completes his or her own time sheet. The job of managing the training operation can be made much simpler if you systematically and regularly collect data regarding the expenditure of time needed to perform the various development and delivery tasks of the department's work.

Because training operations are matrixed in different ways, it is necessary for employees to record time spent doing specific functional tasks. Because training often brings in revenue for both development and delivery efforts, employees need to record time spent in service of particular clients so that proper accounting procedures can be followed for billing (clients are often other internal organizations).

Employee time sheets should be designed to allow clear, differentiated recording of time and type of task accomplished for each client. (Add to this the typical time sheet sections for total hours, overtime, vacation, holiday, and sick time expended.)

The following example illustrates what an employee's time sheet might look like:

Client Codes			Mon	Tues	Wed	Thurs	Fri	Sat	Sun
Task Code	Course Number	Client Number	(Enter hours(1.0) and half hours(0.5) only)						
W	M201	CL 05	3.0	1.0			8.0		
J	—	CL 15	5.0	2.5					
W	M204	CL05		3.5	5.0	1.0			
E	—	Z 100		1.0					
K	T600	Z 100			3.0	7.0			

Training tasks might be represented by this kind of coding (task code):

A	Analysis	V	Delivery
D	Design	E	Evaluation
W	Writing	S	Sales
J	Project Management	K	Marketing

WORKSHEET 19—4

TRAINING TIME SHEET

Client Codes			Mon	Tues	Wed	Thurs	Fri	Sat	Sun
Task Code	Course Number	Client Number	(Enter hours(1.0) and half hours(0.5) only)						

Use the following task code:

-
-
-
-

-
-
-
-

405

HOW TO SET UP TRAINING FILES

Each training department is comprised of many different functions, each of which needs to be accounted for and filed separately. A common troublesome filing problem, for example, is the separation of courses and clients—often a course becomes identified with a client (e.g., "Developing Market Channels" is usually taken by persons in the marketing department and charged to the marketing account). A departmental filing system has to be carefully designed so that each operation of training can be properly documented for planning and billing purposes. A secretary usually creates and maintains the department's filing system, in consultation with the training manager.

Good management of training includes an easy-to-access file system that takes into account the many variables of a training operation. The main categories of training files are:

- General Information (budget, facilities, insurance, personnel, and so on).
- Planning
- Schedules
- Clients
- Courses (objectives, topic outlines, lessons, evaluations)
- Marketing
- In-house Computer Systems Usage Schedule
- In-house Computer Systems Maintenance (specs, diagrams, contracts)
  Hardware
  Software
- Outside Professional Development for Staff (trip reports, brochures, agendas)
- Consultants.

Numbering System for Training Files

Avoid the use of the letter *I*, which can be mistaken for a one (1), and the letter *O*, which can be mistaken for a zero. Choose an alphanumeric system which introduces each file by a letter or combination of letters that are suggestive of the content, for example, CL-- for the client files, or MK-- for the marketing files. Give each file a number, using increments of five so that there is some space left in the numbering system to add new files if necessary. For example:

CL05	Frederick George, Inc.
CL10	Biscuits Internationale
CL15	Federation of Savings Institutions
MK35	Visitor Services
MK36	Guest List
MK37	Visitor Follow-up
MK40	Marketing Plan
MK45	New Products

WORKSHEET 19–5

TRAINING FILES

Main categories of training files:

-
-
-
-
-
-

Numbering system for training files:

-
-
-
-
-
-

TRAINING MASTER SCHEDULE

This is the large master schedule that often appears posted on the training manager's wall or in the registrar's office. Generally, the registrar maintains the master schedule. Typically, the master schedule is created for a three-month period. Be sure to enter a room location or location code in each citation.

The example below is for one month only, to illustrate the format for the entire master schedule. Add more sheets as needed.

Curriculum	Course Number	Number of Days	April 1234567891011121314151617181920212223242526272829 30
Management Courses	M 100	5	N101 N101 N101
	M 102	6	N102 N102
	M 201	2	N102 N101 N102 N101
Sales Courses	SL 10	2	N103 N103 N103
	MK 33	6	S101 S101
Technical Courses	T 04	3	E101
	T 05	3	E102
	T 06	3	E103
	T 07	3	E103
Office Support Courses	S 100	4	W101 W101
	S 200	4	W102

(Attach more sheets here as needed.)

N = North Wing   S = South Wing   E = East Wing   W = West Wing

WORKSHEET 19–6

TRAINING MASTER SCHEDULE

Curriculum	Course Number	Number of Days	123456789101112131415161718192021222324252627282930

(Attach more sheets here as needed.)

(Reproduce as many copies of this as you need. A minimum quarterly presentation of the master schedule is recommended.)

TRAINING MONTHLY SCHEDULE

Issue a monthly schedule of courses to all interested persons. This schedule serves as a current update to the master schedule (which often has to be printed months in advance of training, and frequently has to be changed due to changes in location, timing, and instructor).

Example

OCTOBER 19XX

MONDAY	TUESDAY	WEDNESDAY	THURSDAY	FRIDAY
			1 1.3 2.1 3.1	**2** 1.3
5 1.2 1.3 2.2 3.2	**6** 1.2 1.3 2.2 3.2	**7** 1.2 1.3 2.2 3.2	**8** 1.2 1.3 2.2 3.2	**9** 1.2 1.3 2.2
12 1.2 1.3 2.2 3.2	**13** 1.2 1.3 2.2 3.2	**14** 1.2 1.3 2.2 3.2	**15** 1.2 1.3 2.2 3.2	**16** 1.2 1.3 2.2
19 1.2 1.3 2.2 3.2	**20** 1.2 1.3 2.2 3.2	**21** 1.2 1.3 2.2	**22** 1.2 1.3 2.2	**23** 1.2 1.3 2.2
26 1.1 1.2 1.3 2.2 3.2	**27** 1.1 1.2 1.3 2.2 3.2	**28** 1.1 1.2 1.3 2.2	**29** 1.1 1.2 1.3 2.2 2.3	**30** 1.2 1.3 2.2

Course Codes:

Curriculum 1 Hardware Maintenance

1.1   Memory Boards
1.2   Disk Drives
1.3   Basic Wiring

Curriculum 2 Software

2.1   Avoiding Faults in Software Design
2.2   Software Testing
2.3   Software Design Inspections

Curriculum 3 Quality Control

3.1   Fundamentals of Quality Control
3.2   Basic Statistics
3.3   Using PC Graphics for Quality Analysis

WORKSHEET 19–7

TRAINING MONTHLY SCHEDULE

NAME OF MONTH, YEAR				
MONDAY	**TUESDAY**	**WEDNESDAY**	**THURSDAY**	**FRIDAY**

Course Codes:

WEEKLY COURSE SCHEDULE

The weekly course schedule is prepared by the instructor. Its major purpose is to provide a course overview for the students who are taking the course.

During training, most adult students feel psychologically exposed. Therefore, they need to be as comfortable as possible, especially at the start of training. One key to establishing this comfort level is making the trainee feel that he or she has "the big picture" regarding the schedule, and that he or she can therefore exercise some control over choices regarding the time expended in class.

Example

WEEKLY COURSE SCHEDULE

Course Number and Title: WP3:On-Line Files

This Week's Training Dates: January 25, 26, 27, 19XX

Room Number: 130

Instructor: Charles Johnson

	Monday	Tuesday	Wednesday	Thursday	Friday
A.M.	9–10 Welcome & Intro.	9–10 Input Form Layout	9–10 Principles of File Maintenance		
	10–10:15 BREAK				
	10:15–12 File Structure	10:15–12 How Data Is Collected	10:15–12 How to Add, Delete, and Modify Data Within Files		
	12–1 LUNCH				
P.M.	1–3 Exercises in File Management	1–3 Exercises in Using Input forms	1–3 Lab #3 Adding and Deleting Data Within Files		
	3–3:15 BREAK				
	3:15–5 Lab #1 Creating Files	3:15–5 Lab #2 Input Problem Solving	3:15–4:30 Lab #4 Modifying Data 4:30–5 Course Evaluation		

WORKSHEET 19—8

WEEKLY COURSE SCHEDULE

WEEKLY COURSE SCHEDULE

Course Number and Title: _____

This Week's Training Dates: _____

Room Number: _____

Instructor: _____

	Monday	Tuesday	Wednesday	Thursday	Friday
A.M.					
			10–10:15 BREAK		
			12–1 LUNCH		
P.M.					
			3–3:15 BREAK		

413

DAILY COURSE AGENDA

Post this on the door of the classroom, turn it into a page of a flip chart, or write it on a chalkboard at the start of each day of class. Post a new daily agenda for each day of class.

Have a pile of daily agendas available for students to take to their seats at the start of each day.

Example

Course Number and Title: MFG 607 Cable Design

Date(s): February 16, 17, 18, 19, 20, 19XX

Room Number: 6

Instructor: Sandy Field

Monday, February 16

8:30– 9:15	Unit 1
9.15–10:20	Unit 2 and Exercise
10:20–10:30	Ten-Minute Break
10:30–11:30	Unit 3
11:30–12:30	Unit 4
12:30– 1:30	One-hour Lunch
1:30– 2:30	Problem Definition Lab
2:30– 2:40	Ten-Minute Break
2:40– 4:30	Project Design Lab

WORKSHEET 19–9

DAILY COURSE AGENDA

Course Number and Title: _____

Date(s): _____

Room Number: _____

Instructor: _____

_____

COURSE REGISTRAR'S "TO DO" LIST

Worksheet 19–10 is a handy guide for the course registrar to use in preparing to run a specific course. The registrar has the responsibility for getting students into a course, and following through to getting them to pay for having taken it.

Generally the registrar receives a request to schedule a course from the training manager or sometimes from a regular staff instructor (i.e., not from a consultant instructor). This "To Do" list is one of the registrar's basic tools and can be used by anyone with a registrar's responsibilities—secretary, manager, or real-live registrar.

This "To Do" list is used at the very earliest stages of registration for each course. It is also useful at the end of a course because it is the registrar that often is responsible for handling the paperwork that the instructor needs to record attendance, the billing information, and course evaluations. A registrar is usually very adept and competent at keeping paperwork straight—instructors sometimes are not so good at this. If the registrar can be responsible for these paperwork tasks, the instructor can be freer to attend to the tasks of instruction. It is generally to the registrar's advantage to assume total responsibility for getting students into classes, and this means having classrooms ready for the next group of students who want to use them.

WORKSHEET 19–10

COURSE REGISTRAR'S "TO DO" LIST

15 weeks before the course	Receive request to schedule a course from the training manager or instructor.
14 weeks before the course	Reserve a room and enter the course on the master schedule.
12–6 weeks before the course	Promote the course through targeted mailings, electronic networks, and company bulletins.
12–6 weeks before the course	Send out and receive course enrollments.
5 weeks before the course	Review enrollment data. Decide to run or cancel the course.
4 weeks before the course	Mail out to each person enrolled a confirmation notice, cancellation notice, or waiting list notice.
3 weeks before the course	Talk with the instructor to verify specifics regarding trainee materials, classroom setup, daily timing, and total duration of the course.
2–1 week before the course	Generate course roster; send to instructor.
2–1 week before the course	Coordinating shipping, assembling, and temporarily storing all materials at the course site.
2–1 week before the course	Reserve and test equipment to be used in course.
2–1 week before the course	Order refreshments for breaks and lunch if needed.
The day before the course	Show instructor the classroom, the equipment, and the materials.
The first day of the course	Hand course attendance form to instructor for recording attendance and billing information.
The last day of the course	Hand course evaluation forms to instructor to distribute to trainees before they leave the classroom. Collect completed attendance and billing forms and completed course evaluation forms and mail them to training manager.
The day after the course	Send back to storage or discard unused course materials. Return equipment to storage. Set up classroom for the next course.

COURSE ATTENDANCE AND BILLING RECORD

The instructor generally hands out a course attendance and billing record as soon as it is clear that all students are present and should be charged for the course.

It's easy to forget to do this as the excitement of the course content and student interactions build. It is usually a helpful reminder to the instructor to have the course registrar deliver a pile of these forms to the classroom on the morning of the first day of class.

Students can be expected to fill out a form something like this:

Example

Trainee Name *Rob Scott*	Account Number to Be Billed *T 530*	Company Name *Metal Crafters Ltd.*	Department Name and Number *Process Control 0711*
	Employee Number *539*	Telephone *215-3496*	Job Title *Tester*
Trainee Name *Arnie Todd*			

WORKSHEET 19–11

COURSE ATTENDANCE AND BILLING RECORD

Course Number and Title: _____

Course Dates: _____

Course Location: _____

Instructor: _____

(Note: Reproduce as many of these forms as you need.)

Trainee Name	Account Number to be Billed	Company Name	Department Name and Number
	Employee Number	Telephone	Job title
Trainee Name	Account Number to Be Billed	Company Name	Department Name and Number
	Employee Number	Telephone	Job Title
Trainee Name	Account Number to Be Billed	Company Name	Department Name and Number
	Employee Number	Telephone	Job Title
Trainee Name	Account Number to Be Billed	Company Name	Department Name and Number
	Employee Number	Telephone	Job Title

WORKSHEET 19–12

COURSE ENROLLMENT FORM

This is the form that gets a course rolling. It is sent by the registrar to any potential student after an inquiry has been made. These forms are often included in brochures or course catalogs as tear-off sheets to be completed by the student (and his or her supervisor) and returned to the registrar.

COURSE ENROLLMENT FORM
(Please print or type all information.)

Course Number and Title: _____

Course Dates and Location: _____

Have the prerequisites for this course been met? __ YES __ NO

Name: _____ Job Title: _____

Employee Number: _____ Telephone: _____

Work Location: _____ Room Number: _____

Department Name: _____

Account Number to Which Training Should Be Billed: _____

Approval

I approve this employee's taking this course, and understand that the account number specified above will be charged for this course.

Supervisor's Name: _____ Telephone: _____

Supervisor's Work Location: _____

Company's Name: _____

Supervisor's Signature: _____

Mail this completed form to:

REGISTRAR
Company Name   telephone (XXX) XXX-XXXX
Street Address
City, State, ZIP

This course is accessible to handicapped persons. If you require special services, please indicate the kind of service you need.

_____

_____

WORKSHEET 19–13

COURSE ENROLLMENT CONFIRMATION

This is the notice that guarantees the student a place in the course (or notifies him or her that the course is cancelled or rescheduled). The registrar sends this confirmation notice to the student as soon as the Course Enrollment Form has been received—with the supervisor's signature.

The Course Enrollment Confirmation is a good memory jogger. People often sign up for training before their work schedules are determined, and they forget that they made a commitment to training. (The supervisor's approval for charging helps guarantee that the student will be in class.) Protect your "bottom line" by attending to this important administrative detail.

COURSE ENROLLMENT CONFIRMATION

Name of Enrolled Trainee: _____

Telephone: _____

- -

___ Course Is Cancelled   Course Is Rescheduled for _____ .

- -

You are enrolled in the following course:

Course Number and Title: _____

Course Dates: _____

Daily Time: _____

Course Location: _____

Please retain this enrollment notice. It is the only notice you will receive.

If you have questions, please contact the Registrar at (XXX) XXX-XXXX.

If you cannot attend this course, please notify the Registrar at least 15 days before the course is due to begin or the full tuition fee will be charged.

Trainee substitutions are permissible provided the substitute trainee has met course prerequisites.

Thank you for your interest in the Training Center courses. Attached is a three-month master schedule for your future training needs.

BIBLIOGRAPHY _____

Alessi, S.M., and Trollip, S.R. *Computer-Based Instruction Methods and Development*. Englewood Cliffs, NJ: Prentice-Hall, 1985.

American Society for Training and Development (ASTD). 1630 Duke Street, Box 1443, Alexandria, VA 22313.

Banathy, B.H. *Instructional Systems*. Belmont, CA: Fearon, 1968.

Birnbaum, H. (ed.). *Handbook for Technical and Skills Training*. Alexandria, VA: ASTD, 1985.

Bloom, B.S., ed. *Taxonomy of Educational Objectives, Handbook I: Cognitive Domain*. New York: Longman, 1954.

Federal Register. Washington, DC. August 25, 1978.

Finch, C.R., and Crunkilton, J.R. *Curriculum Development in Vocational and Technical Education*. Boston: Allyn & Bacon, 1979.

Gagne, R.M., and Briggs, L.J. *Principles of Instructional Design*. New York: Holt, Rinehart & Winston, 1979.

Greenwood, K.B. *Contemporary Challenges for Vocational Education (1982 Yearbook)*. Arlington, VA: American Vocational Association, 1981.

Kaufman, R. *Identifying and Solving Problems*. LaJolla, CA: University Associates, 1976.

Mager, R.F., and Beach, K.M. *Developing Vocational Instruction*. Belmont, CA: Lear Siegler/Fearon, 1967.

Mager, R.F., and Pipe, P. *Analyzing Performance Problems, or 'You Really Oughta Wanna.'* Belmont, CA: Fearon Pitman, 1970.

National Society for Performance and Instruction (NSPI). 1126 16th Street NW, Suite 102, Washington, DC 20036.

Rossett, A. *Training Needs Assessment*. Englewood Cliffs, NJ: Educational Technology Publications, 1987.

Simpson, E.J. *The Classification of Objectives, Psychomotor Domain*. Urbana, IL: University of Illinois, 1966.

Smith, J.K. *The Role of Measurement in the Process of Instruction*. ERIC TM Report 70. Princeton: Educational Testing Service, 1979.

Stufflebeam, D.L., and Shinkfield, A.J. *Systematic Evaluation*. Boston: Kluwer-Nijhoff, 1985.

Thorndike, R.L., and Hagen, E.P. *Measurement and Evaluation in Psychology and Education*. New York: John Wiley & Sons, 1977.

Tracey, W.R. *Designing Training and Development Systems*. New York: AMACOM, 1984.

U.S. Department of Labor, Employment and Training Administration. *Dictionary of Occupational Titles*, 4th edition and supplements of 1982 and 1986. Washington, DC: US Government Printing Office.

INDEX